MAMMALS
OF
BRITAIN & EUROPE

RICHARD ORR

MAMMALS
OF
BRITAIN & EUROPE

TEXT BY JOYCE POPE

Pelham Books

First published in Great Britain by
Pelham Books Ltd
44 Bedford Square
London WC1 3DU
1983

Produced by Charles Herridge Ltd
Tower House, Abbotsham, Bideford, Devon
Typeset by Lens Typesetting, Bideford, Devon

ISBN 0 7207 1426 5

Printed in Italy by New Interlitho SpA, Milan

CONTENTS

INTRODUCTION

The 39 argumentative nations of which it is composed remind us that Europe, alone of the continents, is a political rather than a geographical or biological entity. With a total area of 4,929,000 sq km, it is substantially smaller than the other continents, with a comparatively long and indented coastline. The western part may be considered to be a series of great peninsulas; Scandinavia and Iberia jut their chins to the Atlantic from north and west, while to the south, Italy and the Balkans kick into the Mediterranean. Large islands lie beyond these outposts of the mainland, in some cases cut off from the continental landmass by the rise in sea level at the end of the last Ice Age. Iceland and the islands of Great Britain and Ireland are the most important, while those in the Mediterranean include Corsica, Sardinia, Sicily, Crete and Cyprus. The intimate proximity of the sea affects the climate of much of Europe, the warm waters of the North Atlantic Drift and the prevailing west and south-west winds which cross the continent bring relatively mild weather, with no great extremes of heat or cold, to much of the western part of the landmass. Further east, away from the moderating influence of the ocean, the climate becomes continental, with intensely cold winters and blisteringly hot summers.

As the climate of Europe is not uniform, the continent can be divided into five basic zones (see map p.171) which mainly extend across the continent from west to east, each finding expression in differences in vegetation. Starting in the north, they are: tundra; coniferous forest or taiga; broadleaved forests; grassland or steppe regions, which are most extensive in the eastern part of the continent; and the Mediterranean zone. There may be local variations in these zones due to soil differences or the presence of wetlands or mountains.

Mammals, the hairy, warm-blooded creatures which suckle their young, are to be found in all of Europe's climatic zones. A very few, such as the red fox, are ubiquitous, but most of them are more or less specialized to fill niches within the different climatic and vegetation zones.

The tundra, which is found in the most northerly parts of Europe, is an area in which the subsoil is permanently frozen, although the top half metre or so may thaw for a few months during the summer. The frozen depths of the soil prevent trees or other deep-rooted plants from surviving. Because frozen subsoil impedes drainage, the tundra is an area of swamps and lakes.

The largest mammal to be found in the tundra today is the reindeer, which migrates to these inhospitable lands during the summer months. Attendant wolves may make the same journey, but the small Arctic fox manages to survive there throughout the year, probably because of its habit of hoarding in the time of plenty. A number of small mammals, particularly rodents, make the tundra their home. These do not hibernate, but survive by searching for seeds and dry vegetation under the snow which blankets their environment for much of the year.

The seas surrounding the northernmost parts of Europe are rich in nutrients and support a number of species of whales and seals.

A relatively small number of animal species has managed to colonize the Arctic successfully. These are apparently inadequate to ensure stability in the numbers of any species, and thus there are violent fluctuations in the populations of lemmings and several kinds of birds.

South of the tundra a wide band of coniferous forest, or taiga, stretches across

the continent. Here, although the winters are long and cold, the subsoil is not permanently frozen so the growth of large, evergreen trees is possible. A large number of mammal species is found in the taiga, including the elk, which is the largest of European mammals. Rodents, including climbing animals such as birch mice and the flying squirrel, are abundant, and there is a rich fauna of carnivores which preys largely on them. In a few places wolves and brown bears survive, but most of the flesh eaters are small animals, many of them members of the weasel family.

Further southwards, the taiga gives way to broadleaved forests. Here the number of tree species is larger, and includes deciduous forms such as oaks, ash, beech, limes and chestnuts. The leaf litter from broadleaved trees breaks down easily to form a rich humus in the soil. This supports an abundance of small animals which are food for insectivores, while insects found in the foliage nourish bats and a large number of birds, some of which are themselves

food for a variety of carnivorous mammals. Herbivores range in size from the bison through a number of medium-sized creatures, such as deer and wild boar, down to small rodents. Many broadleaved trees produce nuts, and these form the basis of food stores which maintain the smaller animals throughout the winter. Broadleaved forest is the richest of all of the European environments. It has, however, been very greatly altered by Man, whose activities have seriously reduced the numbers of many mammals. Wolves and bears have almost disappeared, but many of the smaller animals and some deer have shown a surprising ability to survive and to modify their behaviour, so they may live near to buildings or even suburbs and towns.

The steppes or grasslands of Europe all lie to the east where there is insufficient rainfall for the growth of forests, although even here bushes and shrubby trees occur in the wetter areas. The climate is more continental than elsewhere; winters are very cold, while summer temperatures

reach a height unknown elsewhere in the continent. At one time, huge herds of wild horses, hardy and well adapted to climatic extremes, lived on these plains, but by the early part of the last century they were all exterminated. Smaller creatures, such as the marmot and sousliks, hibernate deep underground throughout the winter. Some of them spend as little as 3 months of each year awake; into this they must pack all the activities of breeding, moulting, enlarging burrows and making food stores.

In the lands bordering the Mediterranean the heaviest rainfall occurs in the winter and the summer months are hot and dry. The original vegetation of this zone was forest, composed of conifers and other tree species with small, thick leaves capable of withstanding drought. These have mostly been destroyed, for the Mediterranean basin has been the cradle of successive western civilizations each of which, in ancient times, died out as it depleted its

forest resources. Today, Man's destructive influence can be seen here more clearly than anywhere else in Europe; where the great ancient cedars and other warm-climate conifers once flourished, a secondary growth of poor, drought-resistant scrub is now dominant. Virtually all of the large mammals which once lived in the forest have long since disappeared, although wolves still survive in a few remote places. However, many small creatures still flourish. Affinities with the African fauna are more apparent here than elsewhere, for although the hippopotamuses and elephants which once occupied much of Europe died out at the end of the Ice Age, lions existed in southern Europe into early historic times. Today porcupines, mongooses and the Algerian hedgehog survive there, although there is some suspicion that they may have been introduced by Man.

The pattern of climatic variation affecting the vegetation, and in turn the fauna, leads to questions about the origins of the animals and whether there are any restraints, other than climate, limiting their distribution. Since one of the chief characteristics of the large animals is their mobility, why should the mammalian fauna of Europe not be uniform? The answer to the first question lies in the pattern of recolonization of much of Europe after the retreat of the ice at the end of the Pleistocene Period. During this time, when ice sheets had covered much of the north of Europe and a good deal of the south was reduced to an inhospitable tundra, many animals had become extinct and others had retreated to the south and east. Not surprisingly, the fauna of the eastern parts of Europe today has many affinities with south-west Asia, although there are desert and mountain barriers to the movements of animals from much further afield. Other animals returned from the south, to retake lands that had been covered by ice. Some seem to have moved north with the climatic zone which suited their way of life and, as with lemmings and the mountain hare, are restricted to the more northerly or upland parts of the continent. Others, such as the pigmy shrew, hedgehogs and the wood mouse, seem to have followed close behind the ice front, for they are to be found almost everywhere suitable habitats occur, including the islands of Britain and Ireland. A few, more laggardly, managed to reach mainland Britain, but were prevented from going further by the rising waters produced as the ice melted. Thus species such as the common shrew, water voles and the weasel did not reach Ireland. Many of the others, slower still, were prevented by the barrier of the English Channel or the North Sea from reaching any part of Britain, although there is no reason why they should not thrive there. The dormice, with the exception of the hazel dormouse, come into this category, as does the beech marten.

Animals compete with each other for living space, shelter and food, but because each species makes slightly different demands on its habitat, many kinds can live within a single area, although no two species with exactly the same requirements can co-exist. This may limit the distribu-

tion of some creatures, although much remains to be discovered of their lives in the wild before definite statements can be made to account for their presence or absence in what appears to be a suitable habitat for them.

Man has also affected the distribution of many species. A few have been exterminated such as the wild aurochs and the horse and many have been brought to the edge of extinction over much of their former range, including the wolf, the brown bear and the beaver. Stringent conservation measures have allowed the survival of others, including ibex, which might otherwise have died out, but the decline of many mammals has gone uncharted because they are small, nocturnal and secretive. Some species owe their distribution to human intervention in another way, for Man has often removed animals from their normal living places and taken them elsewhere. The Barbary ape was probably taken to Gibraltar in ancient times and the groups which survive there today do so thanks to human feeding and protection.

The fallow deer, initially a southern European species, is reputed to have been taken to the northerly reaches of their empire by the Romans, who wished to have their usual quarry for the hunt. Other species of deer have been brought from further afield — the muntjac from south-east Asia, and the white-tailed deer from North America, for instance, were brought to alien lands to beautify the landscape and perhaps to add to the supply of food. Some mammals were relocated because they had valuable fur. The rabbit, a native of the Iberian peninsula, was probably the first. Later arrivals include the North American mink and musk rat and the South American coypu

In Britain, species such as the grey squirrel and the fat dormouse were introduced as amusing pets, and later escaped or were liberated into an environment which could sustain them, although it was not their true home. Those which survived (and there have been many unsuccessful introductions) generally found themselves without any of the normal predatory con-

straints on their success, and because of this many have increased enormously in numbers to become pests in their new homes, sometimes ousting the native inhabitants.

In spite of our newly acquired knowledge of the environment, there is still much to be learned about how and why animals should live in certain places. In the meantime, the outlook for many kinds of large animals is bleak. Although conservation laws have been widely passed, they are in many places equally widely flouted. The conservation of carnivores lags behind that of other animals, due perhaps to a deep-seated belief that they are by nature always inimical to Man's interests. Even in reserves, populations become isolated and inbred, a danger to ultimate survival. However, at present these are the best hopes we have that future generations may see something of the grandeur and diversity of our native European mammals.

INSECTIVORES

Order Insectivora

While it is easy to recognize some groups of animals from a general description alone, the insectivores defy any such simple identification. All are small — the largest is the size of a cat and most are much smaller than this — and all share certain basic features, but these are so overlaid by specializations which fit them for many ways of life that they are superficially very dissimilar. This multiplicity of form is probably due to the fact that they are the most ancient order of placental mammals — the group in which the unborn young are nourished through a special maternal organ, the placenta. The direct ancestors of today's insectivores evolved as far back as 100 million years ago. They shared their world with the dinosaurs, and must have scurried into the trees or dashed for safety into water or under the shelter of a rock when the tread of their heavyweight neighbours shook the ground.

From these ancient beginnings all later placental mammals have evolved, some as runners, some as climbers and some as swimmers. Many have developed to a large size, which makes it possible for them to occupy new and different niches and to use food resources unavailable to the early insectivores. Most of them have changed radically in their physical structure and dentition to give us the range of mammals in today's world.

Beside these newcomers the insectivores have remained little changed in the essentials of their being, in spite of the adaptations which enable them to survive in a wide range of habitats throughout the world, apart from southern South America, Australia, New Zealand and some oceanic islands. Many of them have ways of life which must be similar to their ancient ancestors, though some of them have become specialized to fill particular niches, especially as burrowers. Externally, they may be distinguished from other small mammals by the fact that they have five toes on each foot; rodents, with which they are most likely to be confused, usually have four toes or less. Most species have a very pointed snout and small eyes. Their sight is generally poor although the senses of smell and hearing are usually acute. The sense of touch, enhanced by large, stiff whiskers or vibrissae round the snout, is often excellent and is probably the most important aid to the discovery of food. Insectivores' coats are often dense and velvety, although in some groups there is a tendency towards the production of spines. In some insectivores these may be no more than stiff hairs, while in others they may form a hidden defence within the fur, and they are occasionally more prominent, as in the hedgehogs. Internally, insectivores usually have a collarbone or clavicle, which is an inheritance from the earliest vertebrates; the brain has large olfactory lobes and is considered to be a relatively primitive structure; and the placenta is also of a simpler form than that found in most other mammals.

Whatever their way of life, the insectivores, as their name suggests, are small-scale predators, feeding on insects, grubs, snails and occasionally helpless vertebrates, such as young rodents, small reptiles, or the eggs and young of ground-nesting birds. Some species may feed on larger animals which they find as carrion. To deal with their food, insectivores carry up to 44 teeth in their jaws, the maximum number normally found in placental mammals. In some the teeth in the front of the mouth are powerful stabbing weapons, and the molars are crowned with sharp, pointed cusps, suitable for slicing and crunching their prey. The form of these teeth has, in some instances, changed little from the triple cusped teeth of the earliest mammals. Many insectivores are extremely active creatures and this restless way of life must be fuelled by relatively huge amounts of food, amounting in some of the shrews to a weight equal to the animal's total body weight each day. It is possible that in some species toxic saliva may help them to subdue their prey. For those hedgehogs which live in temperate regions, the difficulty of obtaining sufficient food during the winter may be overcome by hibernation. During this time, the animals fall into a deep torpor, their bodies using the resources gathered during the rich feeding period of the late summer, which are stored internally as fat.

There are 22 species of insectivore native to Europe. All are small and the pigmy white-toothed shrew, with a head and body length of less than 45 mm, is one of the smallest of all mammals. Although no European insectivore is specialized as a climber, a variety of niches on and under the ground and in water have been colonized successfully, and insectivores are to be found from the tundra to the Mediterranean, wherever there are sufficient insects or other small prey. Many species are themselves food for bigger creatures, their numbers being maintained in most cases by their high reproduction rate.

Man's relationship with the insectivores is generally one of unwitting tolerance. They generally go unobserved — or at least ignored — and the shrill squeaks of shrews, should they be heard, are often thought to be noises made by insects. Hedgehogs are said by some gamekeepers to take the eggs of ground-nesting birds and they may be persecuted accordingly, and in some parts of the world they are eaten by people. The velvety fur of moles is no longer used widely for clothing, although the animals incur the wrath of gardeners and horticulturalists when the mounds of earth which they throw up damage plants or machinery. At worst, however, the insectivores are only a local nuisance, and overall they are probably helpful to Man, because they destroy huge numbers of insects and other invertebrate pests. In general, their numbers seem to be fairly high and in Europe only the desman appears to be seriously endangered, largely through careless pollution of its environment. So it is likely that insectivores will survive in a changing world as they always have done.

HEDGEHOGS
Family Erinaceidae

One of the most easily recognized of European wild mammals, hedgehogs or urchins are to be found almost everywhere there are trees or shrubs, although they are absent from the highest mountains and the coldest places. They are less common in coniferous woodlands, where the soil tends to be rather poor, and they do not thrive in damp places, but they are abundant elsewhere, finding suitable habitats even in some towns. Two species, the eastern hedgehog (*Erinaceus concolor*) and the western hedgehog (*E. europaeus*) are found over most of the continent, the range of each species ending at a line running due north of the Adriatic. The Algerian hedgehog (*E. algirus*), which was probably introduced by Man, maintains a toehold in the south of France and Spain and on the Atlantic coast of France. The three species are similar in general appearance and overlap in size. The eastern hedgehog can be distinguished from the western species by details of the skull and by the white bib which runs from the chin to halfway down the chest. The Algerian hedgehog, which is generally smaller and overall paler than the northern forms, is identified by a broad parting in the spines on the top of the head.

The most characteristic feature of the hedgehogs is their spines. Several thousands of these modified hairs replace the normal pelage from the top of the head to the base of the tail, and can be erected to turn the creature into a prickly ball when danger of any kind threatens. Each sharply pointed spine is 20-30 mm long and 1 mm in diameter. Although more widely spaced than normal hairs, the spines are largely hollow, and must offer a good deal of insulation to the body. Certainly they must deter some predators, but hungry foxes and badgers both devour hedgehogs, defeating them, it is said, by rolling or carrying them to water and tearing at the soft underparts when the unfortunate creatures uncurl to swim. An even greater danger to hedgehogs which venture on to roads is the motor car, for the creatures' main reaction to danger is to remain perfectly still and to present their spiny backs to the world — a form of defence which is utterly useless against a vehicle.

The possession of spines seems to give hedgehogs a high level of confidence for they are unusually noisy animals both while foraging and courting. One disadvantage of spines is that they make grooming by the normal method of scratching difficult and, perhaps because of this, hedgehogs carry a larger number of obvious parasites than most other animals. Fleas are the most noticeable, up to 500 having been recorded from one animal. These, however, are highly host-specific, and will not move from their normal habitat to bite humans or domestic animals.

Although hedgehogs are abundant over much of Europe, little is known about the population in any given area. They seem to lead solitary lives, with little contact with others of their kind. In close captivity, males are aggressive, and they may develop a hierarchical society, but this has not been observed in the wild. Some studies suggest that the size of each hedgehog's territory is quite small — a single animal patrolling a length of hedgerow of about 300 - 400 m. It has been further suggested that droppings are used as scent markers, and that several individuals may use the same area at different times of day.

The hedgehog's skull and jaw carry 36 sharp, pointed teeth.

The fore (upper) and hind (lower) feet of a hedgehog. Each foot has five toes and pads which leave a distinctive footprint.

Hedgehog piglets are born with soft white spines. Their mother will carry the helpless young to another place if she feels their safety is threatened.

Young hedgehogs leave the nest to join their mother on her nightly hunting expeditions when they are about 3 weeks old.

Most hedgehogs mate in the late spring or early summer. The courtship is simple, and consists mainly of the male walking round the female, snorting and sniffing at her. She will generally repulse him for some hours at least by butting him, with the spines on the front of her head erect. The problems inherent in mating are overcome by the male's very long penis being placed far forward on the underside while the female's vagina is positioned very far back. When she is ready to accept the male, the female stands with her hind legs stretched out behind, and the spines of her back flattened. After mating, the pair remain together for about a week. At the end of this time the female drives her mate away and from then on he plays no further part in making the nursery nest or rearing the young.

The female makes a football-sized nest of leaves and grass lined with moss or other soft plant material, and after a gestation period of about 6 weeks she produces a litter of up to ten young, although five is the usual number. Blind and helpless, they may weigh anything between 12 and 25 g at birth. On the back they have a sparse coat of soft, white spines, but these are replaced by darker, sharp spines which begin to show as soon as 36 hours after birth. Although still blind and with closed ears, the young are very active, butting and squeaking as they push to feed. By the time they are a week old they can erect their fast-growing spines to some extent, although they cannot roll up completely until they are about 11 days old.

Their eyes open when they are about a fortnight old, and they first venture from the nest about a week after this. Weaning may take place as early as 4 weeks, but may be delayed until the young are 6 weeks old. At this stage, they have grown their permanent teeth and have moulted the first white spines so that only the sharp, dark armour remains. Their length at weaning is about 160 mm and their weight about 120 g. They grow quickly on the abundant food of the summer months, and those from early summer litters will be full grown, reaching a length of 200 mm or more and a weight of over 1 kg before the autumn, although they will not be sexually mature until the next year.

Some female hedgehogs produce a second litter late in the summer, but the outlook for these young ones is poor, at least in the more northerly part of their range, for although they tend not to hibernate until late in the season, some remaining awake until December, they will not have been able to make sufficient growth to enable them to survive the rigours of the winter and hibernation. When they leave the nursery, the young hedgehogs do not stay together, but wander off to live solitary lives. As with all young animals on their own, the first year is a perilous one, and up to 70 per cent die before they are a year old. Those that survive that long may well live for another 6 years and, exceptionally, for another 9 years.

To fuel this growth and maintain their high level of nightly activity, hedgehogs have, like the other insectivores, a prodigious appetite for almost any high-protein food. Beetles, caterpillars, snails, slugs, worms, grubs and carrion are all sliced and munched by their sharp, pointed teeth. They occasionally eat the eggs and young of nesting birds, and are also recorded as taking young rodents and small reptiles, including snakes, although there is no truth in the folk tales that they are immune to adder venom. Food appears to be located chiefly by the sense of smell and is captured entirely by the mouth. They may take a small amount of fruit, and also drink a good deal of water or milk, if this is available.

Unlike their relatives the moles and shrews, hedgehogs do not make food stores, so when the weather cools and the supply of cold-blooded prey on which they mainly rely dwindles, hedgehogs must hibernate. They prepare for hibernation, which usually starts in October, by making a large nest in a sheltered spot, sometimes among the roots of a tree or even in a rabbit burrow. Heavy feeding enables them to lay down thick deposits of white fat beneath the skin and round the viscera, and brown fat, which is a special high-energy tissue, round the shoulders. During hibernation, they lie tightly curled with spines erect; their temperature matches that of their surroundings, their heartbeats slow from about 190 to about 20 per minute and their breathing rate falls to about 10 per minute, often with long pauses between a series of breaths.

In the past hedgehog skins were used for wool carding and as clothes brushes and even today hedgehogs are eaten by a few people, but on the whole Man has ignored them. Gamekeepers may persecute them for the few eggs they eat, but overall they do little damage. Indeed, they probably do much good in the number of insects and other pests they eat. In folklore, the hedgehog is credited with collecting apples and other fruit on its spines, and with taking milk from cows lying chewing the cud. Both of these activities are fantasies, perhaps invented to fill gaps in observation and knowledge, for there is still much that remains to be learned about hedgehogs.

The eastern hedgehog has a bib of white fur beneath the chin and across the chest. This distinguishes it from the western hedgehog, in which the whole of the underparts are greyish in colour.

The mating female flattens her spines and stretches her hind legs, so that the male will not be damaged by her armament.

Hedgehogs often climb banks and walls. If they should slip, their spines break the fall and they are rarely hurt.

Hedgehogs sometimes produce large amounts of frothy saliva, which they smear over their flanks. This is called 'self annointing'.

Diagram to show the muscle (orbicularis) which lies just below the skin and enables the hedgehog to erect the spines.

Hedgehogs feed on many kinds of small animals, and occasionally even kill adders.

A spine is about 22mm long. In cross-section large air spaces can be seen.

When it is certain that there is no danger a hedgehog unrolls, relaxing the orbicularis muscle gradually, so that the head and feet can be extended and the animal can walk away.

15

SHREWS
Family Soricidae

Despite the fact that Europe's 15 species of shrews are found in most parts of the continent, except for mountains above the snowline and heavily built-up areas, and that they maintain their restless activity, with only short breaks, throughout the 24 hours of the day, very few people have ever seen a live one.

Shrews are small creatures with dark-coloured, velvety fur, long snouts well furnished with vibrissae or tactile hairs, small

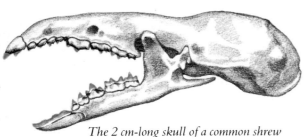

The 2 cm-long skull of a common shrew shows the sharp, pointed teeth tipped with dark red enamel.

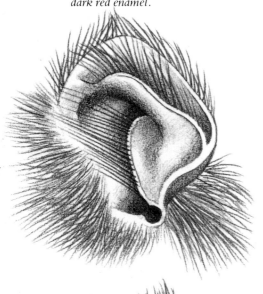

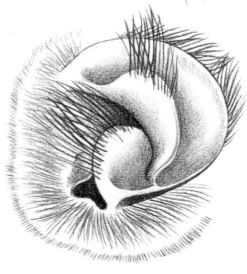

The ears of most red-toothed shrews, which are barely visible in their fur, are quite complex with special valves for guarding the ear. Ears of pigmy shrew (top) and water shrew (bottom).

eyes and ears. Males, and females also in some species, have well-developed stink glands on their flanks, giving them an unpleasant smell at close quarters. They tap an almost limitless food resource of small insects, grubs, and soil invertebrates which are ignored by other mammals. In general they are ground surface dwellers and, although they may climb into the lower branches of bushy trees and shrubs, they do not ascend above a metre or so. Water shrews and other large species make burrows in the surface of the soil, which can be distinguished from the tunnels of mice and voles by their oval cross-section, wider than they are high. Apart from being a safe place in which food might be found, squeezing through the tunnels seems to have a grooming function, scraping and combing the hairs into good condition. All species may make use of the burrows of other animals, such as moles, but they must avoid a confrontation with the rightful owners, which may well kill them if they are caught.

European shrews can be divided into two groups, best distinguished by the

The fur of a swimming water shrew traps numerous air bubbles, giving it a silvery appearance, instead of its usual dark grey colour.

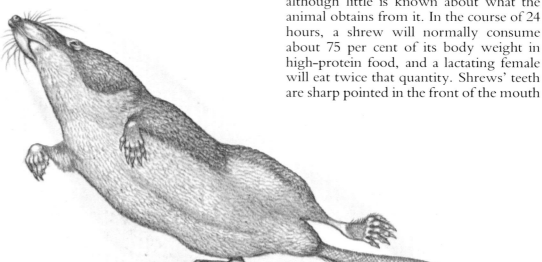

colour of the enamel on their teeth. Red-toothed shrews include the two kinds of water shrews and most of the species with a northerly distribution, while most of the southerly species are known as white-toothed shrews. Tooth colour can be discerned easily in a captive or dead animal, as can some of the more subtle differences between the two groups. Identification in the wild must often depend on the locality, although unfortunately there is much geographical overlap between the species.

The major impression given by a shrew is one of restless energy, and they may be seen fighting or hunting at any time of the day or night. When hunting, the creature bustles along its runs, pushing its long nose into the earth or vegetation in its incessant search for food. Should it encounter a worm or grub, the prey will be seized and worried. The front paws are not used rodent fashion to take the food up to the mouth, but rather to hold it down, more in the manner of a dog

The meal finished, the shrew is quickly on its way again, looking for more. This is vital to its survival, for shrews digest their food very quickly and because they carry little in the way of bodily reserves, they can starve to death in about 4 hours, should no more food be forthcoming. This is particularly true of the smaller species. Very hungry shrews may feed from a secretion obtained by everting the anus. This seems to be a last-ditch reserve, although little is known about what the animal obtains from it. In the course of 24 hours, a shrew will normally consume about 75 per cent of its body weight in high-protein food, and a lactating female will eat twice that quantity. Shrews' teeth are sharp pointed in the front of the mouth

The common shrew (top) will attack almost any invertebrate, even one with a body bulk larger than itself. The water shrew (bottom) is more sociable than most other shrews, and several may be seen together by a stream.

and knife edged further back, so they are well adapted to cutting and slicing the chitinous armour of their prey. They usually drink rain or dew drops, lifting their heads in a rather bird-like fashion as they swallow.

Although water shrews may tolerate the presence of others of their own kind nearby, the other European shrews are solitary, territorial animals. The territory is honeycombed with runs which the owner knows well and which are probably scent-marked to warn any intruders that the area is occupied. Somewhere, usually fairly centrally placed, a nest is constructed of pieces of grass or other soft material. The shrew sits in a chosen spot and pulls such fragments as it can reach towards itself, and tucks them round to make the basis of the bed. Later, material may be brought from further away.

When working their runs food is detected by the vibrissae and seems to be rejected, if it is unpalatable, as a result of its smell. Eyesight appears to play no part in hunting, and shrews seem to be exceedingly short sighted. Hearing is probably acute, for they are highly vocal animals, often twittering and squeaking softly as they work. Should the owner of a territory encounter another shrew, it will squeak loudly, and this may be enough to make the intruder turn tail. If it does not do this, a squeaking match will take place, which will occasionally lead to a fight.

By the spring young shrews are fully grown and the sex organs develop to functional size. The males then abandon their territories to look for a mate. The females are receptive to the males for a very short time, and within 24 hours of pairing they will have parted again. Ovulation is stimulated by mating and by late April all females in a population will be pregnant. In the common shrew, the gestation period is about 3 weeks, at the end of which time a litter of about seven naked, blind, helpless young will be born each weighing about 0.5 g. In the pigmy shrew the gestation period is about the same, but the young weigh only 0.25 g at birth. Immediately after giving birth the female mates again, so that for much of the summer of her adult life a female shrew will be simultaneously pregnant and lactating. The strain of finding enough food for herself and the developing embryos, as well as providing milk for her family, is somewhat reduced in the common shrew, and probably in other species, by the ability of the nestlings to become cold and torpid for much of the time. In this way they use little energy, although they warm up and are ready to feed within minutes of their mother's return.

Young shrews are weaned within 22 days, by which time a new litter will have been born. However, they may remain with their mother for up to another 3 weeks, when they may accompany her on foraging expeditions. Occasionally a 'daisy chain' of young has been reported, each baby holding on to the tail of the one in front of it, but it is more usual for the family to keep together as a group. After the young have started to hunt for themselves, they venture on longer journeys and finally do not return home. Later in the summer, the female's receptiveness to the male decreases, her litters are smaller and are born at greater intervals. None the less, she may well have produced 30 young in the course of the summer. Her offspring will generally not be sexually mature until the next year, although a few females born in the first litter may breed the next September.

The prodigious increase in numbers which such fecundity implies does not in fact occur, and shrew populations do not reach plague proportions as may happen with some rodents. Doubtless the limitations of the food supply may partly explain this, but another reason is the short lifespan of shrews which never exceeds 15 months. Adult shrews which have survived the summer die in autumn. Juveniles which survive the winter are smaller than the adults and more uniform in colour. They can also be recognized by the hair on their feet and tails. In the autumn moult the body hair will grow longer, but there is no further growth on these extremities, which are practically bald by the time old age is reached.

Dead shrews are often found in autumn, mainly because their stink glands make them unpalatable to mammalian scavengers. In the summer many fall prey to domestic cats and dogs, although they are rarely eaten. Wild mammals avoid them but birds, which have no sense of smell, will sometimes take them, and the pellets of owls and the smaller birds of prey often contain the bones of shrews. Apart from this they have few enemies. They are not persecuted by Man, who does not regard them as pests, although he may make changes in their habitats which affect them adversely.

Shrews will almost certainly fight when they meet but much of the contest consists of bluff and squeaking and even when tail-biting occurs, no damage is done.

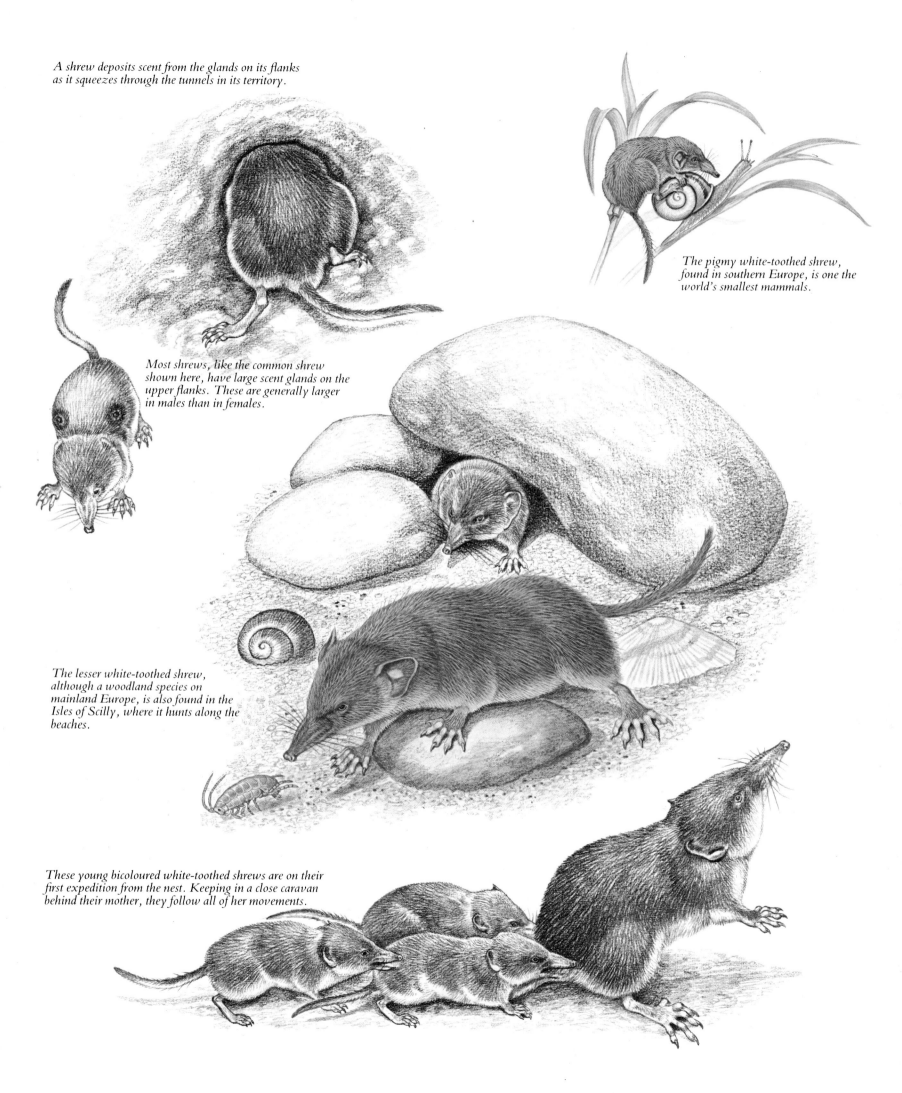

A shrew deposits scent from the glands on its flanks as it squeezes through the tunnels in its territory.

The pigmy white-toothed shrew, found in southern Europe, is one the world's smallest mammals.

Most shrews, like the common shrew shown here, have large scent glands on the upper flanks. These are generally larger in males than in females.

The lesser white-toothed shrew, although a woodland species on mainland Europe, is also found in the Isles of Scilly, where it hunts along the beaches.

These young bicoloured white-toothed shrews are on their first expedition from the nest. Keeping in a close caravan behind their mother, they follow all of her movements.

DESMANS
Family Talpidae

Desmans, which are aquatic relatives of the moles, are among the rarest of European mammals, as well as being among the strangest. There are two known species: the Russian desman *(Desmana moschata)*, which lives in slow-flowing rivers and lakes in the western parts of the Soviet Union; and the Pyrenean desman *(D. pyrenaicus)* which is found in the clear, tumbling trout reaches of Pyrenean streams, and in some rivers and canals in north-west Spain and northern Portugal. The latter species dislikes cold, and so is not found above 1,200 m. Nor is it found below about 300 m where the water becomes too silty. Like most insectivores, they lead solitary lives, marking their territorial boundaries with scent from musk glands below the tail.

Desmans are unmistakeable in appearance. Overall, they are thick set and short necked, but the face is drawn out into a remarkable long snout, which widens at the tip to accommodate the nostrils. The skin round these is naked, and is richly endowed with nerve endings. With their snouts desmans constantly explore their environment — twitching and sniffing to discover the whereabouts of food or possible danger. The eyes are small and vision plays an unimportant part in sensory detection, but the sense of hearing is probably quite keen. The fur is dense, with thick guard hairs which keep the animals dry. They swim using the large, webbed hind feet, and the somewhat flattened tail acts as a rudder. The Pyrenean desman is the smaller of the two species. It has about the same bulk as a mole, with a head and body length of up to 135 mm, which is doubled by the long tail. The Russian desman is about twice this size.

For most of the day, desmans remain in their den, which may be a crevice among rocks or a hole under tree roots, or they may make a short tunnel with an underwater entrance which leads upwards to a nesting chamber near the surface of the ground. Air filters into this through cracks in the ground and via the holes made by tree roots, but there is neither a bolt hole nor a passage through which air can enter the lair, for this might give their presence away to enemies. When desmans need to breathe, only the tip of the snout is pushed above the surface; below water, the nostrils are tightly closed by special valves. Occasionally they may leave the water and search for insects, but they are comparatively clumsy on land and do not stray far from the water's edge. Any surplus food will be taken to the lair and stored. Desmans hunt at night, searching with their sensitive snouts for any small water creatures, particularly those which live on stream beds. The enlarged incisor teeth can even deal with hard-shelled molluscs and crayfish. They are also reputed to eat some vegetable matter, although this may be obtained 'second hand' from the gut of their prey.

During the breeding season (late January or February), the males leave their territories to search for a mate. Groups of males and females may congregate, and courtship chases take place in the water, usually round a submerged tree stump or boulder. The gestation period is about 6 weeks in the Russian desman, but may be less in the Pyrenean species. Up to five young are born. At first naked, blind and helpless, they grow quickly and are weaned within a month, after which they soon set out to lead a solitary life.

Although there have been schemes to transfer Russian desmans to other parts of the Soviet Union, for they are valued as fur-bearing animals, the Pyrenean desman has little importance to Man. Yet it is not safe even in the remote areas in which it lives, for pollution and the alteration of river systems to produce hydroelectric power have taken their toll of its habitats. We know from fossil evidence that desmans were once much more widespread, but their prospects for regaining lost ground seem, for the moment, to be dim.

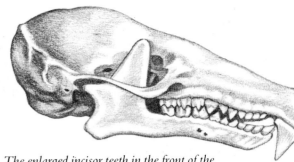

The enlarged incisor teeth in the front of the desman's jaws enable it to deal with hard-shelled. prey.

The broad, sensitive tip of the desman's muzzle informs it, by smell and touch, of the world about it.

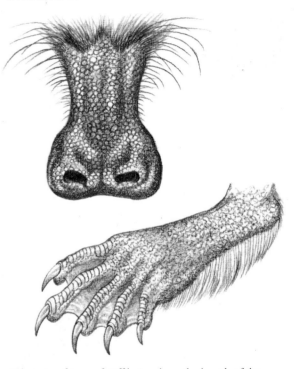

There is a fringe of stiff hairs along the length of the webbed hind foot which makes it a more efficient paddle for swimming.

A desman's lair may have an underwater entrance, with a tunnel sloping up to the sleeping chamber. Air filters to the resting animal through holes made by tree roots.

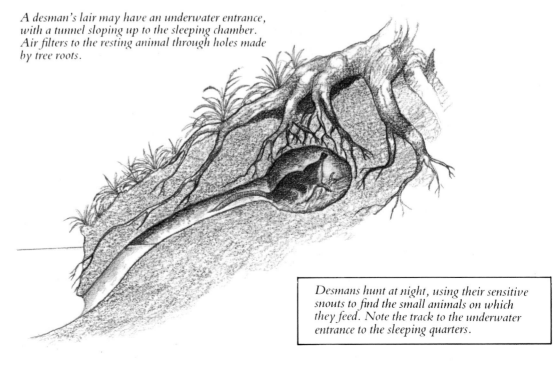

Desmans hunt at night, using their sensitive snouts to find the small animals on which they feed. Note the track to the underwater entrance to the sleeping quarters.

MOLES
Family Talpidae

Many vertebrate animals rely on earthworms and other soil invertebrates for a large proportion of their food, but none is as dependent on them as the moles. These voracious hunters do not attack their small prey from the surface but follow it underground, venturing into the open air only rarely, being poorly equipped to deal with its dangers when they do so. Nevertheless, moles are highly successful predators found within a wide range of environments in Britain and Europe.

Small but stoutly built, moles have strongly muscular shoulders which disguise the neck, giving the body a cylindrical shape overall. The heavy forelimbs are twisted, so that they may be used most effectively when digging, although this means that when walking, moles place only the inner edge of their forelimbs on the ground, leaving a very characteristic footprint. The front paws are huge, when compared with the size of the animal, and their width is increased by a bone which arises from the wrist and is, in effect, an extra finger. Some moles are totally blind, while others can only distinguish different intensities of bright light. All have fine, velvety fur. Although the ears are not visible, moles are capable of hearing quite well. The tactile senses are particularly well developed. Special cells at the end of the hairless pink snout enhance the sense of touch, which probably helps to detect and catch prey. The tail is normally carried erect when the animals are active and it is probable that the hairs on the tip, which brush against the roof of the moles' tunnels, give information about their surroundings.

There are three species of mole in Europe. The smallest is the blind mole (*Talpa caeca*), with a head and body length of between 100 and 130 mm and a hind foot length (without the claws) of less than 17.5 mm. The eyes are totally closed by a membrane, preventing even rudimentary sight. It is found in Spain, southern France, northern Italy, Albania, Yugoslavia and Greece, but does not occur on any of the Mediterranean islands. The Roman mole (*T. romana*), another sightless species, may occur alongside the blind mole in Greece, but it is otherwise found only in southern Italy and some of the major islands of the Mediterranean. It is larger than the blind mole, with a head and body length of over 130 mm and a hind foot length of over 17.5 mm. The northern mole (*Talpa europaea*) is the most widespread. It is found from southern Sweden to northern Italy, and eastwards into Asia. Although it occurs on mainland Britain, it is not found in Ireland or most of the Scottish islands. It has small but functional eyes, and a head and body length of between 120 and 150 mm. All three species of mole are very similar in their habits and ways of life.

Although moles spend most of their lives underground and are rarely seen, they leave evidence of their presence, especially in open country, where little tumps of freshly excavated earth show the pattern of their recent excavations. Occasionally a larger heap may be found. This is the mole's fortress, which may contain a network of tunnels, a nest and a food store.

The front paws are covered with very tough skin and are used for digging. The skeleton of the forelimb shows how an extra bone (the radial sesamoid) grows from the wrist and enlarges the width of the hand.

The mole's skull is about 35mm long, with 44 teeth in the jaws.

A cartilage, which extends from the front of the skull, supports the pointed snout.

In order to drink in dry summer weather, moles may have to leave their tunnels to find dew drops on surface vegetation. At such a time they are in great danger from hunting owls.

Moles usually only construct a fortress in damp places, where underground nests are likely to be flooded. There are three kinds of tunnel. The most superficial is an open furrow on the surface of the ground, made when hunting for worms or grubs living in the upper layers of the soil. Others are made just below the surface and throw up a ridge of soil, easily visible for the whole of their length. A third type is made completely below ground, down to a depth of about 70 cm. The surface runs and tunnels tend to be abandoned quickly, but the deeper runs may survive to be used by successive generations of moles. Where there is no fortress visible, the nest will be made in an enlargement of the deep tunnel.

Tunnels conceal moles from most predators, making them some of the best protected of small mammals in their environment. Moles appear to have three main periods of activity and three periods of rest within 24 hours. It would seem that individuals living near each other are often active at slightly different times, which may allow for some sharing of the tunnels. During their active periods, moles will patrol their tunnel system, picking up worms or insect grubs. Worms form the major part of the diet in winter, but in the summer, when they retreat to lower levels in the soil, insects are taken, along with centipedes, millipedes and molluscs.

Moles have huge appetites and each day they must consume about half their own body weight in food. The difficulty of capturing so much food at all times of the year is to some extent overcome by their habit of storing any surplus food, particularly worms. These are bitten near the head, immobilizing them until required.

Moles use their forefeet to enlarge and repair their burrows. They brace themselves with their hind feet and one forefoot against the side walls of the tunnel, and with the other forefoot scrape at the earth in front of them, probably alternating forefeet after a few strokes. The loosened earth is pushed back under the body and scraped away to the rear by the hind feet, although some of it is consolidated against the side walls of the tunnel. When enough loose material has accumulated, the animal turns round and, with one broad paw in front of its nose, pushes the soil ahead to an opening at the surface, where it is forced out to form a molehill. Moles are fiercely territorial and will attack any other individuals in their domain.

Moles' sex organs regress after the breeding period, but in late winter and early spring they develop to functional size and for a short time males and females pair for mating. Little is known of how a mate is found, or if there is any courtship. Mating has been observed only rarely, for it normally takes place underground. Gestation lasts for 4 weeks, and the young are born in mid-April in a nest furnished with dry grass and dead leaves. Up to seven young have been recorded, but four is the usual number.

At birth the young weigh 3.5 g and measure 35 mm in length. Their early development is very rapid, and they are covered with fur by the seventeenth day, although their eyes do not open until they are 22 days old, by which time they are very nearly fully grown. In spite of this, they continue to be suckled until they are about a month old and remain with their mother for 2-3 weeks after this, although they start to make forays for themselves during this time. The body temperature of baby moles drops while their mother is away from the nest on her frequent feeding trips. This enables them to save energy and presumably prevents too great a drain on the resources of their mother, who at this stage must find it difficult to provide sufficient food to maintain herself as well as her growing family. Young moles that survive their first winter breed during the next spring. They may survive for another 4 years, but they are not believed to be very long-lived animals.

Moles come to the surface for a number of reasons. Juveniles may do so because they are harassed if they try to use the tunnels of established moles. The search for food, which may occasionally take them into the light, and the search for nest lining, have also been observed on several occasions. Moles are reported to push their head and shoulders from the ground and probe about for a leaf or a piece of grass which is quickly pulled back into the hole. This is repeated a number of times until they have enough material to line their resting or breeding chamber. Moles may also be forced into the open in times of flood when their tunnels become waterlogged.

Above ground, moles fall victim to many predators, particularly owls and herons, and even underground they are not always safe from foxes and dogs. However, humans are undoubtedly their greatest enemy. Farmers destroy large numbers because molehills can damage agricultural machinery and the moles' excavations can reduce the fertility of the soil by bringing subsoil to the surface. Even so, the reservoirs of moles in undisturbed woodland mean that they are in no danger of disappearing from the European countryside.

Cross-section of a mole's fortress, containing a nest and young.

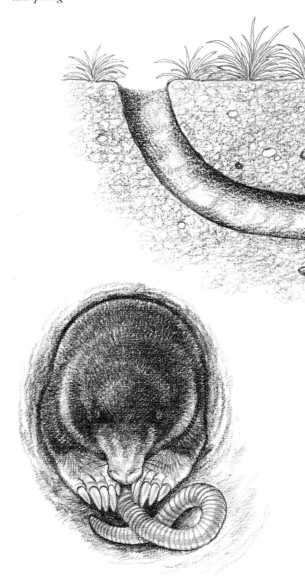

A captive worm is held down firmly by the mole's front feet both to control it, and to squeeze out much of the soil it contains before it is eaten.

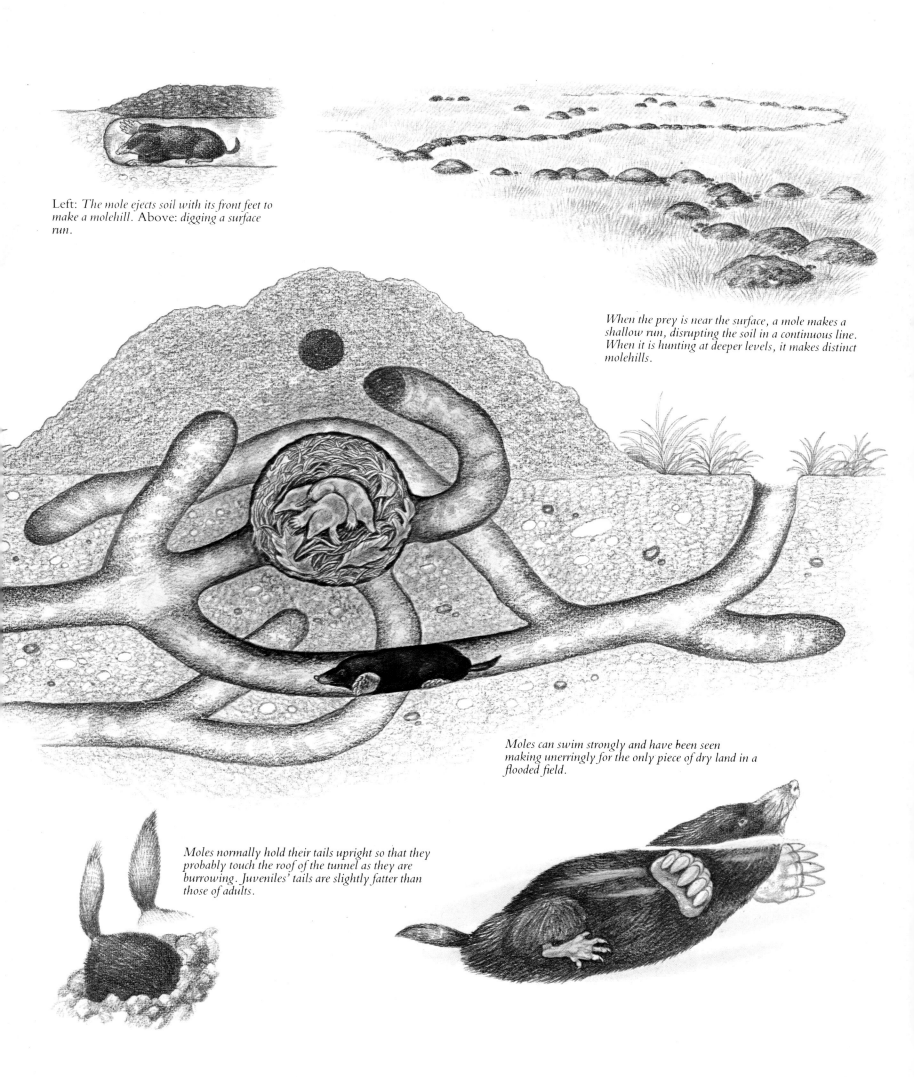

Left: *The mole ejects soil with its front feet to make a molehill. Above: digging a surface run.*

When the prey is near the surface, a mole makes a shallow run, disrupting the soil in a continuous line. When it is hunting at deeper levels, it makes distinct molehills.

Moles can swim strongly and have been seen making unerringly for the only piece of dry land in a flooded field.

Moles normally hold their tails upright so that they probably touch the roof of the tunnel as they are burrowing. Juveniles' tails are slightly fatter than those of adults.

BATS

Order Chiroptera

Although many mammals are capable of becoming airborne in extended, gliding leaps, only bats are capable of true or flapping flight comparable to that of insects or birds. This ability has enabled them to occupy a large number of niches in tropical and temperate environments. A gauge of their success is the large number of species of bats, which account for over 20 per cent of all known mammals. Their diet includes insects, fruit, nectar, blood and fish. In Europe, where the treeless north is a hostile environment for bats, there are 33 species, making up about 16 per cent of the total mammal fauna of the continent.

Europe's bats are all insectivores and belong to three families — Molossidae, Rhinolophidae and Vespertilionidae. The Molossidae is a group found mainly in the tropics, but one species, the free-tailed bat (*Tadarida teniotis*), occurs in southern Europe. It is a large bat easily recognized by its long tail which projects beyond the wing membrane.

The five species of horseshoe bats belong to the family Rhinolophidae. They can be recognized at close quarters by the flaps of skin around the face which have the function of focusing the navigational ultrasonic squeaks which they emit through the nose. At rest they can be distinguished from other groups because they hang free from projections in a roof, wrapping their wings round the body, so that they are enfolded in a cloak of skin. Perhaps because this wing posture leads to the possibility of greater heat and water loss than that of other bats, horseshoe bats tend to hibernate in caves and be highly intolerant of temperature change and water loss during the winter. They also differ from other bats in details of the skull and skeleton, physiology and behaviour.

The third and largest group of European bats belong to the family Vespertilionidae, the smooth-faced or evening bats. Their faces, which are almost dog-like, carry no flaps of skin. The ears are generally large and have an inner appendage, the tragus, which stands erect in front of the main part of the ear. Its size and shape are important for identification. At rest, smooth-faced bats generally hang against a wall, with wings close against their sides, so that the furry body is visible. Some hibernate in caves, while others are tree bats, roosting and hibernating in tight clusters in holes in trees. Within this family,

Myotis bats have medium-sized ears with long, pointed traguses. The noctules have rounded ears and short, rounded traguses. Pipistrelles, which have similar ears to noctules, are small bats with a tail membrane extending outside a supporting spur of cartilage (the calcar) which is attached to the ankle. Long-eared bats are easily recognized by their outsized ears which are folded back when they are at rest, although the long, pointed traguses remain erect.

Although all of these bats are insect eaters and catch their prey in flight, they do not compete with swallows, martins or swifts — which are also aerial feeders — because these birds are diurnal hunters and utilize day-flying insects, while bats, which may compete to some extent with nightjars, fly and feed at night. Within their nocturnal environment, bats seem to have carved the ecological cake into very small slices, since there are more than twice the number of species of bats than there are of swallows or swifts. In autumn and winter, when the supply of insects falls greatly, most insectivorous birds migrate to places where they can continue to find an assured food supply. Although some bats migrate for quite long distances — mouse-eared bats from Poland regularly flying to spend the winter in Italy for example—in general, bats survive the winter by hibernating.

Like birds, bats fly with wings which give power and lift. Both groups use their forelimbs, which have been transformed for this function, but here the similarity ends. A bat's wing is mainly supported by the long forearm and first finger bones, and further strengthened by the bones of the other fingers to which it is also attached. In most bats a small triangle of wing membrane runs from the wrist up to the neck, and the trailing edge instead of being free — as in birds — is attached to the ankle, and from there on is supported by the calcar to enclose the tail (although there are some species of free-tailed bats). This means that the hindlimbs are also involved in flight and have to be spread to maintain the necessary tension of the flying membrane. To facilitate this, the femur has, in effect, swivelled, so that at rest a bat's knee joint does not fold under the body, but faces upwards and alongside it. These adaptations make bats clumsy, though not helpless, when on the ground. The thumbs, which are free and clawed, help the smooth-faced bats to obtain a hold when roosting, or to hang

head upwards so that they can defecate or give birth.

The wing membrane is made of a double layer of very fine skin which in some small species is only 0.03 mm thick. It encloses muscles, nerves, blood vessels and also many elastic fibres which have the effect of ruching or pleating the membrane when the wing is folded, so that a resting bat does not have great loops of wing to impede its movements. In spite of its apparent fragility, the membrane is surprisingly strong and has a number of uses other than flight. A tropical fruit bat may use it to cradle a fruit as large as a mango, which it cannot manipulate with its mouth. European bats may use it like a hand to 'field' an insect in flight, and bring it to the mouth. Horseshoe bats use the part of the wing nearest the body to hold an intransigent insect, while smooth-faced bats make a pouch of the membrane which is brought up hard against the abdomen. They can hold even a large beetle with a surprising amount of strength, until they reach a roosting place where they kill and eat it. If the wing is torn a bat can still fly, unless the injury is very severe, and the membrane repairs itself in a few days.

Bat flight, which is often described as fluttering, is slow when compared to that of birds. The highest speed recorded is 64 km per hour, and among European bats half this speed is normal. However, they can hover and fly with great accuracy, moving through restricted spaces, by minute changes in the shape and camber of the wing. In order to be able to do this, bats use a far greater number of muscles in flight than do birds: The flying muscles, which account for about 12 per cent of a bat's total body weight, are attached to a skeleton modified to give them sufficient anchorage.

Although all bats fly at night, most have characteristic patterns of activity. Some fly intermittently throughout the night, while others often spend a relatively short time hunting early in the evening and again just before dawn to provide enough food for the rest of the day. Most have a definite territory over which they hunt. Each species tends to have its individual pattern of flight. Horseshoe bats usually fly fairly slowly, and may glide between wingbeats, although the lesser horseshoe bat's flight includes many erratic turns. Noctules fly higher and faster than most other European species, and they may dive spectacularly

after a large beetle or moth. The pond bat *(Myotis dasycneme)* and Daubenton's bat *(M. daubentoni)* usually hunt near water, while the long-eared bats hover close to foliage, picking off insects or spiders. Observation of flight pattern cannot give positive identification of a species. It is necessary to examine the bat more closely or to use a bat detector which picks up the ultrasonic sounds characteristic of each species.

Beetles and moths are the major prey of bats, but other insects may be of local importance. It is difficult to tell what a particular bat has eaten by analysing faecal remains because, although the chitinous skeletons of the insects are hardly touched by the digestive system, the bats' sharp, pointed teeth crunch them so small that they are unrecognizable. Some bats, especially small species, feed on very small insects. Bats have been killed with several of these in their mouths, and it is possible that they merely fly through swarms of, for example, midges, trapping them as they go. In general, however, bats pursue larger prey, and this can sometimes be identified as it is carried to the feeding roost, where the hard wings and legs are discarded and only the soft bodies are eaten. Piles of these rejected fragments can indicate the major part of some bats' foods and show the importance of bats in controlling the number of insects.

For centuries Man has puzzled over the bats' ability to navigate and find their prey in the dark. The answer is not to be found in their proverbially poor sight — they cannot distinguish potential food until they are within 3 or 4 cm of it. Early workers suggested that their ears, which are always large and complex, helped them to avoid obstacles at night, but this idea was rejected because nobody could understand how any animal could hear the presence of inanimate objects. It was not until instruments were devised which enabled us to detect sounds of a pitch higher than can be heard by the human ear (ultrasonic sounds) that the answer to the bats' success in navigation and hunting was revealed, for they use a form of sonar like that developed during the First World War to track enemy submarines.

Foraging bats emit a series of high-pitched sounds, of very short duration, at a rate of 4–5 per second, the actual sound and its pitch varying with the species. This is known as the search phase of the hunt. Occasionally the rate of squeaks rises to 200 per second, which is called the approach and terminal phase. This increase occurs when the bats approach an obstruction, which may be a static part of the environment, such as a tree, or an insect in flight.

These squeaks are of a lower frequency than during the search phase, and although each one lasts for only about 0.005 seconds, it changes pitch during this time. Bats decide the position of an object in their path by the echoes of the sounds emitted. The change in pitch allows them to gauge whether the echo is coming from a static or a moving object and, if the latter, in which direction it is travelling. The nearer the object the more vital it is for the bats to be aware of it, and so the greater the number of squeaks emitted. Sound travels at 340 m per second. During the search phase, bats fly about 3 m between squeaks, but while closing in on an insect they fly only about 7.5 cm between squeaks, giving the prey little chance of escape. Very high-pitched sounds die away quickly, so the bats are not confused by echoes from distant objects.

Some moths are capable of detecting ultrasonic sound and may escape by means of a diving zig-zag flight or, in some instances, they can reply with clicking noises which have the effect of jamming the bats' system. Many night-flying beetles can produce high-pitched squeaks and it is possible that they use these to foil bats. Unpalatable insects are rejected by bats in captivity. These are unlikely to be detected by the bats' poor sense of smell, but it has been observed that many distasteful beetles have iridescent bodies which may affect the quality of the echo and warn the bat that pursuit is not worthwhile. In spite of these devices moths and beetles play an important part in the diet of bats. Bats also

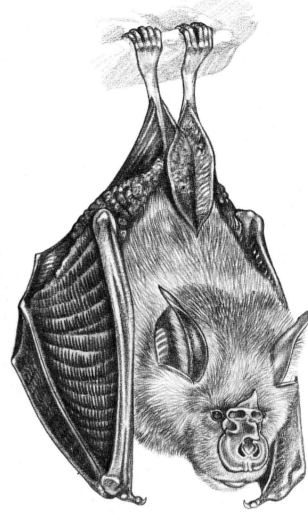

Horseshoe bats, like the lesser horseshoe (above), *hang free from a projection in a cave roof. When they are at rest they wrap their wings entirely round themselves.* Below: *head of Mediterranean horseshoe bat.*

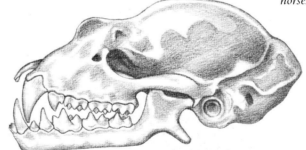

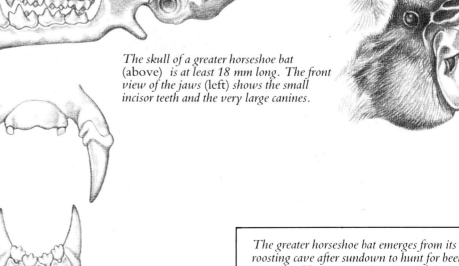

The skull of a greater horseshoe bat (above) *is at least 18 mm long. The front view of the jaws* (left) *shows the small incisor teeth and the very large canines.*

The greater horseshoe bat emerges from its roosting cave after sundown to hunt for beetles or moths. Here one uses its wing to bring an angle shades moth towards its mouth. A baby clings to the false nipple in its mother's groin.

use echo location to build up a sound picture of their surroundings which will be remembered when they are flying in the same area again although it may be at a much later time.

As a method of locomotion, flight requires a great expenditure of energy and needs a large amount of high-quality food to fuel it. Studies in Finland, where it is light enough to watch bats during their evening hunting, have shown that the hunting territory of individual bats increased as autumn approached, suggesting that they found it more difficult to find food as the season wore on. In winter, the food supply of insectivorous bats falls almost to zero over

much of Europe. This problem is overcome by hibernation, a condition to which bats seemed predisposed as, even in summer, a resting bat economizes on energy expenditure by becoming torpid — its temperature drops to near that of its surroundings and its bodily functions are reduced.

Bats cannot make protective nests for themselves, like hibernating hedgehogs and dormice, and so they must find places where they are sheltered from harsh weather. The most usual places are caves (or their man-made equivalents, mines or cellars), or holes in trees. Bats are sometimes referred to as cave bats or tree bats because different species show a preference for a particular hibernating place. Because trees give less protection than caves, tree bats often hang together in dense groups to obtain some mutual warmth. In caves, horseshoe bats hang from projections in the roof. Studies have shown that, within the same cave system, the Daubenton's bat preferred to tuck itself into narrow crevices and did not mind if it was in a horizontal

position, while the whiskered bat *(Myotis mystacinus)* and the Natterer's bat *(M. nattereri)* always chose a position in which they could remain vertical against a wall.

Many hibernating bats wake briefly and move about, some travelling several kilometres. The energy expenditure of a fully active bat is so high, with a heartbeat of over 800 per minute and a breathing rate of over 550 per minute, that there must be some advantage to make them undertake such activity. It is possible that bats start to hibernate in places where the temperature is most favourable to their own temperature drop. Later such a place, for example the entrance to a cave, would be too cold so they retreat into the depths of the cave where it is warmer. Moisture loss may also be important, especially in horseshoe bats, whose enveloping wings can cause greater desiccation than in smooth-faced bats. They have been observed to wake up, lick a few drops of water and return to full torpor. Tree bats are able to withstand greater water loss than cave bats.

Towards the end of the summer bats increase in weight, putting on considerable growth of brown fat, a tissue which gives rapid heat production. This is gradually used up during the winter months and a slow weight loss occurs during hibernation. Bats wake and become active again when the temperature rises in spring, although this may be partly triggered by physiological changes, such as the depletion of fat reserves or the accumulation of urea in the system. Awakening starts with a sudden increase in the rate of heartbeat, and within an hour the bat can fly and hunt again. The hibernating roosts are

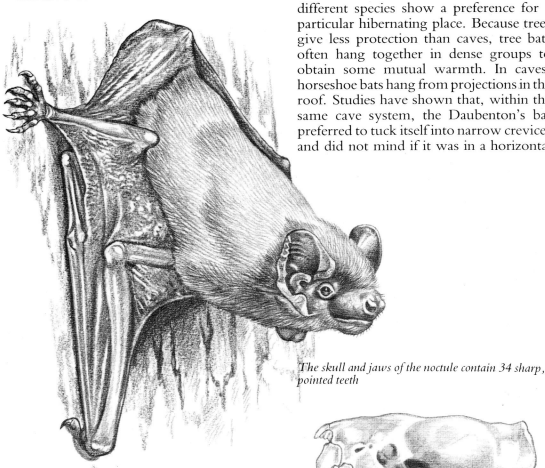

When at rest noctules and other smooth-faced bats hang against a vertical surface with their wings folded at their sides. This one is just preparing to fly and is testing the air for any echoes which might indicate obstructions.

The skull and jaws of the noctule contain 34 sharp, pointed teeth

The long-eared bat has larger ears than any other European species. At rest they are tucked back, leaving the pointed tragus standing up.

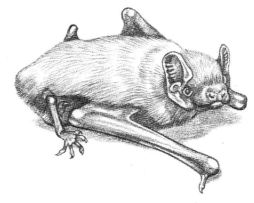

On the ground a bat, such as this noctule, can scuttle rapidly, its wings folded out of the way. A healthy bat can take flight from a horizontal surface.

One of the commonest tree-roosting bats, the noctule (right) has a wingspan of about 35cm. The entrance to a hollow tree where bats roost is usually stained with their droppings. The long-eared bat (left) often hovers to pick insects off foliage.

abandoned; the females depart to breeding sites, often in old buildings, and the males scatter to roost singly or in small groups.

Bats differ from most other mammals in many features of their reproductive lives. Most European species do not have an elaborate courtship. Mating is promiscuous with little or no prenuptial ceremony. A very unusual feature is that sperm formed in the autumn does not fertilize the ovum until the spring. Horseshoe bats mate in autumn and the sperm is stored in the female throughout the winter, for ovulation does not take place until the next year. Sperm storage also takes place among smooth-faced bats, but in these species it is often stored in the male's body through the winter, for mating has been observed during periods of waking from hibernation.

In either case, the development of the embryos does not start until the females resume their active life after hibernation, and is probably triggered by an increase in the ambient temperature and food supply. Even then gestation may be extended by low temperatures and shortage of food. Foetal development is slow, and even with uninterrupted growth, the gestation period for a pipistrelle is 44 days, and for the larger species longer still. The young of most European bats are born in midsummer. British bats produce only one offspring, although females of the same species in continental Europe normally produce twins. Baby bats are usually born during the day, the female hanging head uppermost and catching the baby in the pouch made by the interfemoral membrane. They are very large at birth, often weighing one third of their mother's body weight. Bright pink in colour, and with closed eyes, they have outsized feet and drooping ears.

Although part of a huge nursery colony, the mother will only care for her own offspring, at first carrying it when she leaves the roost. Horseshoe bats have a pair of false nipples in the groin, which the baby grips in flight. Smooth-faced bats do not have these and the young have to cling on as best they can, head uppermost, unlike horseshoe bats which are carried tail forwards. Both mothers and young tend to be noisy and a nursery roost, full of chattering, squeaking bats, can easily be heard by human ears. Bats that roost and breed in trees, such as the noctules, can often be detected by the noise coming from a hole in a tree and also by their dark-coloured droppings which may stain the edge of the hole.

In a short time the baby is too heavy for the mother to carry on her hunting expeditions, and so it is left in the nursery. It is likely that each female has her own place within the roost, where she leaves her young. If they stray she may recognize them by the calls they make, and she will then check that she has approached the right one by smelling it — the scent glands are well developed in many insectivorous bats.

The young are weaned by the time they are 3 to 4 weeks old and are capable of independent flight. Their first flights are taken when insect populations are at their highest so that, even if they are not very proficient at first, they have time to build up experience, expertise and resources before winter comes. Many young bats go into hibernation weighing less than adults, and it is these that are likely to die from depletion of their resources if they wake up too often in the winter or if, as occurs in some areas, they are disturbed by human cavers or those studying bats.

In a few species, young females born in June are sexually mature before their first winter and may produce their first baby the next summer. In most cases maturity is delayed by at least another year, however, and some females are not ready to breed until their third winter.

If a young bat survives its first winter, it is likely to have a long life ahead of it. Although a pipistrelle is no bigger than a shrew in body size, it will probably survive 10 years, and it is known that some European bats have lived for twice this length of time. The reason for this could be the bats' long periods of torpidity, not only in winter but also when resting during summer. It has been shown that bats kept at artificially low temperatures have a longer life span than those allowed to be normally active.

The pattern of reproduction and life span of bats have been discovered largely through bat banding schemes. Banding is

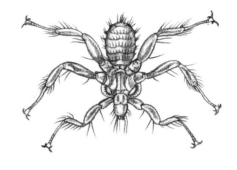

The nycteribiids — 5 mm-long, blood sucking, wingless flies — are parasitic on bats. They run nimbly through the bat's fur to escape its tongue and claws when it is grooming.

The roosts of rare species of bat are sometimes protected by a grille, which allows the bats to enter but prevents inquisitive humans from doing so.

There is a great variety in the appearance of bats' faces and ears:

a Bechstein's bat has long ears, placed far apart.
b The northern bat has small, rounded ears, with a small tragus.
c The long-eared bat has very long ears which meet on the top of the head.
d The barbastelle has fairly short ears, which join on the top of the head, and the face has a snub-nosed look.
e Schreiber's bat is another very short-faced species; its small ears have upstanding hair between them.
f The greater horseshoe bat carries complex lobes of skin called a 'nose leaf' on the face.
g The free-tailed bat has a long muzzle and forward-pointing ears.

The free-tailed bat's tail extends well beyond the tail membrane. It is found only in southern Europe and most of its relatives live in the tropics.

33

similar to the ringing of wild birds but the numbered band, which is recorded together with details of the species, sex, age and position in the cave, is placed on the forearm rather than the leg. In the past many of these bands were badly applied and damaged the bats' wings. Worse still, they were usually put on during winter hibernation when the bats were easy to catch. This disturbance caused them to wake and use resources that they could not afford to squander, and so many young bats died as a direct result of handling. Today this practice is much more strictly controlled and disturbance is kept to a minimum.

The low reproduction rate of bats is typical of a long-lived animal, for if populations are to remain stable each female only has to produce enough offspring to replace herself and her mates. Bats have few natural enemies. Birds of prey and owls may take a few, but on the whole they are immune from the normal predators. Most bats carry some parasites, including large, blood-sucking, wingless flies, but they are rarely numerous enough to cause death.

Humans are the chief enemies of bats. Bat numbers can achieve pest proportions, but in Europe this is only likely where their droppings become excessive and attract scavengers. In some countries bats are known to carry diseases, including rabies, but no European bat has been implicated in the spread of this disease. None the less, Man has reduced the number of bats in recent years to the extent that several species are in danger of local extinction. This reduction is largely accidental, resulting from the demolition of old buildings which have been traditional bat roosts, and the building of new ones with no places for bats, and from changes in agricultural methods which leave little room for wildlife.

The most damaging effects have been caused by the extensive use of insecticides. In some places these have reduced the insect populations to such an extent that far fewer bats can be supported. Some pesticides can be taken in sub-lethal doses by insects, but are then passed on and accumulate in the bats' tissues until a lethal level is reached. The effect of a reduction in population in slow-breeding animals like bats can be very long lasting. Although most insecticides with long-lasting activity are now used with great caution throughout most of Europe, bat populations are still falling in many places.

In some European countries bats have been protected animals for many years. In Britain, the protection which was originally given only to the greater horseshoe and the mouse-eared bats has now been extended to all species of bat. Known bat roosts in caves and tunnels are sometimes protected with specially designed grilles which allow free access of the species of bat which inhabit the area, but which exclude the main danger — the interested but often harmful human. Bat boxes have been used in some places to give the bats suitable winter and breeding roosts. These are similar to the nest boxes put up for titmice, but with a slit-like entrance in the bottom.

Through a better understanding of the lives and needs of bats it may be possible to stabilize, or even increase, the numbers of these animals which are, in almost all cases, completely harmless.

The site of a bat's roost is often indicated by droppings, and the inedible wings of moths and other insects.

Most bats drink by licking drops of water from leaves or walls, but the pond bat can scoop up a mouthful as it flies over a lake or stream.

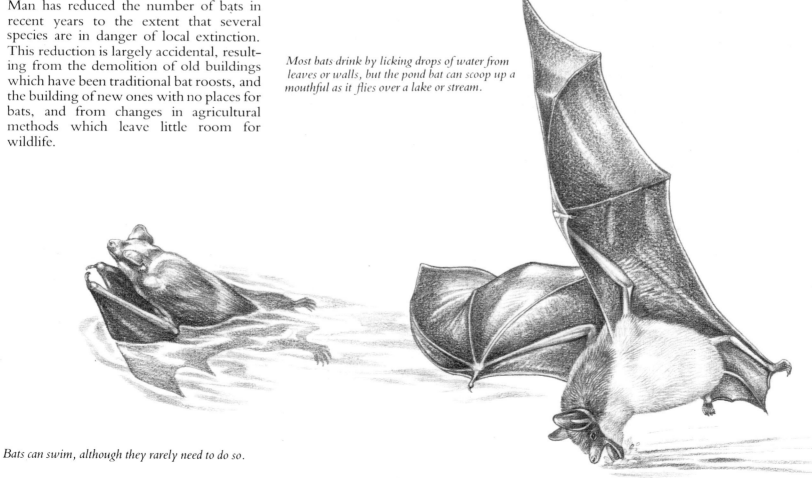

Bats can swim, although they rarely need to do so.

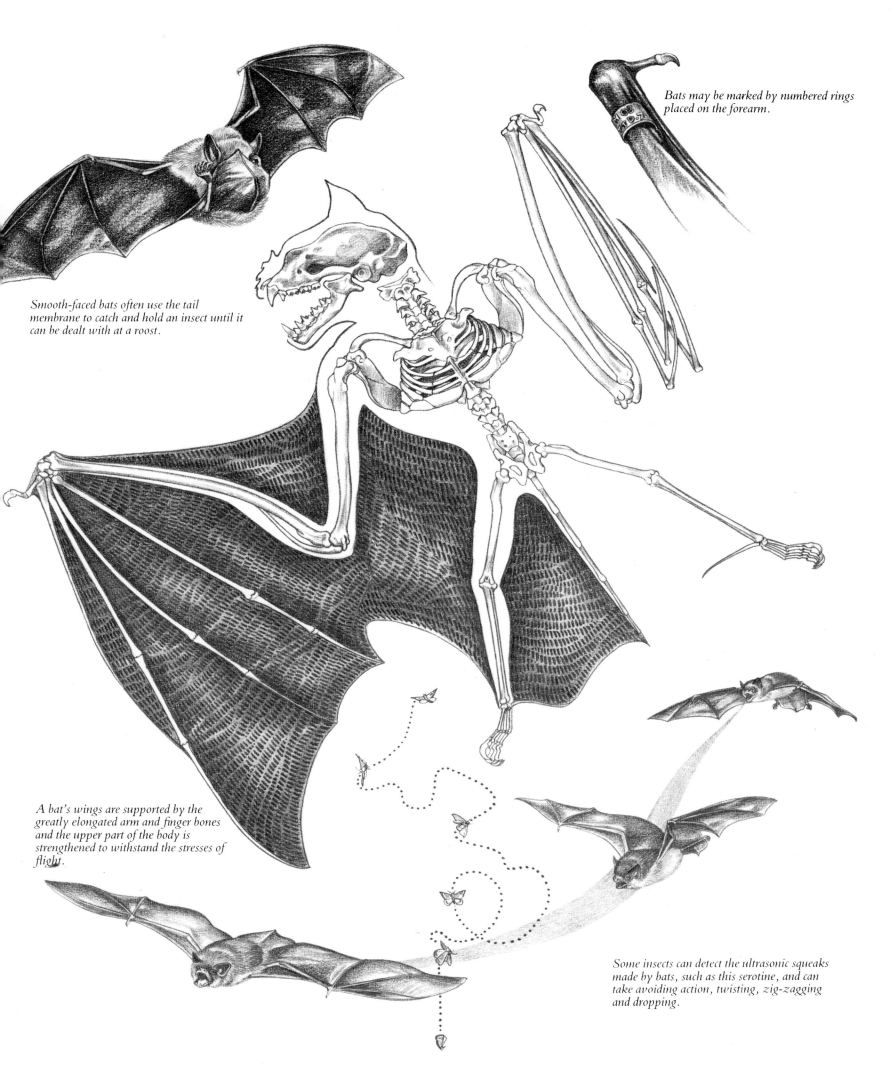

Bats may be marked by numbered rings placed on the forearm.

Smooth-faced bats often use the tail membrane to catch and hold an insect until it can be dealt with at a roost.

A bat's wings are supported by the greatly elongated arm and finger bones and the upper part of the body is strengthened to withstand the stresses of flight.

Some insects can detect the ultrasonic squeaks made by bats, such as this serotine, and can take avoiding action, twisting, zig-zagging and dropping.

RABBIT AND HARES
Family Leporidae

Rabbits and hares are among the most familiar of wild animals, not only because of their size but also because they tend to inhabit open country and so are easily observed — the more so since they are often active during the day. Their compact bodies with long hind legs, and round heads with long ears, make them unlike any other European mammals, and even in uncertain light their hopping movements distinguish them from other animals.

Rabbits and hares are gnawing animals, and because of this they have some features in common with rodents. However, there are also some basic differences, which are present in even their oldest known fossil ancestors, dating back at least 45 million years, which have led zoologists to classify them in a separate order of mammals, the Lagomorpha. One important difference is to be found in the teeth. At first sight these appear similar, for both rodents and lagomorphs have gnawing incisors in the front of the mouth in the upper and lower jaws, followed by a long, toothless gap called the diastema, behind which lie grinding premolars and molars. However, a rabbit or hare has a second, smaller pair of teeth tucked behind the large first upper incisors. These teeth have a complete covering of enamel, thicker on the front than the back, and are open rooted and so continue to grow throughout the life of the animal. Growth is kept in check by the teeth being worn down as they chop tough and often abrasive food against the incisors in the opposite jaw. Normally tooth wear proceeds at a speed consistent with tooth growth and, since it is very rare for anything to upset this pattern, it is an excellent mechanism for maintaining very sharp teeth. However, should the incisors not meet as the animal gnaws — perhaps due to some injury — they continue to grow, and soon become unusable, curving tusks which prevent normal feeding and cause the death of the animal.

Although the Lagomorpha is a small order (including only rabbits, hares and pikas, which are small mountain dwellers from north-east Asia and North America)

it is a very successful one, comprising a great number of individuals. One habit which perhaps accounts for their successful existence in areas where food is not abundant, and their proliferation where it is, is refection. Described as a form of cud-chewing, it differs in that the food is chewed before being swallowed and then passes right through the digestive system. However, at certain times of the day soft, mucus-covered droppings are formed. These are not allowed to fall to the ground, but are taken directly from the anus and swallowed without further chewing, to undergo the process of digestion once more, after which small, hard, dry droppings are formed. This habit enables rabbits and hares to use their food more completely, for B vitamins which are formed in the large intestine cannot be digested there but are absorbed in the upper, small intestine during the second passage through the system. It has been shown experimentally that up to 80 per cent of their food is refected. The main period of refection is in the middle of the day when rabbits are lying up in their burrows, with another shorter period around midnight after the evening feed has been digested.

Rabbits are proverbially fast and successful breeders, yet their reproductive pattern is as limited as that of most other animals, with the majority of the young being born in the first half of the year. Hares have a longer breeding season and, like rabbits, they are comparatively defenceless and are preyed on by many enemies, but their high breeding rate gives the species a chance of survival. Male rabbits are sexually active from mid-winter onwards and mating may take place then, although the females are not at that time capable of becoming pregnant. Their sex organs develop about mid-January, and from then on mating stimulates ovulation, so that young are almost bound to be conceived as a result. In spite of this, the number of litters produced is not quite as large as might be expected, for a high proportion of the embryos break down in the uterus and are resorbed into the mother's tissues, for reasons which are not clear, but it may be related to the number of ova fertilized — very large or very small litters being resorbed in this way. Also, dominant does lose fewer litters than lower ranking females. It has been estimated that in rabbits 60 per cent of the young conceived are lost

in this way. Shortly after a litter is resorbed, the female comes into season once more and will mate again, probably on this occasion producing five or six ova which will allow her to bring a normal-sized litter to term, and she will probably rear 10 to 12 young in the course of the summer. Since these young will be capable of breeding within about 3 months of being born it is easy to see that rabbit populations can withstand the enmity of a great many predators, including Man, without being seriously reduced in numbers for very long.

In spite of this, no animal wishes to be a meal for any other creature, and rabbits and hares are well able to detect possible danger by means of their large eyes and acute hearing. Their sense of smell is also very good. A rabbit or hare testing the air for the scent of possible enemies uncovers special sensory pads which normally lie under the nose flaps and these can inform it that danger is at hand.

The European rabbit *(Oryctolagus cuniculus)*, which is among the most familiar of animals in western Europe, owes its spread — which has taken it as far north as southern Scandinavia, as far east as Poland, Hungary and the Ukraine and beyond the bounds of Europe to Australia, New Zealand and Chile — almost entirely to human intervention. It is fairly certain that the original home of the rabbit was Spain and Portugal and that, like the Pyrenean desman, it was an uncommon creature before the Romans took it about their empire as a convenient source of meat and fur. Even so, it did not reach Britain until Norman times and did not escape from close captivity to become a common animal of the English countryside until the time of Queen Elizabeth the First. It is surprising that an animal originally adapted to the hot, dry Iberian climate should thrive so well in the cold and wet of northern Europe. The reason is probably that it is a burrower, and so is protected against the elements. Even so, it dislikes being wet, and shakes itself frequently if rain falls while it is feeding.

Rabbits are gregarious animals, preferring to live in grassland areas where the soil allows them to make extensive, well-drained burrows, but where there are hedges or patches of woodland to give shelter and cover. Within any warren there is a central area occupied by dominant bucks (males) and does (females). The territories

here are marked by scent from glands under the chin, by urine and by faeces. Lower-ranking animals are to be found on the outskirts of the warren, where territories are less well demarcated. The dominant does produce their young in nests in the central warren, but others are reduced to making short, blind-ended tunnels, called stops, on the edge of the warren to give birth to their young. In a season when rabbits are prospering, these stops are later enlarged to become part of the general warren system, for young rabbits rarely move far from where they were born.

Courtship chases, during which the tail is raised to show the conspicuous white underside, may be seen near warrens in the breeding season. At some point the female may crouch, and as the pursuing male leaps over her, he sprays her with urine. The gestation period is 4 weeks and towards the end of this time the female lines the nest burrow with grass and moss, and about 2 days before the young are due, she plucks fur from her underside to complete the nursery furnishings. It is rare for the litter to consist of less than four, or more than six; young, which when they are born weigh only 30 to 35 g and are blind, naked and helpless. Their mother leaves them in the nursery for most of the time, returning only once during the night to suckle them. In spite of this, they develop rapidly: their eyes open at about 7 days; in about a fortnight they are well furred; they begin to explore the outside world by the time they are about 18 days old; and when they are 3 weeks old their mother stops feeding them. By the time they are fully grown they will weigh upwards of 1.2 kg.

Although rabbits can often be seen during the daytime, particularly in areas where they are undisturbed, they are mainly active at night, wandering furthest from their burrows on dark nights, but being more wary in strong moonlight. They eat a great variety of plant food, often choosing the most nutritious species, including grain, root and garden crops. It is normal for a rabbit to feed by grazing a semicircle which is reached from one position, before moving forward a pace or so to repeat the process. Feeding rabbits will frequently sit up, chewing vigorously, to check for danger. If one detects a possible enemy, it will alert its neighbours by thumping the ground with a hind foot, before scuttling for the safety of its burrow, from where the warning thump may be repeated

The chief predators of rabbits, apart from Man, include foxes, weasels, polecats and some of the larger owls and birds of prey. The average lifespan of a rabbit is unknown, but on the island of Skolkholm, where some of the normal predators are absent, a small percentage survived for 6 years.

Europe's two species of hares are among the most widespread of all wild mammals yet, unlike the rabbits, they owe nothing to Man for their distribution. The larger brown hare *(Lepus capensis),* which may weigh up to 4 kg, is a lowland species, found in open or lightly wooded country from southern Scandinavia throughout Europe and south into the savannahs of Africa. Eastwards, it occurs as far as central China. The smaller mountain hare *(L. timidus),* also known as the arctic hare, the varying hare or the blue hare, replaces the brown hare throughout Norway and most of Sweden, and is found across the north Eurasian and American land masses. Isolated populations occur in the Alps, Ireland and Scotland.

Both species of hare are much bigger than the rabbit, but where distance makes size estimation difficult, they can be recognized by their very long, black-tipped ears and their very long hind legs. In the winter the mountain hare grows a white coat, although it retains the black tips to its ears. In Ireland there may be no change in colour with the autumn moult, or the coat may be patchy brown and white. The brown hare,

The skull of a rabbit is not more than 8.5 cm long. It shows the pair of small incisor teeth placed behind the main biting teeth, and an interparietal bone towards the back of the braincase.

A rabbit suffering from myxomatosis.

Rabbits have scent glands beneath the chin with which they mark objects in their territories.

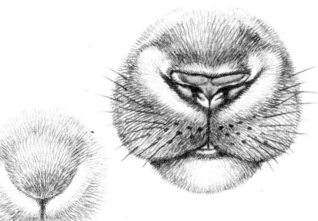

Rabbits have special sensory pads which are protected by nose flaps when they are not in use (left), *and exposed when the animal is testing the air* (above).

The central area of a warren is where the dominant does will rear their young, in nests lined with dry grass and fur. The 3-week-old young are ready to leave their mother, but they remain under cover for much of the time, since many hunters, such as the buzzard, find them easy prey. A predator is usually seen by one of the vigilant adults, which will alert the whole warren.

which is usually a warmer, redder brown than the rabbit, may moult to white in the most northerly parts of its range in Russia.

Both the mountain and brown hare are essentially solitary, territorial, ground-dwelling animals and, although the mountain hare may make a short burrow in peat or snow, it never makes the long, deep tunnels characteristic of the rabbit. Because of their solitary habits, hares are never as abundant as rabbits, and estimates of numbers rarely suggest more than one hare to 3 hectares, although there does appear to be some periodic fluctuation of numbers on a 9-yearly cycle. The mountain hare seems to be slightly more social than the brown hare, and sometimes groups can be seen feeding together — possibly because their territories, which are generally long and narrow, running from the hill tops down towards the valleys, meet at the best feeding places.

During the day hares lie up in slight depressions in the ground known as forms. Because their colour camouflages them, they are prepared to allow potential predators to approach very closely before bursting from cover. Their defence then lies in their speed, for they can outrun all their normal predators on level or uphill ground, although they lose speed if they are forced to run downhill. Young hares may fall prey to small predators such as stoats and adults may be caught by foxes. The mountain hare is preyed on by eagles, wild-cats and lynxes.

Hares are perhaps best known for their exuberant courtship behaviour, which starts soon after the shortest day of the year and reaches a peak in early spring. When the 'mad March hares' (which are really brown hares) first assemble for these social displays they appear quiet, although tense. Suddenly, for no discernible reason, there will be an explosion of activity, which includes chasing and boxing. The mountain hare has a similar, but more subdued courtship. As with rabbits, urine-spraying of the female occurs, and mating stimulates ovulation.

A regular feature, rare in other animals, is superfoetation. This is the conception and development of a second litter before the first is born. It may be a useful method of rearing large numbers of young when conditions are particularly favourable. As with rabbits, resorption of embryos also takes place and this is doubtless an important factor in controlling numbers. The brown hare normally produces four litters and the mountain hare three litters a year. Two or three young, known as leverets, are born after the 6-week gestation period. They weigh about 110 g, are fully furred, open eyed and active, and are taken by their mother to separate forms within her terri-

tory. Here they lie, still and quiet, waiting for her to feed them during the first week of their lives, after which they are weaned and begin their solitary existence. The lifespan of a hare is unknown; the young do not usually breed until the year after their birth, and it is unlikely that many survive to be more than 6 years old.

After a light fall of snow, the footprints of rabbits, criss-crossing fields and parkland, remind us of the abundance of these animals wherever there is suitable living space and food. Their tracks are among the most easily recognized of all European wild mammals. The prints of the forefeet are more or less round, showing the indentations of the four toes which normally touch the ground, while the hindfoot prints are slipper shaped. These are made by the furry soles of the feet, and they also show the marks of four claws. When moving, the forefeet are placed one slightly behind the other, and the hindfeet are then lifted together, outside and ahead of the position of the forefeet in a jumping action. Hare tracks, though similar, are rarer and larger than those of the rabbit. In deep snow, the densely furred hindfeet of the mountain hare may leave an almost pear-shaped footprint.

When there is no snow, signs indicating the presence of rabbits may be slightly less easy to find, although the large burrows in fields and banks are usually obvious

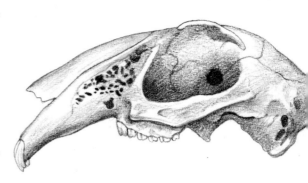

The skull of a hare is larger than a rabbit's (up to 10 cm) and has no separate interparietal bone at the back of the braincase.

Leverets are born fully furred and with their eyes open.

'Mad March hares' often stand on their hind legs, boxing at each other with their forepaws, while the female takes little interest in the contest.

enough. However, the effects of large numbers of rabbits in any area are devastating to agriculture. Rabbits are among the few European animals which can totally alter the ecology of the area in which they live. This was demonstrated in the chalk downlands of southern England, some parts of which changed from grass to scrubland within a few years of the removal of rabbits by myxomatosis in the mid 1950s. Rabbits feed by nibbling grass and other herbs very close to the ground, destroying anything higher than about 3 cm. They also take cultivated cereals and in the early 1950s were estimated to destroy about 6.5 per cent of winter wheat, apart from taking other crops. In sown pasture, other palatable species are taken, and may be eliminated entirely, to be replaced by wild grasses which spread by means of creeping stems.

Young trees in the first year of their growth, before they have developed woody trunks, are eaten by rabbits and thus they prevent regeneration within a woodland area and the spread of trees beyond it. An exception is the elder, which rabbits find distasteful, and it is often the only tree growing in the middle of a warren. In a very heavily grazed area, the grasses will be destroyed completely, and will be replaced by mosses, which rabbits will not eat.

Should a rabbit colony spread to a place where low-growing trees are already well established, the lower branches of these may be eaten and, although the trees may not be killed, they will develop a shrubby appearance. Hares, which are rarely numerous enough to pose a real menace to agriculture, may also feed on the branches of young trees, which they sometimes seem to bite off wantonly, without eating them. Mountain hares, which feed mainly on heather and upland plants such as cottongrass, are most abundant in places where the heather is burned to produce tender shoots for grouse or sheep, so they may be a significant factor in the grazing of these areas. When there is snow on the ground, rabbits and hares do not dig through it to find food, but take anything which they find standing clear of it. The mountain hare, therefore, will often graze the tops of old, unburnt heather bushes which it could not otherwise reach. At this time of year, both rabbits and hares may take to feeding on the bark of trees, often killing young specimens. Since hares will stand on their hind legs to reach as far up as possible, the damage that they do to older trees can also be very extensive.

Natural enemies and some predation from humans keep the numbers of hares in check, but rabbits seem to be capable of surviving in the face of intense predation from many enemies, including birds of prey, many mammals and Man. The traditional ways of killing rabbits were shooting, snaring, trapping, or driving them from their burrows with ferrets, so that they could be killed once they were in the open. These methods were less than totally effective, however. Even the gassing of warrens was rarely completely effective, so when the Australian authorities, plagued by rabbits, introduced a virus disease which afflicts a closely related rabbit from South America, agriculturalists in Europe quickly followed this method of control. Myxomatosis was first introduced into France in 1953, and mysteriously found its way from there to Britain. In South America the disease has little effect on the rabbits which catch it. In Europe, however, where rabbits had at first no natural immunity, it destroyed nearly the whole population. By the end of 1955, only a tiny proportion of the previously huge numbers of rabbits in Britain and western Europe survived.

Rabbits are particularly at risk from diseases such as myxomatosis, which is spread by the rabbit flea, only one of the numerous parasites which thrive because of the rabbit's social, underground life. Hares are remarkably free from parasites and, although there are records of hares having died from myxomatosis, there have been very few casualties among them. A very small number of rabbits survived the initial onslaught from myxomatosis and from these, subsequent populations have developed. The disease is, however, now endemic, and although the virus may have lost some of its early potency and some rabbits have a greater degree of tolerance to it than in 1953, it still causes many rabbit deaths. Where rabbit populations begin to build up to high numbers, conditions are once again suitable for the successful spread of the disease, which is unlikely ever to be eradicated from Europe.

The mountain hare has a brown coat in the summer time (above left). *In the autumn it moults to a second brown coat, and the pale-coloured underfur may show through* (above). *Late in the year it moults again and grows a white coat* (left) *which it loses in the spring.*

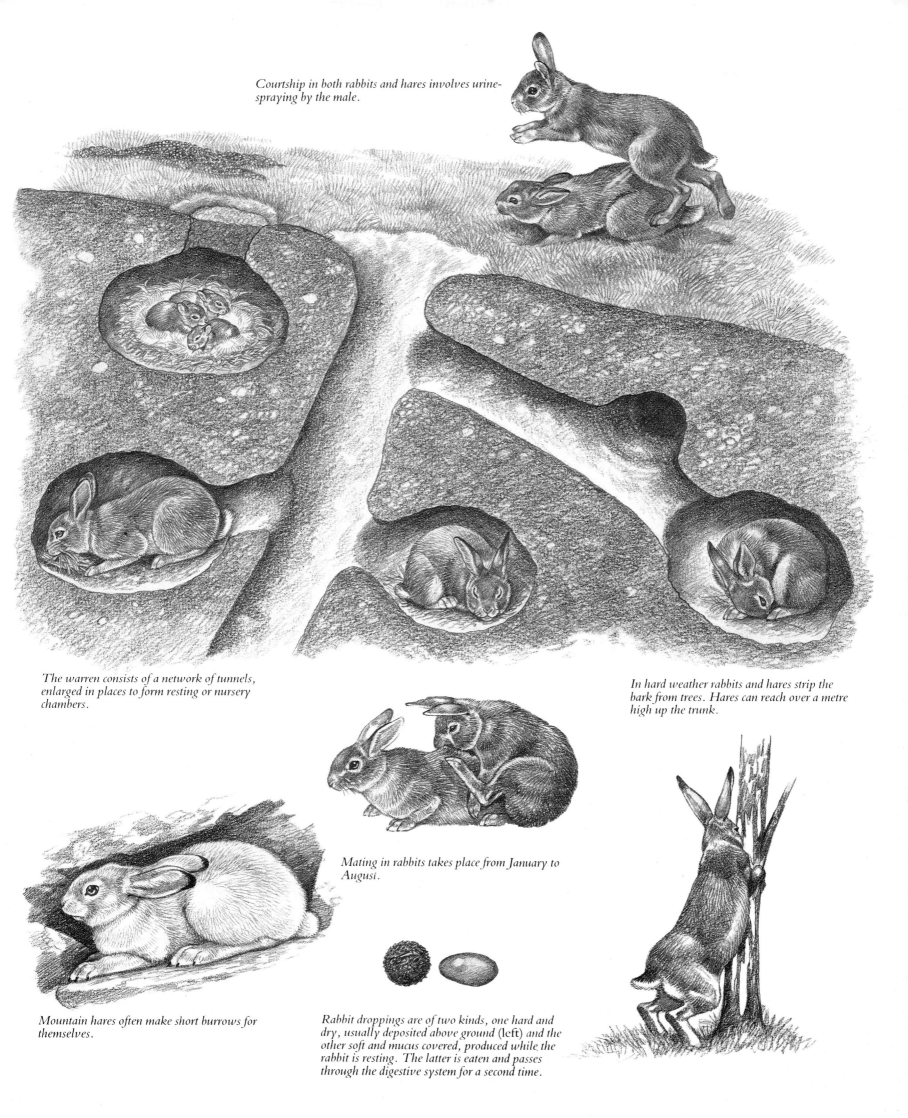

Courtship in both rabbits and hares involves urine-spraying by the male.

The warren consists of a network of tunnels, enlarged in places to form resting or nursery chambers.

In hard weather rabbits and hares strip the bark from trees. Hares can reach over a metre high up the trunk.

Mating in rabbits takes place from January to August.

Mountain hares often make short burrows for themselves.

Rabbit droppings are of two kinds, one hard and dry, usually deposited above ground (left) and the other soft and mucus covered, produced while the rabbit is resting. The latter is eaten and passes through the digestive system for a second time.

RODENTS

Order Rodentia

Another group of gnawing animals, the rodents, make up over one-third of all known mammals, and the 60 species living wild in Europe form an even higher percentage of the European fauna than this. Their variety in size, appearance and way of life is far greater than that found in any other order of mammals. Not only is the number of species very large, but the number of individuals within some species is also huge — wood mice in Britain, for example, outnumber the human population, the only wild mammals to do so. There are many reasons for this success. One is that rodents are almost all small animals; few are as big as rabbits, and several rival the shrews in their diminutive size. This small size means that many individuals can occupy a small habitat without depleting its resources.

One of the ways in which rodents can be distinguished from lagomorphs (rabbits, hares and pikas) is by the number and structure of their teeth. In the front of the mouth of rodents, the upper and lower jaws each carry only two incisor teeth. These work against each other as in the lagomorphs, although the jaw movements are somewhat different, for they operate with a forward and backward motion and not just with a side-to-side grinding action. Also, like those of lagomorphs, the teeth of rodents grow constantly — a rat's incisors, for instance, grow at about 0.27 mm each week, but this growth is kept in check as the animal gnaws at tough food. A difference in the teeth of rodents, however, is that the enamel, which is often yellow or orange in colour, is to be found on the front of the teeth only while behind this lies the very much softer dentine. It is, therefore, only the hard enamel which forms the actual cutting edge of the teeth, which are kept at razor sharpness. Behind the incisors is a long gap or diastema, followed by a short row of grinding teeth. These vary in shape and complexity and, in some species which feed on particularly harsh food, they also are open rooted and continue to grow throughout the life of the animal. A feature which increases the efficiency of the rodent dentition is that the sides of the lips can be sucked behind the incisors, effectively cutting them off from the rest of the mouth. A rodent such as a mouse can thus gnaw continuously at the outer casing — say a nut shell — of possible food and the parts which are inedible will fall away without having to be taken into the mouth at all.

Rodents have occupied every European environment, from the tundra to the Mediterranean. Some dwell by water, for they are adept swimmers, and others climb trees. One species spans the distance between one branch and the next by gliding, using as a wing a spread of skin stretching from the wrists to the ankles. Almost all of the smaller species make runs among the roots of vegetation, and some have become burrowers to rival the mole, rarely seeing the light of day. Apart from all of these specialists, there are some opportunists which are capable of occupying a wide range of habitats, and among these are the house mouse and the rats, which are now the most widespread of all animals other than Man. Most rodents are seed eaters, although almost all will take some herbage as well, and in some cases this has become the dominant part of their diet. Others will feed on insects when these are available although none is entirely carnivorous and some, including the rat and house mouse, are truly omnivorous, rivalling Man in the catholicity of their tastes.

Although some rodents (the beavers and marmots, for instance) are long-lived and slow-breeding animals, the majority have short lives. However, within 12 months, which is the lifespan of most species, many display an amazing fecundity. The house mouse and brown rat may, in suitable circumstances, breed virtually throughout the year, during which time a house mouse can produce 10 litters of young, which quickly achieve sexual maturity themselves. Other species have more restricted breeding seasons, but even so may produce enough young to cause violent fluctuations in the population. These can build up to plague proportions, with thousands of animals per hectare, all jostling for living space, food and mates. Yet strangely such a plague is always followed by a crash in numbers to a low level once more. It is known that in some species territorial behaviour prevents overpopulation, but the mechanisms which control numbers remain to be studied in detail.

Rodents have acute senses of smell and of hearing, although eyesight, in spite of the large eyes of some species, is, in general, very poor. Certainly scent plays a part in territorial and sexual behaviour and some species have powerful scent glands.

The importance of rodents in the environment cannot be underestimated, for, as herbivores, they often control the abundance of plants. They do this by nibbling young shoots in the early stages of growth, yet they frequently help the regeneration of these same plants, for many make food hoards, consisting mainly of seeds of the plants which they have damaged in the springtime. If a rodent forgets where it has made its larder, or more likely, does not survive the winter, these seeds hidden in the underground store are in the best possible position to grow into new plants. The rodents themselves are an important food resource and form the most important part of the diet of many predators, including birds of prey and owls as well as almost all of the mammalian carnivores.

It is not surprising that animals so numerous and ubiquitous should sometimes conflict with Man and some of the world's most important vertebrate pests are rodents. Huge sums of money are spent each year trying to minimize the damage they cause, and to reduce their numbers. However, since the pest species are almost always those with the highest breeding rate, it seems like a losing battle. Man may destroy the vast majority of a local population of rodents, yet those which have the ability to survive may pass these qualities on to their offspring. These will then be the progenitors of future generations of pests so that Man, in his ruthlessness, often selects for the qualities which will damage him further. A few species, such as the beaver, the musk rat and coypu are valued as fur bearers. Others may have benefited Man indirectly since their domesticated descendants are the laboratory animals on which many drugs, which help people to survive, have been tested.

SQUIRRELS

Family Sciuridae

The squirrel family is one of the largest of the rodent groups, containing not only the familiar tree-dwelling forms, but also flying squirrels and ground-living, burrowing species. Technically, they are grouped together because of similarities in the structure of their teeth and jaw muscles, but all tend to be medium-sized, large-eyed animals, with rather large, well-clawed feet. In Europe, there are five native squirrels, two of which are tree living (the red squirrel and the flying squirrel) and three of which are ground squirrels (the European and spotted sousliks and the marmot). In addition to these animals one tree squirrel (the grey squirrel) and one ground squirrel (the Siberian chipmunk) have been introduced by Man.

The red squirrel (*Sciurus vulgaris*) is found wherever there are trees, throughout Europe and eastwards across most of northern Asia to Hokkaido. It thrives best where there are large, mature lowland pine forests, although it is found up to heights of 2,000 m in the Alps and Pyrenees. Its body size, a mere 200-240 mm, is almost doubled by the length of its tail, which may measure up to 195 mm. The individual hairs of the tail are controlled by muscles which cause them to stand erect or lie flat. The tail is used for communication, as well as for balance and for helping the animal to maintain its height as it leaps up to 3 m from tree to tree.

The red squirrel's speed and agility in the trees is made possible by its light bones and long hind limbs, which carry curved claws sufficiently strong to allow it to hang on to a branch by only one or two toes, and also by its remarkable eyes. These are large and so placed as to give the animal good vision in front, at the side, above and below the body and, to some extent, behind. The retina is composed entirely of cells of a type called cones, which make the squirrel acutely aware of movement. In tree squirrels, the blind spot in the eye is also reduced to a minimum, for it is pulled into a horizontal line, only one cell wide, high in the back of the eye. This accounts for the absolute assurance with which they can run up the trunk of a tree and leap from branch to branch.

The home range of a red squirrel varies considerably from one area to another, according to the types of trees available. In east Scotland, for example, where trees are about 15 m high, the average area of the territory of the red squirrel is 470 by 285 m. In Sweden and Japan much smaller areas have been recorded. The territory size is larger in summer than in winter and overlaps the fringe of neighbours' ranges. Each animal will build within its home area a number of dreys, which are domed nests made of twigs lined with moss, grass, pine needles or shredded bark. These are generally situated where a large branch forks from an ivy-clad tree trunk.

Red squirrels are never active at night. They dislike strong wind and are hampered by deep snow, but they do not hibernate and cannot survive for more than a few days without food, so they may be seen throughout the year. In summer they leave their dreys to forage soon after sunrise, again at midday and once more before night falls, although in winter these periods tend to become telescoped into one. In spite of their skill in the trees, red squirrels often search for food on the ground, although they give the impression of being ill at ease there, frequently pausing to sit up and look

Squirrels are capable of descending tree trunks head first, securely held by their widespread fore and hind limbs.

Squirrels have five long, flexible, strongly clawed toes on the hind feet (left) but only four on the front feet, where the thumb is reduced to a small tubercle (above).

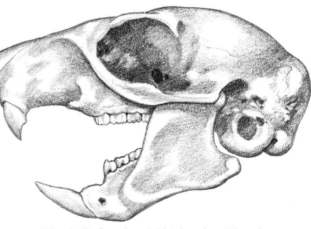

The skull of a red squirrel is less than 55mm long.

The hole in the tree could be the result of squirrel damage in the past. Now, generations later, another squirrel eats the young of a crested tit which has used the hole to build its nest. The dark tail shows that this is a continental red squirrel.

around, and siting their feeding places on tree stumps or other vantage points. The diet is varied, consisting mainly of tree seeds, leaves and fungi, and in spring the sappy tissue beneath the bark of trees. Some animal food is also taken, including insects and the eggs and young of birds. Food is detected by smell, and it is usually held and rotated in the forepaws as the animal feeds, either squatting on the ground or hanging by its hind limbs from a branch. Pine cones are the most important single item in the diet; a red squirrel in Scotland may take between 100 and 150 in a single day. Within 3 minutes, the cone scales are gnawed off and the 30-odd seeds which they protect are eaten. During the course of a day, a squirrel may consume food equivalent to 5 per cent of its body weight in this way. When food is plentiful, its abundance acts as a trigger to cause the squirrel to store some of it, usually by digging a small hole in the ground and scuffing the surface soil over the hidden treasure. It is certain that the squirrel does not remember where it has hidden any particular item, but a strong sense of smell enables the hungry animal to dig up caches when required.

Red squirrels become sexually active soon after mid-winter, a fact signalled by noisy chases with several males pursuing a female at high speed through the branches. Mating may take place in the trees or on the ground, and the young, usually two or three in number, are born 6–7 weeks later. Blind, deaf and naked, and looking as though they are wearing a skin several sizes too large, they weigh only 10–15 g. Before they are 3 weeks old, they have grown their first furry coat, and soon after this their lower incisors erupt. By the time that they are a month old their eyes open. They are capable of eating some solid food at about 7 weeks, but are not fully weaned until they are over 2 months old.

They are reared by their mother alone, for she becomes extremely aggressive towards all other squirrels, including her own mate, as the time approaches for her litter to be born. Should it be necessary for her to move the young during their helpless period, she seizes them by the loose skin on the underside and the young curl up around her chin, to be carried safely, undamaged by jutting twigs. A second litter may be born in mid-summer, and the young do not normally breed until they are a year old, although a few may do so at about 6 months.

In captivity, a red squirrel has survived for 20 years; in the wild they may survive for 5 or 6 years. Their enemies include martens, foxes, some birds of prey and domestic cats and dogs, but above all Man. By destroying their habitat in many areas, he has reduced the numbers of red squirrels more

than any other single agency, although starvation after the failure of a cone crop, and the heavy burden of parasites which they may carry, have decimated numbers, at least temporarily, in certain areas.

In Britain, red squirrel numbers reached a very high level late in the last century, but in the early part of the twentieth century these were reduced by disease, just at the time that the American grey squirrel (*Sciurus carolinensis*), which had been introduced and released in a number of places, was beginning to become well established. The two species are closely related and are sufficiently similar in their general requirements and ways of life to be unable to co-exist for long, so the grey squirrel, which is the larger species (measuring about 250–300 mm plus a tail up to 220 mm long) and is generally more aggressive, tends to be the survivor. However, it is essentially an animal of deciduous woodlands, so where there are large areas of conifers, the native species can hold its own.

The European flying squirrel (*Pteromys volans*) lives only in the taiga in the far north of the continent. This little creature, measuring only 230–300 mm plus about 140 mm of tail, spreads a flap of skin stretched between its fore and hind limbs as it leaps from tree to tree. This skin, which is not obvious as it runs about the branches, enables it to glide much further than it could leap. The flying squirrel is rarely seen, for it rests in holes in trees, and is active only at night. Unlike other squirrels, it hibernates. Already rare, its numbers are declining still further, although the reasons are unknown.

The flying squirrel inhabits the taiga of northern Europe.

Mating in grey squirrels usually takes place in trees in late winter and early summer. Most females have two litters.

The coat colour of the red squirrel changes through the year.

JANUARY. The squirrel hunts for the nuts which it buried last autumn.

SEPTEMBER. Squirrels are noisy animals, chattering with fury or alarm at real or supposed enemies.

JUNE. Stout twigs are cut for making the outer framework of a drey.

The drey of the red squirrel is usually built against the trunk of a conifer, and is over 8 m above the ground.

MAY. Squirrels take the eggs of many forest birds.

Dark coloured forms of the red squirrel occur on the Continent. This one is sleeping among twigs.

MARCH. When feeding, squirrels often sit on a tree stump, which enables them to watch for enemies.

Stripped pine cones, cleanly cracked nuts, bark nibbled from small branches and, sometimes, tooth-marked bones are all signs of the presence of squirrels.

49

SOUSLIKS
Family Sciuridae

Two species of sousliks spread from the steppes of western Asia into Europe, as far as East Germany and Rumania. At first sight their compact, short-tailed bodies seem to proclaim that their greatest affinities are with other burrowing rodents. However, they resemble the squirrels, to which they are more closely related, in their rather large heads, large eyes and diurnal habits. The European souslik *(Spermophilus citellus)* is the more northerly species. It measures 19-22 cm from the tip of its nose to the base of its 7 cm-long tail. The spotted souslik *(S. suslicus)* has a slightly greater range of head and body size, from 18-23 cm, but its tail is much shorter.

European sousliks are animals of dry grassland, and avoid woodlands and marshy places. They may be common in pastures or in uncultivated headlands between arable fields at heights up to 1,300 m in Czechoslovakia and 2,200 m in Yugoslavia. Large numbers may belong to a single colony, occupying a network of underground runs, with many openings to the surface. European sousliks are active only during the daytime, when they forage for the seeds of grasses and other low-growing plants, which are their main food. They move quickly between one feeding place and the next, but pause often to sit upright and take stock of their surroundings. If any sort of danger threatens, they give a sharp whistle, which alerts their neighbours, before diving to safety underground.

At least some of the food which is gathered will be pushed into capacious cheek pouches and carried into the burrows where there are substantial larders. By August or September these stores are sufficient to enable the animals to develop fat reserves in order to survive the winter,

and they then go underground to feed up in preparation for true hibernation. Probably some food reserves will remain to be the sousliks' first meal when they rouse in March or April, for outside at this time there will only be buds for them to feed on.

Sousliks mate very soon after emerging from hibernation, and after a gestation period of 28 days the litter of six to eight young is born. Naked, blind and helpless at birth, they are fully furred by the age of 4 weeks, when they first leave their burrows. The adults do not breed again that year and the young do not produce their first litter until the next summer.

The spotted souslik lives in the more south-easterly parts of Europe, where it leads a life very similar to its northern relative. It probably burrows a little deeper, for ploughing does not disturb it, so it can occupy arable fields as well as pastures. Both species are regarded as serious agricultural pests and little effort is spared in destroying them by trapping, gassing and poisoning. Apart from Man, they are hunted by ground predators such as polecats and weasels and by predaceous birds such as the goshawk and buzzard.

Squirrels of many species used to be popular as pets, but few people keep them today for they need a good deal of space and they can deliver a deep and painful bite.

When danger threatens the spotted souslik gives a shrill whistle of alarm before diving into its burrow.

One small member of the family which is still found as a domestic pet is the Siberian chipmunk *(Tamias sibiricus)*, an attractive creature with five well-defined, dark stripes running the length of its body and a bushy tail, intermediate in thickness and length between that of the tree squirrels and the sousliks. This little animal has escaped from captivity in many parts of Europe and established itself in woodlands where there is a good shrub layer in which it can climb. Like sousliks, it makes large stores of food on which it feeds throughout the winter, for although it does not hibernate, it is less active than the tree squirrels in cold weather.

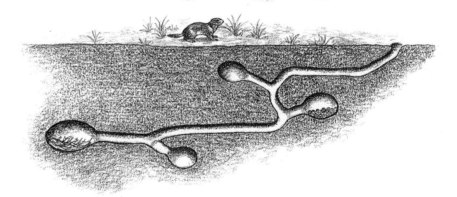

The homes of European sousliks may be very extensive, for each one contains a nest chamber, large food stores and latrine areas. Although many individuals live together, each occupies its own burrow.

Sousliks feed mainly on many kinds of seeds, but in the spring they may augment their diet with the eggs of ground-nesting birds.

Siberian chipmunks have escaped from captivity and become established in many parts of Europe.

The European souslik is an animal of the steppes. It rarely moves far away from its burrow which offers safety in a world of many enemies, such as the steppe polecat.

MARMOT
Family Sciuridae

The Alpine marmot (*Marmota marmota*) makes its home on mountain slopes above the tree line, usually at heights of between 2,000 and 3,000 m. It prefers a warm, southerly aspect, and is rarely active except when the sun is shining. Once widespread, original populations now survive in the Alps, Tatras and Carpathians, and it has been reintroduced to the Pyrenees and Yugoslavia. The largest European member of the squirrel family, the head and body of the Alpine marmot measures about 50-58 cm and the tail a further 19 cm. The animal weighs about 6.8 kg.

Like most ground squirrels, they are social animals, and several individuals share a complex of burrows. These are usually situated in a stabilized scree, where sufficient earth has formed between the blocks of stone to allow them to dig deeply enough for warmth and safety. They may tunnel as deep as 3 m below the surface, although the usual depth of the main resting chambers is about 1 m. These are warmly lined with dried grass, carried down before the start of hibernation and replaced when the animals awake in the springtime.

Alpine marmots feed on grasses, sedges and the leaves and shoots of various mountain plants, but they have no cheek pouches and so do not make underground stores of seeds. They are too large for the smaller predators and avoid the attentions of eagles and high-ranging foxes and bears by constant vigilance, since they are too big to slip into the many small crevices found in rocky places. As they feed they pause frequently to sit up on their haunches and inspect the nearby slopes and sky, for they have keen eyesight and can detect movement from afar. It is sometimes said that a feeding party posts a sentry, but it is more likely that should any individual become aware of danger, it will give a shrill whistle of alarm which sends the whole group bolting to safety below ground.

The long mountain winters start early, and by October marmots are ready to hibernate. They retire to their hay-filled sleeping dens and close the main entrance tunnels with earth dug from small side passages. This task completed, the whole family, huddled together, drops into the coma-like state of true hibernation. They do not wake until the following April, and only emerge when the sun is shining brightly. When the sun is warm they may sunbathe, flattening themselves against a rock to absorb all possible heat.

Marmots mate soon after emerging from hibernation and the litter of two to four young is born after a gestation of about 6 weeks. They do not emerge into the daylight until mid-July, by which time they are weaned and fully furred. The adults do not breed in the next year, but continue to look after the previous litter, which are not sexually mature until they are at least 3 years old. Like all young animals, the juveniles are playful, their games taking the form of mock battles in which two animals will stand up on their hind legs and wrestle with each other. This sparring is quite bloodless, but it probably has the purpose of deciding the position of the young in the family hierarchy. As might be surmised from their slow breeding rate, they are long-lived animals. In captivity, they have been known to survive for 20 years, and it is possible that they may live nearly this long in the wild, protected as they are by the bleakness of their habitat and their own sharp senses.

The fighting games of juvenile marmots are replaced by similar but real battles between rival males, such as those shown here.

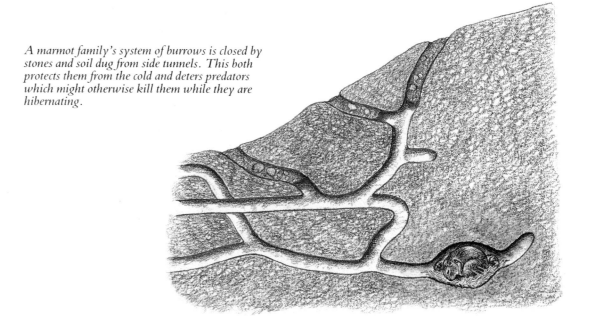

A marmot family's system of burrows is closed by stones and soil dug from side tunnels. This both protects them from the cold and deters predators which might otherwise kill them while they are hibernating.

Marmots are good housekeepers, lining their burrows with dry grass and leaves, which are replaced when they wake from hibernation.

The Alpine marmot inhabits the upper slopes of Europe's high mountains. It loves the fierce sun of these areas and spends much of the summer sunbathing close to its burrow. The young play near at hand, for they are more at risk than their parents from eagles and other birds of prey.

BEAVERS
Family Castoridae

Like so many of Europe's larger mammals, the European beaver (*Castor fiber*) has been exterminated in most of its former haunts, which included virtually the whole of the continent where streams or lakes were bordered by broadleaved woodland. It was easy prey, being slow and clumsy on land, and because of its extreme attachment to its home area a whole colony, once located, could be trapped. Beavers were hunted not only for their beautiful, dense fur, but also for a glandular secretion called castoreum, used by beavers for territorial marking and by Man in medicine and as a basis for perfumes. The beaver had disappeared from most of western Europe by the end of the eighteenth century. Today, small populations survive in Scandinavia, Finland and the valleys of the Rhône and the Elbe and in Russia. They are protected over most of this area, and have been reintroduced to various suitable places within their old habitats, while the closely related North American beaver *(C. canadensis)* has been released in Finland.

By far the largest of Europe's rodents, an adult beaver measures up to 100 cm in head and body length, to which the tail adds up to 40 cm. The animal may weigh as much as 20 kg. Yet, in spite of their size, beavers are rarely seen, for they are extremely secretive, normally living in burrows with underwater entrances and only building the dams and lodges characteristic of American beavers when free from harassment. They may be active in the daytime in places where they are undisturbed but otherwise they are nocturnal and their presence is indicated only by the stumps of waterside trees which have been felled.

Although awkward on land, once in the water a beaver is transformed into an animal of speed and grace. On the surface it swims slowly, kicking the hind limbs alternately, but underwater at speed these are kicked outwards and backwards together and the powerful, flat tail adds to the effort with an undulating motion. This remarkably flexible organ is used as a rudder, and may be twisted at right angles to its normal position so that it has the maximum steering effect. It is also used as a means of communication, for when alarmed, a beaver smacks it noisily against the surface of the water as it dives to safety, though it is perfectly capable of sliding beneath the surface. Many mammals — rabbits, for instance — are capable of altering their environment, but few do so as spectacularly as the beavers. They not only remove large numbers of young trees from their feeding areas, but can change the character of the watercourses by building dams which reduce fast-flowing streams to a series of placid pools. The stimulus for building seems to be the sound of fast-running water, so that a dam may be started where some rocks in a stream cause a noisy flow. The beavers will roll stones along the stream bed, and then place lengths of tree trunk and sticks in the

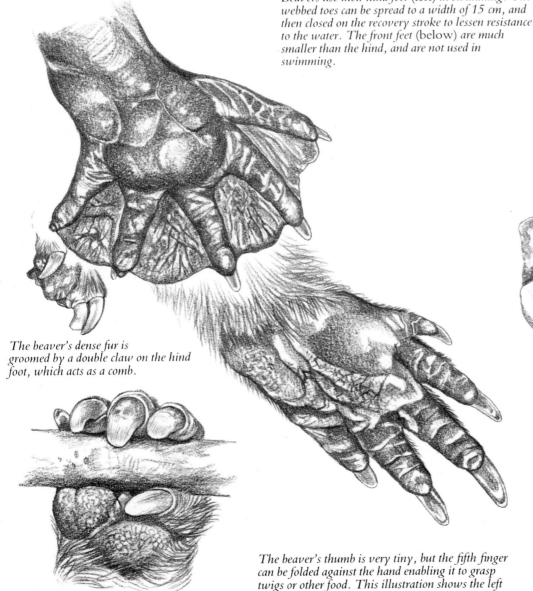

Beavers use their hind feet (left) in swimming. The webbed toes can be spread to a width of 15 cm, and then closed on the recovery stroke to lessen resistance to the water. The front feet (below) are much smaller than the hind, and are not used in swimming.

The beaver's dense fur is groomed by a double claw on the hind foot, which acts as a comb.

The beaver's thumb is very tiny, but the fifth finger can be folded against the hand enabling it to grasp twigs or other food. This illustration shows the left hand.

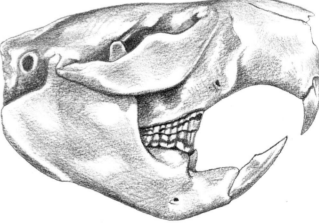

The beaver's skull measures about 14 cm in length. The powerful incisors are the tools with which the animal can fell trees up to a metre in diameter.

Beavers eat the leaves and sweet bark of the trees which they fell, but use the trunks and larger branches to add to the pile of stones and mud with which they dam fast-flowing streams.

dam, finally adding twigs and mud to make a smooth-surfaced structure which may be 3 m wide and over 2 m high, containing several thousand cubic metres of wood as well as stones and mud. The material to make the dam is usually carried in the mouth, but mud and twigs are often brought to the building site in the arms, with the beaver moving awkwardly on its hind legs. In the dam they may build lodges which contain feeding and sometimes living chambers which are approached from under water.

During the summer beavers eat a wide variety of waterside plants, including, if they are available, meadowsweet and rosebay willow-herb, and also the leaves of most deciduous trees except for alder. During the winter, their diet consists entirely of the bark of trees which they have felled and stored underwater. Trees up to a metre in diameter may be brought down, although the size is usually much less. Branches are cut off and dragged to the water's edge, often forming deep furrows along the route, and sometimes canals are dug so that food can be floated to the main store.

When feeding, beavers first cut a twig using their large incisor teeth, then hold it in the forepaws. In these, the thumb is very small, but the fifth finger can be opposed to some extent, so that the food can be rotated as the animal strips off the juicy bark. As with some other animals which feed on fairly unnutritious food, beavers practice refection. The faeces are rich in vitamins which have been released in the appendix and these are absorbed on their second journey through the digestive tract.

Beavers mate for life, and their social organization is based on the stable family unit. Where conditions are favourable, groups of up to 14 may live together, but usually, before such numbers are reached, food resources are overstretched, and some of the younger animals leave to find mates and set up home elsewhere. Within the group, there is no direct co-operation in food finding or dam building, but there is a strong social spirit. In the underground living areas, a wide range of audible contact sounds are used, although when outside, sounds too high pitched for human hearing are general. Young beavers wrestle in play and probably establish their position in the family hierarchy in this way. Older animals solicit attention from each other by 'dancing' movements, and mutual grooming is one of the methods of maintaining close contact between members of a group.

Mating takes place in the water and the young, up to four in number, are born after a gestation of 105 days. Their eyes are open and they are covered with downy fur. The male is not excluded from the nursery and has even been recorded as helping the female to eat the placentas. The young become fully active very soon, venturing first into the submerged tunnels leading from the nursery at 4 to 5 days, although their parents are always on hand to lead them back to safety. They do not swim regularly in open water until they are about 2 months old, by which time they are weaned and capable of collecting their own food.

By autumn, at the age of 4 to 5 months, they share in the task of adding to the group's winter stores. In spite of their advanced state at birth young beavers develop slowly, and remain with their parents for at least 2 years. The earliest age at which they will mate is as they approach their third year. Their parents will by then have produced another litter, and beavers are among the very few animals in which a family includes the immature young of more than one breeding season. As might be expected in an animal with such slow development beavers are long lived, and even in the wild may survive for 20 years.

A beaver dam has a base of stones and mud on which tree trunks and sticks are heaped, and finally it is plastered with more mud. Lodges and living chambers within the dam are approached underwater.

If a beaver senses danger, it slaps the water noisily with its tail as it dives to alert other members of the family, although normally it slides silently beneath the surface.

Baby beavers are active soon after birth, but are carefully watched over by their parents, who may have to rescue them and carry them back to the lodge when they become too adventurous.

The castoreum glands lie in the beaver's groin area. The secretion from them is used to mark territory.

When felling a tree, a beaver gnaws a deep notch all round it and then weakens one side still further so that the tree falls in the right direction.

A dam often curves downstream since during its construction the flow of water pushes some of the building materials downstream. Heavy objects, such as rocks, are rolled along the stream bed using hands and chin.

DORMICE
Family Gliridae

Dormice differ from house and wood mice in their rather rounded appearance, with shorter faces and smaller ears, their dense, almost woolly fur and, usually, hairy tails. All dwell in dense vegetation and are agile and adept climbers. The family is restricted to the Old World, with four species in western Europe and others further east and in Asia.

Only the smallest European species, which measures 11.5 to 16.5 cm overall, almost half of which is the bushy tail, is native to Britain. Here it is known as the common dormouse (*Muscardinus avellanarius*), a most unsuitable name, for it is among the rarer small mammals, occuring abundantly only in the south-western counties of England. It is also found in suitable country from western France, throughout Italy, north to southern Sweden and eastwards into Asia Minor. It is

here known as the hazel dormouse, because it usually lives in secondary woodland where hazel thickets provide it with dense cover and with food.

Hibernation or dormancy is the habit from which dormice derive their name. It sets them apart from other small rodents which survive the winter by making food stores. Dormice avoid the hard season, when the temperature is consistently below 15°C, by means of a deep, coma-like sleep, which may last for over 6 months. The snug hibernation nest is usually at or slightly below ground level, and in this, like a small furry parcel, with its tail wrapped round to cover its head, the dormouse spends the winter. During hibernation the rate of its bodily functions drops and its temperature falls to a little above freezing, so it uses very little energy. So soundly does it sleep that a hibernating dormouse may not wake up even when its nest is disturbed. However, they may rouse several times during the winter, to feed on nearby stores of seed. While asleep, dormice produce a sort of whistling snore. This may guide predators to them, for foxes, badgers and magpies are all recorded as locating and digging out the plump, sleeping rodents. Studies of European hazel dormice have shown that 80 per cent may die during the

winter, although this may be due to insufficient reserves of fatty tissue being laid down before the onset of the cold weather.

During the summer months, when its temperature is between 34°C and 38°C, the hazel dormouse is normally active only at night. The occasional individual seen during the daytime is usually a young one. Its unathletic appearance is belied by its climbing ability. It is entirely at home among slender twigs, which it is able to grasp because it can turn the feet at right angles to the legs — a feature lacking in other mice.

In Britain the hazel dormouse is far rarer than it was a century ago. This may be due, in part, to a reduction of coppiced woodlands, which make a suitable habitat. However, this is not the sole reason, for even where they occur they are patchily distributed, some woods being occupied while others, apparently equally suitable, are empty. Climatic change has also been suggested as a factor, but this cannot account totally for the reduction. Future studies, which will include monitoring

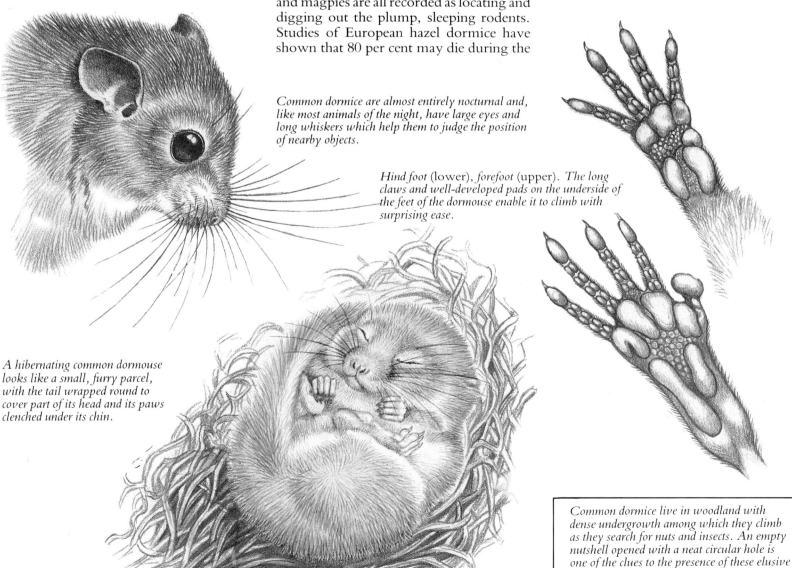

Common dormice are almost entirely nocturnal and, like most animals of the night, have large eyes and long whiskers which help them to judge the position of nearby objects.

Hind foot (lower), *forefoot* (upper). *The long claws and well-developed pads on the underside of the feet of the dormouse enable it to climb with surprising ease.*

A hibernating common dormouse looks like a small, furry parcel, with the tail wrapped round to cover part of its head and its paws clenched under its chin.

Common dormice live in woodland with dense undergrowth among which they climb as they search for nuts and insects. An empty nutshell opened with a neat circular hole is one of the clues to the presence of these elusive animals.

changes in populations of the hazel dormouse, will probably show the decline to be the result of a subtle combination of factors, some of which may not yet have been considered.

Four other species of dormice are native to Europe. One of these, the fat or edible dormouse (*Glis glis*) is found from north Spain across most of the rest of Europe excluding Scandinavia. It was introduced into southern England towards the end of the last century and is now well established there. It is by far the largest of the dormice, with a head and body length of 13 to 19 cm and a tail up to 15 cm long. Its colour makes it look rather like a small grey squirrel, which it rivals in agility. It often spends the summer months in the canopy of woodlands, although the hibernation nest is usually much lower. This species gets its name from its ability to boost its weight by heavy feeding before hibernation, a characteristic noted by the Romans, who used to fatten the little animals as table delicacies.

The garden dormouse (*Eliomys quercinus*) is another western species found from Spain to Austria and east to the Urals, but not occurring in Scandinavia, the low plains of northern Europe or the Balkans. Its head and body length may be as much as 17 cm, to which the tufted tail can add 12 cm more. Although as agile as other dormice, it often descends to the ground, especially in scrub or stony areas, and it also invades houses very readily. Its diet contains more insects and other animal food, such as snails, than that of its close relatives.

The forest dormouse (*Dryomys nitedula*) is an eastern species found in deciduous woodland with thick undergrowth from Poland to the Balkans and east to China. Superficially like the garden dormouse, it is smaller, with a head and body length of up 13 cm and a tail up to 9.5 cm long. Like the fat dormouse, it often occupies the upper layers of its environment, at least during the summer months.

The little mouse-tailed dormouse (*Myomimus roachi*) is the only European species not to have a bushy tail. This could lead to confusion with some other small rodents, but mice have, on the whole, larger eyes and longer tails, and voles have smaller eyes. It is known only from parts of Greece and Bulgaria, and is thought to spend more of its time on the ground than other dormice.

Hazel dormouse nests, made for breeding or resting, may be close to ground level or up to 3 m above it. Oval in shape and about 15 cm across, they may be made of grass but are more usually constructed of the papery outer bark of honeysuckle. First, broad straps of this material are interwoven, to make a scaffolding between which the hazel dormouse can push, for there is no special entrance hole. The inner part of the nest is filled with the same substance, finely shredded. Branches of honeysuckle, neatly stripped of their bark, are a good indication of the presence of hazel dormice, and a nest can often be found within a metre or so of the cleared twigs.

On the Continent, the hazel dormouse often produces two litters of young a year. In Britain, females generally give birth to three or four young in the early summer, although there are records of litters as late as September. Born after a gestation of about 23 days, the babies weigh about 2 g and are naked and helpless. Their first fur, which is grey in colour, begins to grow very soon and is well developed in less than a fortnight. Their eyes open at 18 days but they do not venture from the nest until they are a month old. They leave their parents 10 days later, usually remaining in the area of the nursery nest. Where the species is abundant groups of nests may be found, probably representing dispersed family units.

Compared to most other rodents, the hazel dormouse develops slowly and at its first hibernation may weigh only about 20 g — about half the weight of a fully fed adult before the winter. Early in its second summer it develops the rich, marmalade-coloured coat which is its badge of maturity, for it will then be capable of breeding. In spite of its slow reproductive rate, the hazel dormouse does not appear to be very long lived, for its teeth are badly worn by the time that it is 3 years old and it is unlikely that it normally survives much beyond this, although it has lived for 6 years in captivity. Even in a favourable environment, it is never as abundant as the bank vole and wood mice, although occasionally on the continent it may be so numerous as to be a forestry pest.

The food of hazel dormice consists largely of nuts and berries. During the autumn, the animal grows fat in preparation for hibernation. However, it is likely that in the period immediately after awakening, insects are eaten to a much greater extent than usual. Food may be taken to a favourite spot to be consumed and, occasionally, an accumulation of shells, particularly those of hazel nuts, may be found. These can be distinguished from the food remains of wood mice by the small, very neat opening, compared to the larger, more jagged hole edged with obvious tooth marks, which are the work of *Apodemus*.

All species of dormice eat insects as well as plant food. Here an edible dormouse is seen feasting on a cockchafer, which it has caught high in a tree.

Most species of dormice descend to lower layers of the forest during the winter. Many make use of a hollow tree, where they are saf from the gales which whip the upper branches.

The forest dormouse may climb into the canopy layer of woods, as well as using the dense cover near to the ground.

All dormice are in danger from nocturnal hunters. Here a garden dormouse, which has a tufted tail, with a variable amount of black and white colouring, has been caught by a genet.

The edible dormouse inhabits the upper branches of the forest during the summer months, building neat, compact nests high above the ground.

Common dormice favour honeysuckle bark as a nest-building material, and white twigs, stripped of their bark, often show where common dormice have been at work.

The nest of a common dormouse is usually made entirely of honeysuckle bark, shredded finely to make a soft bed inside the coarse framework.

61

The mouse family forms by far the largest subdivision of the rodents and includes a vast array of small, generally ground-living species, many of which are pests of crops and stored products. Their success is due to their fecundity and their rapid rate of development, which make it possible for large populations to build up quickly in suitable environments. In Europe, there are 44 members of this family, the least mouse-like of them being the hamsters, which are plump, short-tailed, burrowing animals found widely over the continent. They usually occur in grasslands and the moister steppe zones but may survive in open woodlands.

HAMSTERS
Family Muridae

The golden hamster (*Mesocricetus auratus*), which is often kept as a pet, is not a native of Europe. Although escaped golden hamsters sometimes develop into colonies, these are usually short lived. The European common hamster (*Cricetus cricetus*) occurs in suitable lowland areas from Germany eastwards. It is far larger than the familiar pet, being about the size of a guinea pig, with a head and body length of 22 to 30 cm and a tail length of up to 6 cm. It is unusual in that the underside is black, rather than paler than the back. Like the sousliks, it is a solitary burrowing animal, often forced by circumstances to live in close proximity to others of its own kind. The burrows may be up to 2 m deep and ownership is probably proclaimed by scent, for the common hamster has scent glands placed high on the flanks and on the underside, well positioned to rub against the floor and walls of the burrow. Each hamster's quarters include sleeping and larder areas, the latter stocked with up to 14 kg of seeds, including cultivated grains, which are carried down in the animal's huge cheek pouches. Since it also feeds on roots, it is not surprising that it is considered to be an agricultural pest.

Like the ground squirrels, hamsters hibernate, but unlike them may wake several times in the course of the winter and feed on the stored reserves. Unlike the sousliks, hamsters are strictly nocturnal in their activity.

Hamsters mate soon after emerging from hibernation. After a gestation of 20 days a litter of six to twelve blind, naked and helpless young is born. They develop quickly and are weaned within 3 weeks, leaving their mother soon after. This allows her to produce a second family in August. The young do not breed until after their first hibernation.

Two other species of hamsters occur in Europe. The Rumanian hamster (*Mesocricetus neutoni*) lives on the coast of the Black Sea and in lowland areas of Bulgaria. It is closely related to the domestic golden hamster, but is more drably coloured, with black markings on the underside of the neck. It has a head and body length of up to 18 cm with a tail which may be 2 cm long. The grey hamster (*Cricetulus migratorius*) is an even smaller member of the group, measuring not more than 11 cm in head and body length, and with a tail nearly 3 cm long. It is basically an Asiatic animal, which occurs in Europe only in scattered localities throughout the Balkans. Both the Rumanian and the grey hamster lead lives very much like that of the common hamster.

Another animal which has become a popular pet in recent years is the Mongolian gerbil (*Meriones unguiculatus*). This, in common with many small mammals, has escaped from captivity. Since it comes from a place with a far harsher climate than any found in Europe, it has managed to survive in some areas.

All hamsters tend to be aggressive, chattering and showing their teeth if they are threatened. Here a grey hamster defies a dog with teeth and claws.

Hamsters, such as the golden hamster shown here, can carry heavy loads of food in their cheek pouches. Pet golden hamsters often move the entire contents of their feed tray to a place which they consider more convenient.

Section through the burrow of a common hamster, showing sleeping and storage chambers.

Common hamsters cannot climb but, if need be, can swim. They suck air into their cheek pouches which then act as lifebuoys as they paddle through the water.

Common hamsters spend much of their lives in the dark security of a burrow. The female need not leave her young even to feed, for she has stocks of grain remaining from the last harvest.

LEMMINGS and VOLES
Family Muridae

Voles differ from true mice in having blunt faces, small eyes and ears, and short tails. They tend to live in open country and to be dependent on grass as their main food, sometimes to the exclusion of virtually all other nourishment. The molar teeth of some species are open rooted and grow throughout life, to cope with this tough diet. They are often active by day as well as by night, and none, even in the most hostile environment, hibernates. In some species, periodic fluctuations in numbers lead to the build up of gigantic populations followed by catastrophic crashes survived by only a few individuals.

Twenty-five species of voles are known in Europe. These can be placed in five groups:

lemmings have short tails and are found only in the far north;

red-backed voles are widespread, usually occupying more bushy places than other voles;

grass voles are the most abundant animals in open country;

pine voles burrow more extensively than the other species and are often found at high altitudes;

water voles are much larger than all of the other species, and over most of the continent are associated with streams or still water.

Two species of lemming are widespread in Scandinavia and northern Europe. Of these, the Norway lemming *(Lemmus lemmus)* is the better known. It has a head and body length of up to 15 cm plus a tail of about 2 cm. It is a creature of open tundra in the far north and the treeless zone of some mountains. In the summertime, it makes burrows near to the surface of the soil, while in winter its runs lie in the surprisingly warm protection of vegetation buried beneath the snow.

The wood lemming *(Myopus schisticolor)* has a head and body length of up to 9.5 cm, with a tail of about 2 cm. It is found from Scandinavia to Siberia, but is rather local in its distribution, preferring to live in wet secondary growth areas of coniferous forests. Alone of European mammals, it feeds largely on the abundant mosses of its environment.

Norway lemmings normally produce two litters a year. The gestation period is about 20 days and the four to eight young, which are weaned within 3 weeks, are capable of breeding only a fortnight later.

Occasionally, the breeding season may be prolonged and young are sometimes born in winter beneath the snow. This may help to build up large populations, which reach a peak about every 4 years, falling after this to a low level. Occasionally, vast numbers of these rodents, amounting to plagues, build up. Although so abundant, the crowds of animals seem to have no social structure, each being aggressive and quarrelsome on its own behalf. In an attempt to find food, living space and solitude to breed, they migrate from centres of abundance, and may swim large rivers or arms of the sea. Many reach unoccupied areas where they may establish colonies, but these are generally in unsuitable habitats and so are short lived.

The numbers of the wood lemming also fluctuate, but never so wildly as to produce plagues, although migrations occur in times of population excess. This little lemming has a curious breeding strategy — about 75 per cent of the population is female and many of these are apparently incapable of producing male offspring, thus perpetuating the sexual imbalance.

The Arctic lemming is reported occasionally on the island of Spitzbergen, which it reaches by travelling on ice floes from its normal home in northern Asia. It differs from other lemmings in its very broad claws.

A wood lemming feeds under the snow of its damp forest home. It is far warmer here than on the surface, where during the winter no small animal could survive for long.

A heap of droppings reveals the entrance to a lemming's snow tunnel.

Lemmings remain active throughout the winter, feeding on seeds and other vegetation beneath the blanket of snow. When this melts, the pattern of their runs is exposed on the surface of the ground.

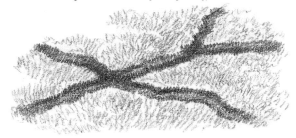

Norway lemming numbers sometimes build up to plague proportions. At such times many animals disperse from the centre of abundance to try to find unoccupied places to live. They often swim across lakes or large rivers and may even attempt to cross the sea, but the suicide urge, with which they have often been credited, is a myth.

Europe's twenty species of small voles occupy almost every ground habitat except those in the furthest south of the continent and their domain includes scrubland, grasslands, wet pastures and mountain slopes.

The bank vole (*Clethrionomys glareolus*) is typical of the red-backed voles. It lives throughout Europe except for the tundra and part of the Mediterranean zone. Northwards it is replaced by the northern red-backed vole (*C. rutilus*) and eastwards by the grey-sided vole (*C. rufocanus*), which extends from Scandinavia to Japan. Intermediate in size between the northern red-backed vole and the bigger grey-sided vole, the bank vole averages 8-11 cm head and body length, plus up to 6.5 cm of tail, which is proportionately longer than in its two close relatives.

All are rather brightly coloured animals, often living in dense vegetation but rarely venturing into fields. They prefer low or secondary woodland for, although they can climb, they are not adapted to life in the tree canopy. Males occupy territories of about 0.2 hectares; females live in areas little more than half this size. Both ranges contain runs which in suitable places are above ground but may be burrowed as much as 10 cm below the surface. These centre on the nest, which is made of leaves or grass and is warmly lined with moss or feathers and, unlike the resting places of many small mammals, has a definite doorway. Nearly two-thirds of their time is spent resting and the active periods are spread over day and night as they search for fruit, seed, leaves, insects and worms.

Bank voles are probably short-sighted. Smell is important and it is said that males prefer the scent of closely related females. They are highly vocal, often squeaking and chattering and also using sounds too high in pitch to be detected by human ears, especially during courtship and between a mother and her nestlings.

The length of the breeding period varies greatly, depending on food supply, temperature and population density, for breeding ceases when numbers grow too large. Four or five blind, naked, helpless young, each weighing about 2 g, are born in each litter. They are weaned in 18 days and each female usually produces several families during her short life. The first young born in April or May are likely to breed before the end of the summer.

The grass voles are similar in size to the red-backed voles, but their tails are shorter, their faces blunter, and their eyes and ears smaller. Several species overlap in Europe and are difficult to identify with certainty, although they may be distinguished by their tooth structure. In general, the field vole (*Microtus agrestis*), which is widespread from the Arctic to the Pyrenees and east into Siberia, inhabits old pasture land. The common vole (*M. arvalis*), which is a more active burrower, is at home in shorter pasture or even in arable land. The root vole (*M. oeconomus*) prefers wetter places, including quite swampy areas.

Their territories are normally small, those of the field vole being estimated at less than 1000 sq m, with most animals moving less than 27 sq m from their nests. They know every part of their home range intimately, and explore it frequently, using primarily their sense of smell to assess whether all is well. Droppings neatly placed in latrine areas probably announce ownership of runs. Encounters with other members of the same species are likely to be aggressive, accompanied by much squeaking and chattering.

The nest, made of finely chopped grass, is usually above ground at the base of grass stems, although it is sometimes protected by a stone or log. A field vole produces her first litter of four to five young in late March, and the last may be born in October. Weaned before they are a month old, the females can mate at 6 weeks.

Population fluctuations sometimes occur and huge numbers, comparable to lemming plagues, may build up. The common vole, which feeds on arable crops, may then be a serious pest. However, the plagues never last for long, for grass voles are the prey of almost every open-ground predator and none survives for more than one winter.

Pine or root voles are similar to, but smaller than, grass voles, from which they differ principally in their small eyes and ears, which are almost hidden in their fur, and their small feet. They are more nocturnal and subterranean than the grass voles, occupying woodlands, pasture and arable land and feeding largely on roots and bulbs.

A number of species are found in small, well-separated areas of Europe. The common pine vole (*Pitymys subterraneus*) is the most widespread, occurring from western France through to eastern Europe, and south to the Alps and northern Greece. It may occupy the same area as the common vole, but when this happens minor features of the habitat combine to tip the balance in favour of one or the other, so they are never equally abundant. Pine voles have a breeding pattern similar to other voles, but their litters tend to be smaller, rarely containing more than four young.

The snow vole (*Microtus nivalis*) and the Balkan snow vole (*Dinaromys bogdanovi*) live in open mountain slopes above the tree line, feeding mainly on the dwarf plants of that zone. Although not closely related to each other, they are similar in general appearance and habits.

The common pine vole is widespread in Europe but it is not seen frequently since it is a burrowing creature, mainly active at night.

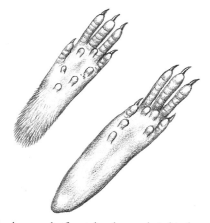

Pine voles have only five tubercles on their hind feet, compared to other voles which have six.

The snow vole is an animal of high mountains, where it tends to be active during the day and can often be seen basking in the sun.

Many voles store food in times of plenty. The bank vole (shown here) often uses the disused nest of a hedgerow bird as its larder.

Many voles are found on islands; some colonies were established in prehistoric times, since when they have developed differences from the parent stock. Subspecies of the common vole (lower) are to be found on Guernsey and Orkney, and on Skomer Island a form of the bank vole (upper) is much bigger than the normal mainland animal.

Baby voles are reared by their mother alone. Here a field vole moves her litter of unweaned young to a safer place.

A hazel nut opened by a bank vole shows clear marks of the animal's teeth on the inside of the hole. Small tooth marks on twigs and minor branches of trees stripped of their bark are usually the work of bank voles.

Grass voles, such as the field vole (above), have blunt faces, small eyes, and ears which scarcely stand above the level of the fur on the back of the head. Red-backed voles, such as the bank vole (below), have slightly longer faces, and larger eyes and ears.

The runs of field voles can often be seen in old pastures but are not usually visible unless the grass is turned aside. Each animal's runway system contains its nest, larders and latrine area.

WATER VOLES and MUSK RAT
Family Muridae

Water voles, often called water rats, have few of the habits which have brought the true rats into conflict with Man. They should not be confused with rats for like all voles they have shaggy coats, blunt faces, small eyes and ears, and tails which are never more than 75 per cent of the head and body length.

In spite of their name and the fact that they are usually found by ponds or slow flowing streams, water voles have no special adaptations for swimming and diving. Their feet are unwebbed and their tails are rounded; although they take readily to the water, they swim high in it and can stay submerged for only about 20 seconds. In some parts of eastern Europe they live away from water, making extensive burrows and throwing up mounds of earth, which can best be distinguished from molehills by the entry holes at their base.

Two species of water vole with very similar habits and behaviour live in Europe. The north-western water vole *(Arvicola terrestris)* is found in lowland areas of the continent excluding Spain, western France and most of Greece. The south-western water vole *(A. sapidus)* is found in Spain, in western France and the Pyrenees, where there is some overlap between the two species. In northern Europe, the north-western water vole may grow to a head and body length of 19 cm with the tail adding up to 10 cm more. Further south, the same species may be 2-3 cm smaller. The south-western water vole is always at least as large as the northernmost forms, often larger, and tends to be darker in colour.

A suitable stream may be colonized by a female water vole shortly before she gives birth to her litter of five or six young each weighing about 5 g. Her territory may extend for 75 m along the bank, defined by droppings in a latrine at either end and by the secretion from powerful scent glands on her flanks. As her family grows they remain with their mother, enlarging the territory. A mated pair will stay together, the male helping his mate to defend the family if need be. Their runs meander into the river bank, with entrances above and below water and feeding holes may be opened into the top of the bank. There is often a resting nest near to the entrance, as well as one deeper in the network of underground runs. Both are lined with shredded grass and the pith from rushes.

Water voles are particularly active around dawn or dusk. If they are startled, they normally dive and swim under water to the shelter of some vegetation. Many sorts of waterside plants are eaten, but grass stems seem to be the staple diet. These are cut with the teeth and manipulated by the paws, which are often shaken to rid them of mud. They are wasteful eaters, often leaving bits of discarded vegetation.

Water voles have many enemies including stoats, herons and pike, and the introduced American mink has destroyed large numbers in some areas. Brown rats not only kill the voles, but take over their burrows. In a few places these voles may damage waterside crops and Man may kill them for this or, occasionally, for their fur.

The musk rat *(Ondatra zibethicus)*, which has a total length of up to 65 cm, is a large member of the vole group. It was imported into Europe from North America in the early years of this century for its fine dense fur, which is marketed as musquash. Many have escaped and, since they produce several litters of up to eight young in a season, their numbers have increased. They have now spread widely through France and much of central and northern Europe, where they have been welcomed as a source of sport, furs and meat, in spite of the fact that they make large and deep holes in river banks, for which reason they were eradicated when they first began to establish themselves in Britain.

They sometimes make large surface nests among dense waterside vegetation. At first sight these look like beaver lodges, but they are smaller and are not plastered with mud. Musk rats are most active early in the day. If they are surprised, they dive and swim expertly under water, aided by their somewhat flattened tails and their partially webbed feet.

Musk rat nests can be distinguished from beaver lodges by their smaller size and the fact that they are not plastered with mud.

The musk rat's fine, long fur, which protects it against the water and cold in its original home, is sufficiently valuable for the animal to be farmed on a commercial scale for its pelt.

When alarmed, musk rats dive noisily to warn other members of the colony. They can stay submerged for longer than water voles.

A swimming water vole uses all its feet to paddle along.

Although their diet is mainly of plant food, water voles sometimes eat fish. It is likely that this is usually carrion washed up, rather than fish which they have caught themselves.

When feeding on grass, water voles often pull it towards them and, especially on a slope, this gives the nibbled ends a 'combed down' look.

Water voles may mate on land or in the water. In Britain only two litters are produced in a year, usually in early spring and summer, but further east females may give birth to four litters in a season.

Water vole burrows usually have entrances above and below water. In the summer vertical shafts are opened up to the river edge. The voles feed close to these holes, mowing conspicuous 'lawns' round them.

HARVEST MOUSE
Family Muridae

The smallest of the European rodents, the harvest mouse *(Micromys minutus),* may be found through most of the continent except for Ireland, Scandinavia, the far north and most of Spain, Italy and Greece. It extends eastwards through much of Asia to Japan. Mainland animals tend to be larger than those in Britain, where the head and body length never exceeds 7 cm and is usually less than this. However, the overall length is almost double this due to the slender, prehensile-tipped tail. The adult weight is about 6 g, pregnant females being heavier.

Although harvest mice are mainly nocturnal, they may also be active during the daytime, seeking the seeds, fruits and insects on which they feed. They are rarely seen, for their sense of hearing is very keen, and if they detect an unusual sound they will either freeze, or leap to safety. They have been banished from the grainfields, which are their traditional home, by modern agricultural methods, but survive in areas of rank vegetation such as may be found on waste ground or in damp meadows. Here, in the summer, they live among the stalks, retreating as the leaves die in autumn to hedgerows and scrubland, where they become ground living. They are one of the most agile rodents, their widely spread toes enabling them to grasp the stems of grasses and other plants. Alone of the European mammals, they have prehensile tails. These are strong enough to support their weight, although they are more commonly used as an extra 'hand' to steady their progress.

The breeding season starts fairly late in the spring when the grasses and other herbaceous plants have made a good deal of growth, since they are the site of the nursery nests. These are built by the females who first weave leaves still attached to the plants into a hammock for shredded leaves which form the bulk of the nest. Since this outer support is still part of growing plants, it remains green and thus helps to camouflage the nest.

Up to seven young are born after a gestation period of 17 to 19 days. Weighing as little as 0.65 g at birth, they are blind and helpless, but by the fourth day the first downy hair appears on their backs. By the ninth day their eyes are open, and they have increased their weight by five times. They make their first exploration outside the nest on the eleventh day and by the time that they are 16 days old, their mother, who may well be preparing to produce another litter, will drive them away. In the course of her short life, a harvest mouse will probably produce three litters, the last of them in the late autumn, although the young from this litter will not survive if there is a sudden cold spell.

In captivity, harvest mice have survived for 5 years. The maximum life span in the wild is only 18 months and there is some evidence to show that in Britain few live for more than 6 months. In general, people do not persecute harvest mice, which do little damage to crops. However, other animals take a heavy toll, and predaceous mammals and birds — even pheasants — eat harvest mice.

Since the outer support of the harvest mouse's nest is made of leaves which are still attached to their parent plants, they stay green, helping to camouflage the nursery.

When building her nursery nest, a harvest mouse pulls the lower leaves into long strips to make the basic support for other shredded leaves which form the bulk of the nest.

The forefoot (upper) and hind foot (lower) of harvest mice have well-separated toes which enable the animals to grasp grass stalks or twigs firmly as they climb.

The summer nests of harvest mice are built among the stalks of cereal crops or coarse grasses. At first only a few centimetres off the ground, by late summer they have been raised by the growth of the stems to which they are attached. Small predators, such as the weasel, may send the baby mice scuttling to safety.

WOOD MICE

Family Muridae

In some parts of Europe the wood mice (*Apodemus spp*) are the most abundant mammals, outnumbering even Man. They may be recognized by their long faces, with large eyes and ears, their long, pale-coloured hindfeet and their very long tails, which usually measure more than the head and body combined. The tail can be a life-saving device, for if it is grabbed by a predator the skin breaks and slides off, to be the flesh-eater's only prize, while the mouse leaps to freedom. There is little tissue surrounding the tail vertebrae, and those which have been exposed quickly dry up and break off. Occasionally, a stump-tailed mouse may be found, bearing evidence of several lucky escapes.

Five species of wood mice occur in Europe. The rock mouse (*A. mystacinus*) is the largest, measuring 27 cm overall. It lives in dry woodlands and rocky places in Greece, along the Adriatic coast and into Asia Minor. The pigmy field mouse (*A. microps*) is the smallest at only 18 cm overall. First recognized in 1952, its distribution may well be far wider than the parts of eastern Europe and the Ukraine in which it is currently known. The striped field mouse (*A. agrarius*) rarely totals more than 19 cm and is the only species in which the tail is shorter than the head and body. It lives in scrubland and forest edges from eastern Europe across Asia to Taiwan. The two most widespread species are the yellow-necked mouse (*A. flavicollis*), in which the head and body length may be up to 12 cm and the tail up to 13.5 cm, and the wood mouse (*A. sylvaticus*), which is slightly smaller, with an overall length of not more than 22.5 cm. These two species may cross open ground, but they usually occur in forests. In Europe, the wood mouse is ubiquitous except for parts of Scandinavia, and it extends south into north Africa and eastwards to Japan. The yellow-neck, found in southern Britain, is absent from most of the rest of western Europe and is found no further eastwards than mainland China.

Male wood mice occupy a home range of about 2,250 sq m, while the females usually use less than 2,000 sq m. As with many territorial animals, the outer part of the range overlaps with that of other individuals. A dominant male may control an area of up to 2.5 hectares, which is also the living space of a number of subordinates and females. These appear not to be aggressive towards each other, although the females will defend their breeding areas. They are almost entirely nocturnal and are less active in periods of bright moonlight than when the nights are dark, when they may leave their nests for up to 2 hours.

Their diet is very varied. During the winter they feed mainly on acorns, chestnuts or hazelnuts, which they store in underground larders. Unlike squirrels, wood mice usually hide a large number of nuts together, and often nibble a corner of each; whether this is to test the soundness of the nut or for some other reason is not known. In spring and summer, the buds and shoots of growing plants are taken and so are insects, earthworms and snails. Their long hind feet enable wood mice to leap and climb well, but not as adeptly as the yellow-necks, which may live in the woodland canopy.

Under suitable conditions, wood mice and yellow-necks will breed almost throughout the year, but normally the first mating occurs in February. After a gestation of 20 days a litter of five to seven blind, naked, helpless young are born, each weighing 1 to 2 g. They begin to show the first brownish-grey fuzz of fur on their backs by the sixth day and their eyes are open by the tenth day, after which they become increasingly active.

If the nest is disturbed by a predator before this time, the young can be carried away together by their mother, for they all hang on to her nipples as she scampers to safety. They seem to be quite undamaged by this, even when they are dragged over rough ground or swung against branches.

The female wood mouse (below) *loses the end of her tail to a predator, but escapes with her life. She can carry her whole unweaned family to safety, for they cling to her nipples as she rushes away from danger. The wood mouse is building up a store of nuts and acorns in a hollow tree, while the yellow-neck eats an acorn.*

Once their eyes are open this behaviour ceases as they are probably too heavy to be carried together. In captivity, a female has been seen taking her young individually to places of safety round the nest, but since they are active and inquisitive, they often move, to the apparent distress of the mother. In the wild this untimely activity would probably bring disaster on them. By the age of 3 weeks they are independent and their mother has probably produced another litter.

Their life expectancy is short for they are among the chief prey of all small mammalian predators and owls. Numbers are maintained by their high breeding rate, for the young born early in the year produce their first litters at the age of about 2 months. In captivity, a Methuselah among yellow-necks has survived for more than 8 years, but in the wild no *Apodemus* can expect to live more than 2 years and most meet their end long before this.

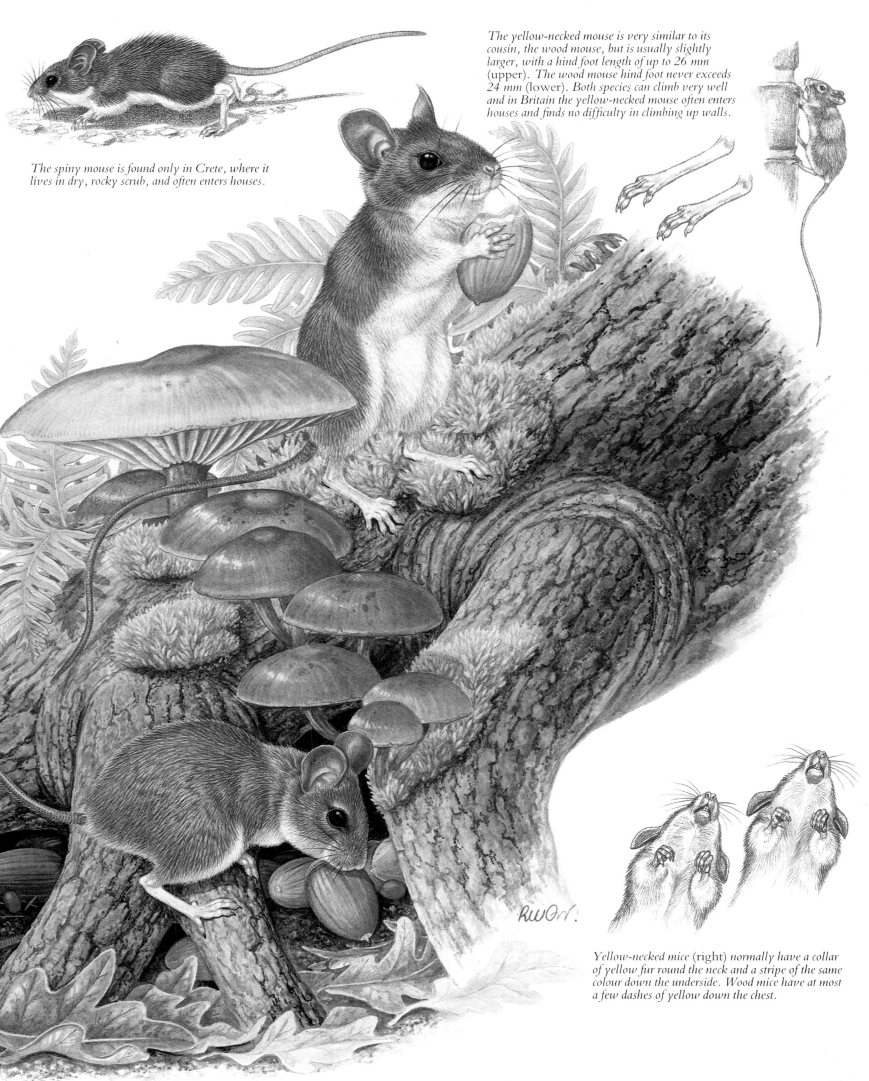

The yellow-necked mouse is very similar to its cousin, the wood mouse, but is usually slightly larger, with a hind foot length of up to 26 mm (upper). The wood mouse hind foot never exceeds 24 mm (lower). Both species can climb very well and in Britain the yellow-necked mouse often enters houses and finds no difficulty in climbing up walls.

The spiny mouse is found only in Crete, where it lives in dry, rocky scrub, and often enters houses.

Yellow-necked mice (right) normally have a collar of yellow fur round the neck and a stripe of the same colour down the underside. Wood mice have at most a few dashes of yellow down the chest.

HOUSE MICE
Family Muridae

After Man, the most ubiquitous mammal is the house mouse (*Mus musculus*). It is likely that it originated in the steppes of western Asia and began its association with Man during the Neolithic period when it joined the earliest settled human communities. As these expanded, the house mouse accompanied them and it is now found almost wherever humans live. The house mouse and its relatives *(Mus)* are smaller animals than the wood mice *(Apodemus)*, with less prominent eyes, smaller ears and hind feet, and stouter, almost hairless tails, which roughly equal the head and body length of 14–19 cm.

Two forms of house mouse occur in Europe. The western form is dark grey-brown on the back and only slightly paler below. The eastern mice, which are found in Scandinavia and east of a line running south from Denmark, are browner with pale underparts. House mice are all-rounders, which can run, climb well and swim if need be. They are probably short-sighted but have excellent hearing and sense of smell, by which they recognize landmarks and other members of their family.

In the warmer parts of their range house mice may live out of doors during the summer, making burrows and also maintaining a network of runs on the surface, but tending to migrate to ricks or buildings with the onset of the autumn. Inside buildings they nibble their way into cavity walls and spaces between floors. In such situations their territories may be very tiny with overlapping feeding ranges. As numbers grow, territorial aggressiveness increases and any mouse not belonging to a family group will be attacked. At very high population densities a small number of males will live polygamously with several females in strongly defended territories, while the bulk of the population crams into a small area in which they survive as non-territorial, non-breeding subordinates.

In a new territory, large numbers can build up very fast provided that there is plenty of food. Nesting material is also vital and may include paper, sacking, grass or leaves and where these are in short supply females will share nests. The litter normally contains five or six helpless young, which weigh about 1 g at birth. They are fully furred at 14 days and weaned within 3 weeks, by which time they measure about two-thirds of their mother's length. They can produce young of their own within a few weeks of this. In good shelter breeding is uninterrupted, and a female may produce 10 litters in a year. In less favourable areas the number of litters may drop to five.

House mice drink very little, but eat almost anything that Man eats, as well as sampling many apparently less edible substances. Outdoor-living mice include some insects and worms in their diet. Feeding takes place mainly at dusk and dawn with snacks in between.

In southern Europe, the house mouse has two small relatives. In the east of the continent, the steppe mouse (*Mus hortulanus*) is a grassland species which lives socially, often forming huge food stores containing up to 10 kg of grain. The Algerian mouse (*M. spretus*) lives in the moister parts of Portugal, Spain and southern France. It is less social than the steppe mouse, and does not make such extensive food hoards.

Dominant male mice are aggressive to others, maintaining their position through displays such as this in which they make themselves look bigger than their opponent.

Pet white mice are domesticated descendants of house mice. The tail in this species is not fragile, and here a tame mouse climbs up its own tail.

The nest of a house mouse may be built of many materials, shredded newspaper being one of the most commonly used components.

Over much of Europe house mice live out of doors during the summer. In cold weather they retreat to the shelter of buildings, where they damage and foul far more than they actually eat.

RATS
Family Muridae

Of all, the rodents, rats are primarily responsible for the group's bad name. Undeniably they eat and contaminate vast amounts of crops and stored products; their powerful jaws can do considerable structural damage to buildings; and also they carry several extremely unpleasant diseases of Man and domestic animals. Their efficiency as pests is increased by their ability to live in a wide range of habitats and to replace by rapid breeding any losses caused by Man's relentless attacks with traps and poison. Ironically, the very insistence of this onslaught has selected those rats which are best able to withstand humans, so that they are among the most adaptable and intelligent of the smaller animals.

Two species of rat are found in Europe. The black or ship rat *(Rattus rattus)* has a head and body length up to 24 cm, a tail of more than this length, and weighs at most 280 g. It is a lightly built animal, with a long pointed face and large, almost hairless ears. The coat may be a wide range of colours, but always has long guard hairs which stand out from the underfur. The common or brown rat *(R. norvegicus)* is a larger, coarser looking animal, with a blunter face and finely furred ears, measuring up to 56 cm overall, of which less than half is the tail. Growth may continue throughout the normal lifespan of 1 to 2 years and a large brown rat may weigh as much as 600 g, although most are smaller.

Both species originated in Asia and arrived in Europe through natural migrations aided by Man, who has now spread them to much of the rest of the world. The black rat probably originated in a warm forested area, for it is an agile climber and sometimes, in the more southerly parts of Europe, it lives in trees, making nests like squirrels' dreys, but it is unable to withstand cold climates without shelter. It is reputed to have spread from its original home during classical times and to have been brought to Europe by Crusaders returning from the Holy Land. The common rat has a more northerly origin. It invaded eastern Europe in the early 1700s and was soon spread throughout the continent. As it became settled in Europe it drove out the ship rat, which now tends to survive in warmer areas, in heated buildings or around ports. Most open country, warehouses, ricks and sewers are inhabited by the brown rat. The two species can coexist and sometimes the upper parts of a building are the domain of the black rat while the common rat occupies the lower storeys.

Where food is abundant and shelter good, brown rats may not need to travel more than 40 m from the nest, although in open country their runs have been traced 10 times this distance across fields. Their runs usually include bolt holes and blind ended tunnels which reach nearly to the surface of the ground and can be broken through in an emergency. They are good swimmers and tend to settle within easy reach of water, which is as vital to them as food, colonizing stream banks in the countryside and sewers in urban habitats. Female brown rats are mature at about 11 weeks and mate soon after this, although they are still far from fully grown. Their early families are small with perhaps only six young. As they grow they may produce a dozen or more in a litter and the record number is 22. The gestation period is 21 to 24 days and at birth the young are hairless, blind and deaf. Their eyes open on about the sixth day and they are weaned within 3 weeks. Normally no young are produced during the winter, and it is rare for a female to give birth to more than five litters in a year.

A small brown rat colony has great cohesion, repelling invaders to its territory, to which it is, perhaps, bound by a colony smell. As numbers grow, a social hierarchy develops, the dominant rats living closest to the source of food, while the underlings are forced to search further afield and even to feed by daylight. The young of subordinates stand a poor chance of survival, and they do not show the same inclination to repel newcomers.

Little is known of the social organization of the ship rat. In Europe it almost always inhabits buildings, which makes it easy to control, so the build up of large numbers is comparatively rare. It swims less and climbs more than the brown rat, moving faster and pausing less frequently as it dashes along a rafter or a branch.

Rats can survive on almost any food, although they prefer a cereal diet with some animal matter. In general, the ship rat is the more vegetarian of the two species. Food is not stored, although it is taken to a safe place to be eaten. Rats are an important food of many carnivores.

The black rat is an agile climber and in southern Europe it may live in trees. Elsewhere in the continent it is found mainly in heated buildings or near to ports.

Although both species of rat are associated with unhygienic conditions, both are clean animals and spend much time grooming.

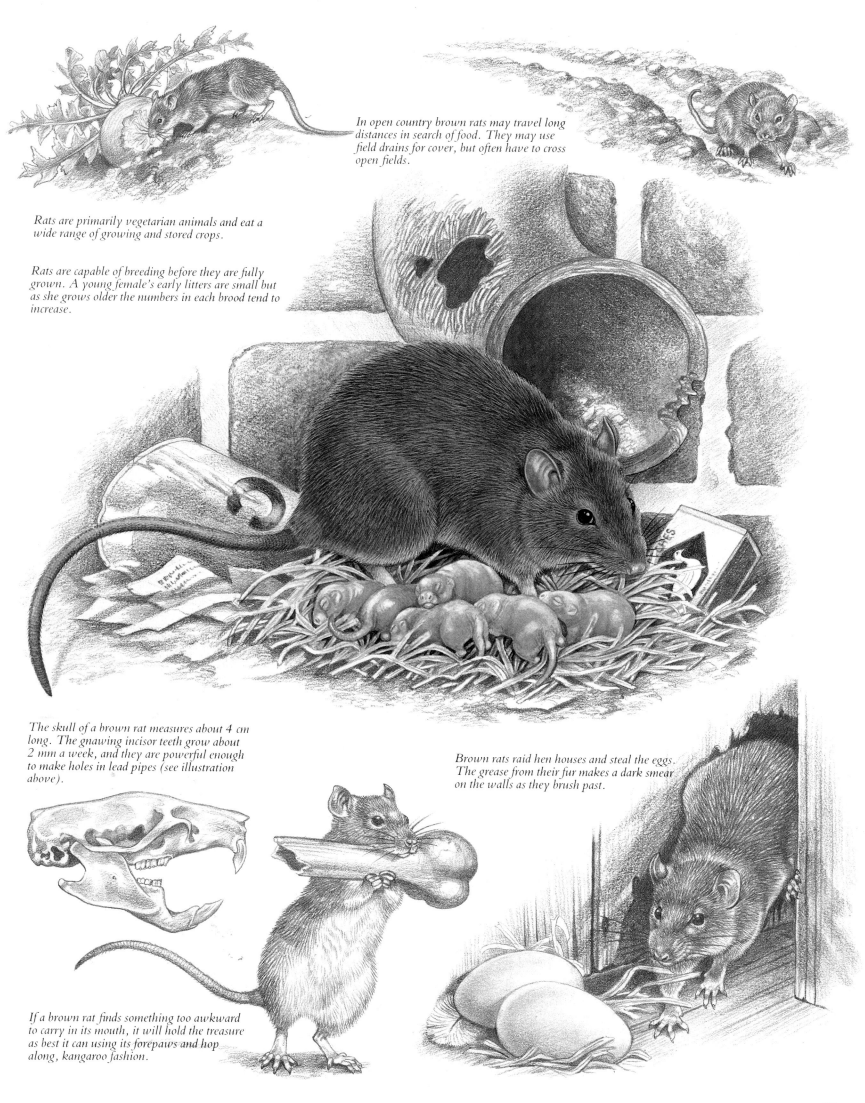

In open country brown rats may travel long distances in search of food. They may use field drains for cover, but often have to cross open fields.

Rats are primarily vegetarian animals and eat a wide range of growing and stored crops.

Rats are capable of breeding before they are fully grown. A young female's early litters are small but as she grows older the numbers in each brood tend to increase.

The skull of a brown rat measures about 4 cm long. The gnawing incisor teeth grow about 2 mm a week, and they are powerful enough to make holes in lead pipes (see illustration above).

Brown rats raid hen houses and steal the eggs. The grease from their fur makes a dark smear on the walls as they brush past.

If a brown rat finds something too awkward to carry in its mouth, it will hold the treasure as best it can using its forepaws and hop along, kangaroo fashion.

BIRCH MICE
Family Zapodidae
and MOLE RATS
Family Muridae

The agile little northern birch mouse *(Sicista betulina)* is found in central Norway, parts of Sweden and Denmark and from Finland and Poland eastwards to central Asia, while isolated populations occur in Czechoslovakia and Austria. It belongs to a group of small rodents which are mainly steppe and semi-desert dwellers, but as its name suggests, it differs from them in that it lives in birch forests, especially where there is a heavy scrub layer. A close relative, the southern birch mouse *(S. subtilis)* is found on the Asiatic steppes and extends into Rumania, with small numbers in Hungary and Austria.

They are very similar in size, with an adult head and body length of up to 7 cm. The tail is very long and in the northern species may be nearly one-and-a-half times the head and body length. It is partly prehensile and helps the animal as it scampers through the undergrowth. The hind feet of this species are also large, although it does not jump like some of its dry country relatives. Both of these birch mice could be confused with the striped field mouse (p.72), which is a rather more robust-looking animal with a far shorter tail and larger ears.

Throughout their range birch mice are thought to be rare, for they are not often seen nor is it usual for their remains to occur in owl pellets. The northern birch mouse is strictly nocturnal, spending the daylight hours in a nest which may lie a few centimetres underground in a system of shallow burrows or in a rotten log. The southern birch mouse is thought to be more active during the daytime, but little is known of its behaviour. Both feed largely on insects. The northern birch mouse eats mainly the beetles and other insects which develop in decaying wood. The southern species apparently specializes in caterpillars and surface-dwelling beetles, but it also eats grain and other seeds at times when these are available.

Towards the end of the summer, the northern birch mouse increases its intake of plant food, building up resources for the cold weather. From October to April both species enter true hibernation, with their bodily functions reduced and their temperature lowered to as little as 7°C.

Pairing occurs soon after they rouse from hibernation and four or five young are born in late May or June. In spite of the long gestation of 4 weeks, baby birch mice are helpless at birth and they develop far more slowly than the young of other small rodents. Their eyes do not open for 25 days and they do not leave their mother's care until they are 5 weeks old. As each pair produces only one litter a year, it is likely that they have a long lifespan comparable to that of dormice, with which they share a number of anatomical features.

Western Europe is one of the few parts of the world lacking subterranean rodents. Only two species, which have spread from the steppes of Asia, are found in the east of the continent. The greater mole rat *(Spalax microphthalmus)* and lesser mole rat *(S. leucodon)* are distinguished by their size, up to 31 and 26 cm long respectively, and in some details of their structure. However, in habits and habitats they are very similar.

They are totally blind and lack external ears but round the head have a row of stiff bristles, which almost certainly has a tactile function. Unlike true moles, mole rats have rather small feet and claws, for they shove their way through sandy ground with their spade-shaped heads, consolidating the walls of their tunnels as they go. Where the soil is firmer, or stony, they use their powerful incisor teeth to loosen it, pushing any surplus to the surface to make molehill-like mounds. Mole rats are active by day and night throughout the year, whatever the weather above ground. Their burrows are very extensive, reaching a depth of 3 m or more. In agricultural land mole rats can be a major pest for they feed almost entirely on the underground parts of plants, including many root crops, and they sometimes also pull green growth down into their burrows.

Like true moles, mole rats are solitary creatures and, after mating in January or February, the male probably does not remain with the female. She prepares a large nursery chamber where her litter of four or five young are born in March. These are naked and helpless at birth, but within a fortnight develop a coat of long, pale fur, quite unlike that of the adult. They disperse as soon as they are weaned at the age of 4 to 6 weeks. They are often forced to travel overland where they are highly vulnerable to predators and their remains are often found in the pellets of barn owls.

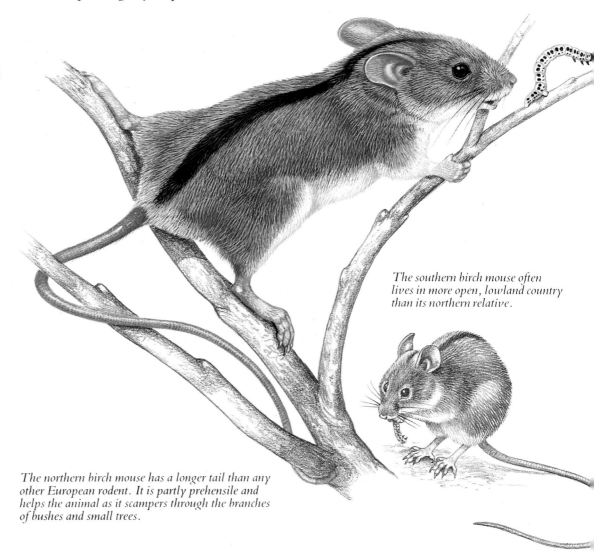

The southern birch mouse often lives in more open, lowland country than its northern relative.

The northern birch mouse has a longer tail than any other European rodent. It is partly prehensile and helps the animal as it scampers through the branches of bushes and small trees.

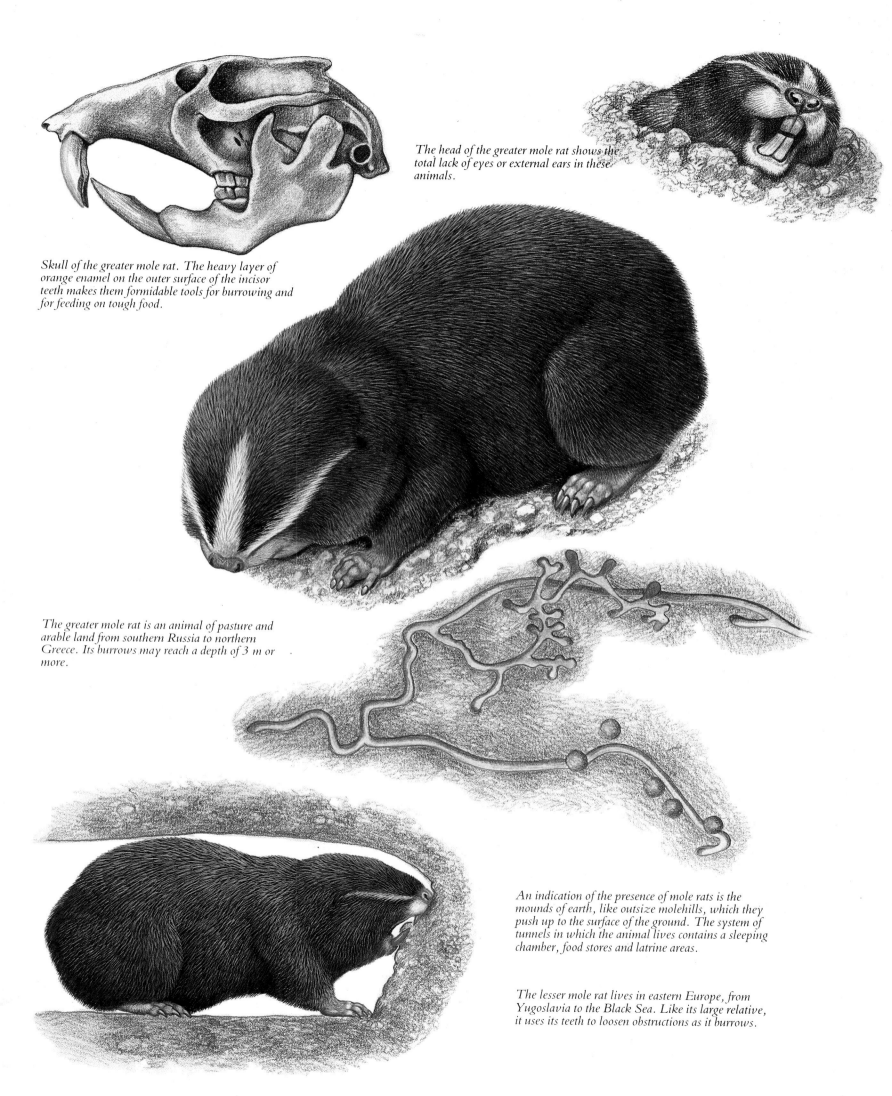

The head of the greater mole rat shows the total lack of eyes or external ears in these animals.

Skull of the greater mole rat. The heavy layer of orange enamel on the outer surface of the incisor teeth makes them formidable tools for burrowing and for feeding on tough food.

The greater mole rat is an animal of pasture and arable land from southern Russia to northern Greece. Its burrows may reach a depth of 3 m or more.

An indication of the presence of mole rats is the mounds of earth, like outsize molehills, which they push up to the surface of the ground. The system of tunnels in which the animal lives contains a sleeping chamber, food stores and latrine areas.

The lesser mole rat lives in eastern Europe, from Yugoslavia to the Black Sea. Like its large relative, it uses its teeth to loosen obstructions as it burrows.

CRESTED PORCUPINE

Family Hystricidae

The crested porcupine *(Hystrix cristata)* is to be found principally in steppe and savannah areas in the northern half of Africa, and it was probably released in southern Italy and Sicily in the remote past for, although it is not common, it is well established there. More recently, the crested porcupine has been freed in the Balkans. Occasionally, this and other porcupine species escape from zoological collections further north in the continent, but they are rarely allowed to remain at large for long.

After the beaver, the crested porcupine is the largest European rodent, reaching a head and body length of 70 cm and a weight of 20 kg although this is less than in the warmer part of its range. In spite of its size it is not often seen for it is nocturnal, and little is known of its social life. It seems that several individuals, perhaps the members of a single family, share a den. This is made in a deep crevice in rocky country, or in extensive, deep burrows, sometimes taken over from badgers, in other places.

If sighted it is unmistakable, for the long spines and conspicuous black-and-white colouring set it apart from all other animals. The spines vary on different parts of the body — those on the head are long and slender; those on the upper back are very much thicker and banded with black; and those on the lower back are predominantly black. Most extraordinary are the hollow tail spines, the ends of which break off soon after they have developed leaving long, goblet-like structures. When alarmed, a crested porcupine shakes its tail and these spines rattle loudly, giving warning that here is an animal not to be trifled with. If an inexperienced or hungry predator ignores this advice, the porcupine runs backwards into it to give it a sharp reminder of the fact. A crested porcupine cannot shoot its spines as is claimed in folklore, but the quills of the back are very loosely attached and transfer themselves readily to the snout or paws of an attacker. This gives it absolute security from most enemies other than Man, against whose snares this rodent has no armour.

Like other well-protected animals, crested porcupines are noisy, grunting and scuffing as they search for food. They are mainly vegetarian and hunt for roots, tubers and bulbs. Their powerful jaws and teeth allow them to chew bones, which they often collect and carry to their dens. In farmland they may be considerable pests since, apart from attacking sugar beet, they will eat grain, including stored crops. More serious and widespread, however, is the damage which they may do to trees, especially in the springtime, when they remove the bark to get at the sweet and sappy cambium below.

Crested porcupines mate early in the year. In captivity, a gestation period of about 100 days has been recorded. The litter of two to four young are born in a nest warmly lined with grass and leaves. It is not known how long they remain with their parents in the wild.

Porcupines do not hibernate, but after the rich feeding of summer and autumn they become less active during the colder weather.

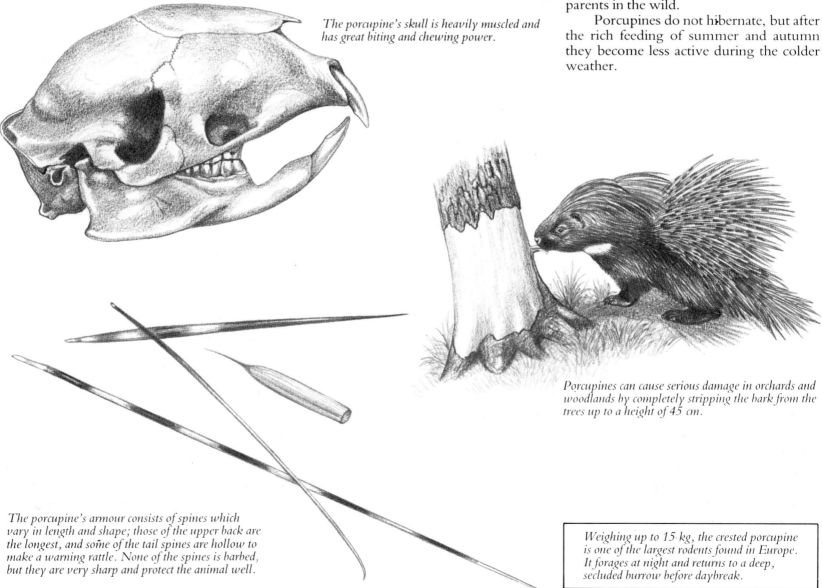

The porcupine's skull is heavily muscled and has great biting and chewing power.

Porcupines can cause serious damage in orchards and woodlands by completely stripping the bark from the trees up to a height of 45 cm.

The porcupine's armour consists of spines which vary in length and shape; those of the upper back are the longest, and some of the tail spines are hollow to make a warning rattle. None of the spines is barbed, but they are very sharp and protect the animal well.

Weighing up to 15 kg, the crested porcupine is one of the largest rodents found in Europe. It forages at night and returns to a deep, secluded burrow before daybreak.

COYPU
Family Capromyidae

The aquatic coypu *(Myocastor coypus)* is protected in the water by its fine, dense coat. This has been its downfall in its native South America, where hunting and disease have reduced its numbers greatly. However, it can be kept easily in captivity and has been widely farmed for its fur, which is marketed under the name of nutria. Many specimens have escaped, and in some places it has been deliberately released, so it is now widespread in Europe. Except for parts of France, Germany and eastern England, colonies tend to be short lived, as they cannot stand the harsh northern winters.

A male coypu is almost a metre in length, one-third of which is the cylindrical tail, and it may weight over 7 kg. The females are slightly smaller. When swimming, the webbed hind feet are kicked alternately, and paddling movements are made by the forelimbs. The forefeet are strongly clawed and are used for grooming and manipulating food.

The coypus' preferred habitat is slow-flowing streams, in the banks of which burrows about 20 cm in diameter and 6 m long can be dug. During the day they rest in the nest chamber at the end of the main tunnel, while at night they are intermittently active. When high populations build up, colonies develop which are dominated by a clan matriarch and her mate. Her female offspring occupy ranges partially overlapping that of their mother, while the males tend to migrate at puberty. In a rich, mixed environment the home range of a clan matriarch is 4 hectares and that of a male may be up to 5 hectares, but it may be very much larger where grazing is poor. The ranges are marked with a secretion from a large gland which lies just above the rectum.

Studies in East Anglia have shown that at different times of the year coypus feed on different plants, so that they utilize their environment very fully. In spring, the shoots of many waterside plants are eaten; later in the year, the lower stems are taken; and in winter the roots and storage stems of water plants are most important. They also plunder arable crops, especially cabbages and sugar beet. In order to digest their food fully, coypus practice refection during their daytime rest periods.

In Britain, coypus may breed throughout the year, most litters being born in the autumn and winter, although a few older females may give birth in the spring. About five young are produced after a gestation of 127 to 138 days. Their weight is variable, ranging from 120 to 330 g. They are fully furred and active at birth with functional incisor and molar teeth, and can feed themselves within a few days. However, they are at least partially suckled for 6 to 10 weeks and they are not fully grown until they are about 2 years old. Their mother's nipples are placed high on her sides so that the babies can suckle in the water, but she normally feeds them on land.

In Europe the coypu has many enemies. Apart from Man, the most severe of these is probably the weather, for hard winters certainly reduce the numbers of young. Even in a good season they are vulnerable to many predators including dogs, foxes, mink, hawks, owls and pike.

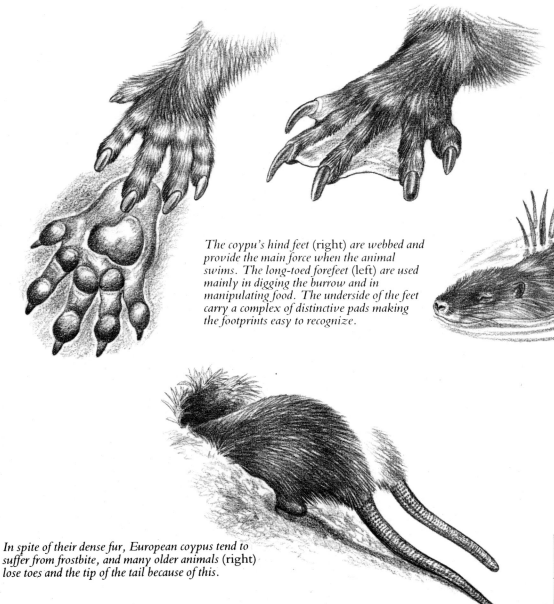

The coypu's hind feet (right) *are webbed and provide the main force when the animal swims. The long-toed forefeet* (left) *are used mainly in digging the burrow and in manipulating food. The underside of the feet carry a complex of distinctive pads making the footprints easy to recognize.*

Female coypus can suckle their young while swimming for their nipples are placed high up on their sides.

In spite of their dense fur, European coypus tend to suffer from frostbite, and many older animals (right) *lose toes and the tip of the tail because of this.*

The South American coypu was brought to Europe as a fur-bearing animal but has escaped from captivity on numerous occasions and is now well established by slow-flowing streams and in swampy places over much of the western part of the continent.

CARNIVORES

Order Carnivora

Many animals eat some flesh but only one group of mammals, the carnivores, habitually feeds on vertebrates which cannot be subdued easily and need to be partially dismembered before swallowing. They are never abundant in the way that rabbits and voles may be, yet they exert a very important controlling influence on the herbivores. By removing the weak, the injured, the old and a proportion of the young, which are their primary food targets, they ensure a degree of fitness in the survivors.

In Europe, 19 species of native carnivores are augmented by a further six species which have been introduced by man, and by feral populations of ferrets, cats and, sometimes, dogs. They range in size from the bears to the weasel and they are divided into six families by structural details which are, in part at least, a reflection of their hunting techniques. In spite of differences in appearance, all share certain characteristics associated with their flesh-eating habit. All carnivores are capable of running at high speed, at least over short distances, for while the ways of making a kill may vary, they almost always involve a chase of some sort before the prey is caught. All have fairly generalized bodies, with medium to long legs, and most have five-toed feet. Some, such as the cats and dogs, walk on their toes (digitigrade). Many of the rest place the sole of the foot on the ground (plantigrade). Some are variable and may use the whole foot or only part of it as the occasion and their gait demand.

In order to be sure of a meal, the carnivores have to be able to outsmart their prey, so their brain is relatively large and complex. All carnivores are intelligent animals and among land mammals only the primates have a larger brain size in relation to their body bulk. This allows them to adapt their hunting techniques to suit particular circumstances, such as the temporary abundance of a certain prey, and to learn by experience.

The method of making a kill may vary, but the large stabbing canine teeth, which all carnivores possess, usually play a part. Behind the canines, in both the upper and lower jaws, is a row of sharp, pointed premolars which mesh with each other. Behind these, the fourth upper premolar and the first lower molar are elongated teeth, with narrow, knife-like crowns, which cut like the blades of a pair of scissors. They are called carnassials and are one of the hallmarks of the carnivores. The position of the carnassials, well back in the mouth and near the jaw hinge, gives them the power to cut through even the hard skin and tough muscles of large, old animals.

In order that the carnassials may work to their maximum advantage, the jaw hinge in carnivores allows very little sideways movement and a carnivore typically champs, rather than chews, its food. Many carnivores include some plant food in their diet and this is crushed by broad molar teeth which lie behind the carnassials.

All carnivores tend to produce large quantities of saliva, which helps them to bolt their food. Meat does not require the intense chewing needed by plants, especially grass, and huge pieces of flesh can be swallowed and digested. The length of the carnivore gut is small compared with that of herbivores, which gives the flesh-eater a lean look in comparison with the round-bellied plant feeders.

Most carnivores are solitary animals and courtship and mating are brief episodes, after which the partners return to their territories and do not meet again. The females generally give birth to several young early in the year, although a few species produce a second litter. In some, the gestation period is prolonged by delayed implantation. In these animals, mating takes place long before the birth of the young. The fertilized ova, after a very short period of development, remain as pinhead-sized bundles of cells for several months. These do not continue their growth until some stimulus causes them to become implanted in the wall of the uterus, after which foetal growth continues in a perfectly normal manner. The reason for delayed implantation is unknown, although it has been suggested that it enables both mating and birth to take place at the most advantageous time of the year.

The young of carnivores are generally born in an isolated, well-protected burrow or den, and at first are blind and helpless. In most cases they are reared by the mother alone. However, in foxes the father helps to provide food and in wolves, the whole pack helps with caring for and feeding the cubs once they have been weaned. Whatever the family structure, young carnivores develop slowly and, as they grow, they learn the techniques of hunting and escape. This is mainly through the play-fighting which makes all young carnivores such engaging creatures to watch. These scuffles have an important function, not only in developing a dominance hierarchy among the young, but also in teaching them the basic movements of attack and defence. Later, they accompany their parents in food searches. A young carnivore deprived of parental example is a less successful hunter, at least during its first season.

Most carnivores have well-developed senses of smell, which may be used to track down food and in the animal's social life. All carnivores possess paired stink glands just below the root of the tail and the secretions from these may be used in marking territorial boundaries or in proclaiming the ownership of hidden food. Most carnivores have excellent hearing and are capable of detecting sounds of a higher pitch than can be heard by humans. They also have the ability, important in a hunting animal, to determine very accurately from which direction a sound is coming. The acuity of vision varies. Most do not have colour vision and the rest probably see little more than tinted greys. Carnivores have a good sense of touch enhanced by thick whiskers called vibrissae, which are situated mainly on the snout, but also above the eyes and, in some species, under the chin and on the sides of the face.

The beautiful fur of many carnivores and the fact that some of them conflict with Man's interests, have led to them being persecuted more than any other group of animals, and a few are now in serious danger of extinction. Most of these are now protected, many surviving almost entirely within the bounds of reserves. A more widespread understanding of their ways of life and a curbing of persecution should, however, enable them to survive into the next century.

WOLF and JACKAL

Family Canidae

The wild dogs of Europe include the wolf, the jackal, the foxes and the introduced raccoon dog. In general they are long-legged hunters, which capture their prey after a prolonged chase. Fox cubs remain with their parents throughout their first summer, but young jackals and wolves may stay longer and form a pack, for the family unit is the nucleus of a well-organized social life. Packs rarely include more than about 10 animals and generally less, for if too many hunt together a single prey animal will not satisfy them. A large pack usually breaks up into two groups occupying mutually exclusive areas. Very rarely, under the stress of hard weather and food shortage, family packs may temporarily amalgamate.

In prehistoric times, the wolf *(Canis lupus)* lived throughout lowland Europe and Asia and over much of North

The front foot of a wolf is very much like that of a dog. When they walk, wolves do not 'crab' with the hind quarters in the manner of many dogs.

America. This large, intelligent hunter came into conflict with Man when he began to farm and replaced the wild herds with domestic stock of which the wolves took their toll. They have been virtually exterminated in western Europe, although tiny isolated groups survive in Spain and Italy. In the east of the continent, they are more numerous, but even here they tend to occupy upland and forested areas rather than the open lowland plains which are their natural habitat.

It is not surprising that an animal which once lived over so large an area should differ somewhat across its range, and the northern wolves are usually larger and paler in colour than the southern forms. A wolf resembles a German shepherd dog, although the ears are smaller, the tail carriage is often lower, and there is a large facial ruff which may make it look bigger than it really is. The maximum recorded weight for a European wolf is over 50 kg and the overall length is up to 180 cm, 40 cm of which is the tail. Even a small wolf is likely to be more powerful than a domestic dog. It will also have a brain about 30 per cent larger than a dog of comparable bulk, for the wolf is among the most intelligent of all land mammals.

Wolves are social animals, a family pack usually occupying a territory greater than 30 sq km. The method by which such ranges are maintained is unknown, although it is probably by scent marking with urine. Wolves apparently advertise

The wolf's skull shows the large braincase, a long row of uncrowded teeth, and a wide arch of bone through which large chewing muscles, attached at one end to the lower jaw and at the other to the top of the skull, pass.

their presence near to the boundaries of their territory by howling, and since their voices can carry over several kilometres, others know of their presence and avoiding action can be taken. They will criss-cross their territory when hunting, and during the summer they may travel 50 km or more during a single hunting expedition.

Wolves are monogamous and are reputed to remain celibate if their partner dies. It is normally only the dominant bitch in the pack which mates, usually, although not always, with the dominant male. However, large packs may break up with one female in each group mating. This takes place in the early spring and is prolonged, with the pair becoming tied, as with the domestic dog. Other members of the pack often remain close by, since mating couples are helpless to defend themselves. The gestation period is from 61 to 63 days, and towards the end of this time the bitch finds a suitable spot to dig a whelping burrow, generally on a well-drained ridge near to water, and usually with some outlook so

Dogs have descended from wolves which were first domesticated by Stone Age Man. A dog is usually less powerful than a wolf of similar bulk, its teeth are smaller and its jaws are weaker, as can be seen from the front of the dog's jaws (upper) *compared to those of a wolf* (lower).

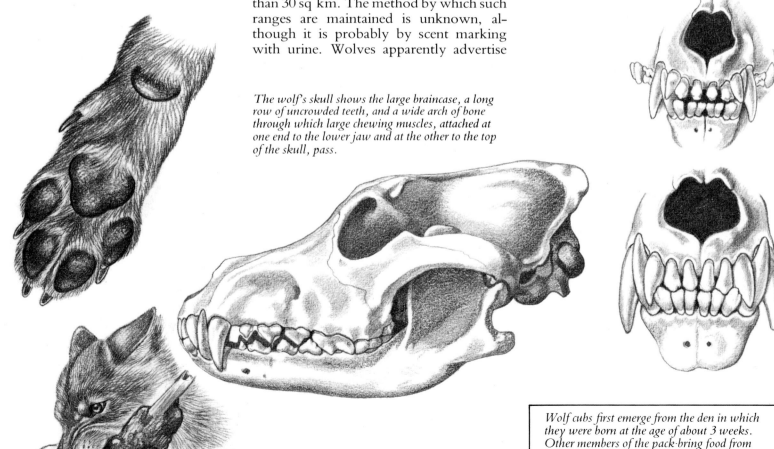

The most powerful teeth of a wolf are the slicing carnassials, which lie towards the back of the jaw and are used for cutting tough flesh from the prey.

Wolf cubs first emerge from the den in which they were born at the age of about 3 weeks. Other members of the pack bring food from kills, probably made a long way away. The meat is regurgitated so that the cubs' first solid meals are partly digested for them by the adults.

that the approach of enemies can be observed. She often takes over a badger hole or enlarges a fox earth. The actual chamber in which the cubs are born is at the end of a tunnel beteen 2 and 10 m long.

The litter usually consists of five or six young, which weigh just under 0.5 kg at birth. At first they are blind and deaf, although their bodies are covered with short, dark fur. They grow rapidly in the first 14 weeks, gaining more than a kilogram in weight per week. Their eyes open at 11 to 15 days old, although they cannot see clearly until some weeks later. Within days of this their first teeth erupt, and when they are about 3 weeks old they begin to hear. Until then their mother remains with them in the den being fed by her mate, and leaving only to drink. She keeps the cubs clean by licking them and maintains the hygiene of the nursery by eating their faeces.

At about 3 weeks, a cub can walk and may leave the den to take its first foray into the outside world, romping with its brothers and sisters on the playground in front of the tunnel entrance. Like puppies, wolf cubs tumble and play, learning the rudiments of hunting techniques in their mock battles, and establishing dominance. Also, they begin to use the complex repertoire of posture and expression with which they maintain their position in the pack. The pack is rigidly hierarchical and a low-ranking cub is unlikely ever to become a pack leader.

Weaning starts soon after they first leave the den, although they may continue to nurse until they are 7 or 8 weeks old. Since they are growing prodigiously at this time, their parents alone cannot provide enough food for them, and other members of the pack help by bringing loads of meat which they have swallowed and which they regurgitate for the cubs. This behaviour has a dual function, for the cubs become socialized to all members of the pack, who are, in any case, likely to be their aunts and uncles, and it gives these non-breeding adults some of the satisfaction of bringing up the family.

During the summer months when the cubs are growing, the wolf pack may be fairly sedentary, although the adults may have to travel long distances to make a kill. As winter approaches they become more nomadic, following whatever prey they can find. In North America, where wolves have been intensively studied, some hunts have been watched from start to finish. As with most prey species, the deer which formed the major quarry did not seem to be alarmed by the mere presence of wolves, although a mother with young was always alert and vigilant. Often the prey was hidden in a belt of trees and the wolves became

aware of its scent before they saw it. Almost any animal detected was chased but if a deer managed to maintain a head start of 100 m or so for more than about 10 or 15 seconds, the wolves gave up and looked for other prey. Usually they ran in a line behind the animal. Occasionally, if it ran in a curve, they cut across to intercept it. Sometimes, the chase would go on for 2.5 km, but was usually less than this, as a healthy deer can outrun a wolf. A few of the deer turned to face the wolves, which inhibited the attack, for wolves apparently need the stimulus of running prey.

The capacity of a wolf's stomach is about 5 kg and the animals normally bolt their food, so that a pack of six animals will eat the greater part of a deer very quickly. The gut content, although usually not the stomach, is eaten first and if anything is left when the pack is sated, they will return to demolish it completely, apart from a few of the largest bones. If wolves are forced, by lack of their normal food, to kill domestic animals, these are often left after one meal. This may be due to the relative ease with which these slower and more docile animals can be killed, or the proximity of humans may cause the wolves to be extra wary.

The future of the wolf depends on Man and it seems at present that conservation measures may be taken in enough areas to prevent this beautiful and complex animal from becoming extinct. In the remote areas in which it lives, it benefits the prey species by removing the old, the surplus young and injured animals.

In south-east Europe, the golden jackal (*Canis aureus*) survives in the Balkans, European Russia and parts of Hungary. Far smaller than the wolf, with a total length of less than 130 cm and a weight not exceeding 15 kg, it looks like a slender, long-muzzled dog. Its preferred home is dry steppe or semi-desert, where there is some scrub to give it cover. In its search for small prey or carrion, it sometimes comes into villages or towns, where it scavenges for refuse. Its main food is rodents and birds, and in some places chickens or even lambs come under attack, which makes it as unpopular as the wolf. Like the wolf, it is a social pack animal, maintaining hunting territories by marking with urine. It has been intensively studied in Africa, but whether the social bonds and behaviour patterns are the same in European populations is unknown.

With their musical howls, wolves maintain social contact within a pack and warn neighbouring packs of their presence.

Wolves mark the boundaries of their pack territory with urine, a habit still found in domestic dogs.

The elegant golden jackal is found in south-east Europe, where it often scavenges round the edge of villages.

Facial expressions are an important part of wolf language: upper, a dominant animal has ears forward, eyes open and mouth in normal position; lower right, expresses aggression but not fear; and lower left, the ears back, the eyes partly closed and the mouth drawn back but closed express submission.

Wolves are able to subdue prey much larger and stronger than themselves by working as a group. They normally kill weak animals, and a healthy moose can escape in most cases.

Like dogs, wolves often rub the sides of their faces in specially strongly scented substances, such as the droppings of prey animals.

Mating wolves become tied; while in this position they are helpless, so other members of the pack remain on hand in case danger should threaten.

RED FOX

Family Canidae

A glimpse of the tawny coat and the white-tipped brush of the fox *(Vulpes vulpes)* may reward the country lover or surprise the townsman almost anywhere in Europe, for this animal is not only among the commonest but also one of the most widespread of Europe's mammals. It can make its living in all but the most barren of Arctic wastes or the highest mountains, and in recent years it has discovered that urban areas are a source of easy pickings. Beyond Europe, the red fox occurs throughout temperate Asia, over much of North America, into North Africa, and it has been introduced into Australia.

The fox may be up to 125 cm long, over 40 cm of which is the long, bushy tail. The weight of a male may be as much as 10 kg, although most are smaller than this, weighing less than many domestic cats. Foxes are active at dusk and at night, although where they are not persecuted by Man they may be seen during daylight hours as well.

For most of the year they are solitary animals, occupying a range defined by the scent of urine, and at all times scent from the foxes' powerful stink glands announces their presence. The size of their territory varies with the type of environment; in poor upland country it may be as much as 15 sq km, while in a rich and varied lowland habitat, a pair may survive in 0.5 sq km. If there is enough cover, foxes will not normally make underground dens, but will lie up under thick hedges or in hollow trees. In the breeding season vixens will enlarge rabbit holes or take over disused parts of badgers' setts to give their cubs safe unlined nurseries. Foxes are opportunist feeders. Rabbits and rodents are probably their favourite fare, but insects, worms and other invertebrates are also important. Like all dogs, foxes can digest a good deal of plant food and in the autumn apples, plums and blackberries form an appreciable part of the diet. Carrion is eaten, and early in the year sheep placentas and stillborn lambs are an important part of the food of hill foxes. Foxes also kill birds, ground-nesting species, their eggs and young being particularly at risk, but overall probably little harm is done to wild populations. However, where woodlands are reserved for game birds, foxes can do considerable damage. If a fox discovers a way into a hen house, it may kill every bird there. This has often been cited as proving the animal's blood lust, but it is more likely to be the result of an over-stimulation of the animal's hunting instinct by the flapping, squawking birds. Any surplus food is normally cached, to be used later when hunting has been unsuccessful.

Some authorities suggest that foxes pair for life, but this is uncertain. However, the courtship is prolonged and in the late winter the high-pitched barks and screams of the red foxes serenading their prospective mates may often be heard. The cubs are born after a gestation period of 52 or 53 days. At birth they weigh 100 to 130 g and are covered with fine dark fur. For the first 3 weeks of their lives their mother remains with them, the dog bringing food to her. After this, she leaves them during the daytime, although she returns to feed them. They are given regurgitated meat from about 4 weeks old, although they are not fully weaned until 6 to 7 weeks old. Shortly after their eyes open, they leave the den to play under the watchful eyes of their parents. They remain as a family unit until the autumn, when they wander away, perhaps travelling long distances before they find an unoccupied territory. Foxes are hunted, shot, trapped, snared, poisoned and gassed, yet despite this many survive for over 10 years.

Where game birds are preserved as a woodland crop, foxes find easy food and become pests in the coverts.

Many foxes have discovered easy living in towns, where they raid dustbins and rubbish dumps for food.

Cubs are born in early spring in secluded nursery dens. They emerge to play at the age of 4 to 5 weeks, at which age they begin to be weaned.

A fox needs about 500 g of food a day. It kills small prey, such as wood mice, with a high pounce. It prefers voles to wood mice, and will only eat shrews or moles when it very hungry.

ARCTIC FOX
Family Canidae

The Arctic fox (*Alopex lagopus*) is the largest land mammal living throughout the year in the tundra regions of Europe, Asia and North America. It also occurs in the mountains of Scandinavia and, probably by travelling on ice floes, has reached Iceland and many other northern islands. Protected by its dense fur, the Arctic fox is a more compact-looking animal than the red fox, and looks larger than it actually is,

Some Arctic foxes have a bluish grey coat all the year round. They are found mainly on particular islands, and have become rare, for they are a special target for trappers.

measuring up to 110 cm, including the 35 cm tail. Its shorter face and tail, and its small, rounded ears are all adaptations to reduce the risk of frostbite in the intensely cold winters through which it is fully active. Usually its coat colour changes from greyish brown with white underparts in summer to yellowish white in winter. Between 1 and 5 per cent have bluish grey fur throughout the year. This form is known as the 'blue fox' and is the dominant variety on some islands.

Perhaps because of the harshness of the environment, Arctic foxes are even more flexible in their behaviour than red foxes. They may be active by day or night, since in the summer there is no real darkness over much of their range, while in the winter there is no more than twilight even at midday. They do not have fixed territories and may migrate long distances to find food, some even entering the northern forest zones. They are more tolerant of their own kind than other foxes; groups of animals may travel together, although they do not develop the tight social bonds of the wolves and jackals, and in summer several families will live in peace near to each other. Arctic foxes eat whatever is available. The summertime may be a period of plenty, for huge numbers of ducks, geese and waders travel to the tundra to breed, and such ground-nesting birds are easy prey. Sea birds in their millions come to nest on cliffs, which are a Mecca for Arctic foxes, especially when their young are nearly fledged. Many birds do not survive their first jour-

ney to the sea and this carrion, as well as the sitting birds and the eggs of some species, provide plentiful food. On the seashore many molluscs and sometimes fish may be found, while the stranded carcass of a whale or the remains of a polar bear's meal are riches indeed for the scavenging fox. Inland, lemmings form a major part of the food, and so great is the Arctic foxes' dependence on these animals that their survival and abundance fluctuates with the 4-year cycle of this prey. Any food which cannot be eaten at once is cached in the den, in a crevice, or shallowly buried, and in the cold of the Arctic climate will remain fresh for long periods. In common with many animals which have little contact with Man, the Arctic fox shows little fear of him and Arctic travellers have often seen these animals stealing things from their camps.

Arctic foxes pair for life, and probably maintain contact with each other throughout the year. Soon after the spring equinox, the males establish territories, which they mark with urine, and mating takes place soon after this. The cubs are born after a gestation of about 53 days and within a week the female may mate again, producing a second litter in about mid-July. The den, dug into a moraine, usually has several side branches and may interconnect with the tunnel system of an adjacent family. The cubs grow fast; their eyes open when they are a fortnight old and a week later they leave the den to play. At 6 weeks old they are weaned.

In the summer time Arctic foxes haunt cliffs where seabirds nest, the eggs and chicks providing them with easy food.

Arctic foxes store anything which they cannot eat immediately. They will sometimes take things which are of no use to them as food, such as empty tins and other rubbish from travellers' camp sites.

In the winter months, the Arctic fox's completely white fur matches its snow-covered environment. It hunts any small creatures which it can find, and even the wary ptarmigan may become a meal for it.

RACCOON DOG
Family Canidae

The original home of the raccoon dog *(Nyctereutes procyonoides)* is the wide tract of temperate and subtropical broadleaved forest from the Amur River in Siberia to Vietnam. Because of its dense, thick fur it was introduced into European Russia and has spread westwards throughout Germany and into Switzerland in the south and Finland in the north, thriving even in coniferous forest and wetlands.

In some places the raccoon dog overlaps with the raccoon, which has also been introduced into Europe. The two animals have a similar black mask across the upper face, but the raccoon dog has a blunter muzzle, and is more solid-looking, measuring up to ·82.5 cm including the 17.5 cm long unbanded tail. It is not easy to see, for it is usually nocturnal except in the most northerly part of its range, where it is forced to be active in the twilight of the long Arctic days. Generally, it spends the hours of daylight lying in dense reed beds or in thick scrub. When more protection is needed, it may take over part of a badger's sett, or even excavate a lair, which is usually a simple chamber at the end of a tunnel up to 2 m long, with at least one bolthole.

Like foxes, raccoon dogs are solitary hunters for most of the year. In other respects, they resemble badgers, for they are the most omnivorous of the dog family in Europe. Like badgers their carnassial and molar teeth are adapted to crushing vegetable food rather than slicing flesh, and the canines are much smaller than those of other dogs. Similarly, they have a longer gut than most other carnivores, which enables them to digest the large proportion of fruits, grain and bulbs in their diet.

They are essentially small game hunters, taking ground-nesting birds and voles, amphibians, molluscs and some fish, but otherwise concentrating on still smaller prey, such as crickets and slow-moving dung beetles. Carrion is eaten whenever it is available, and they have even been reported to feed on dung. In autumn, raccoon dogs feast on various fruits and acorns, and on this rich diet, like the badgers and bears, they build up a store of fat which enables them to be relatively inactive throughout the winter. During this period they are merely dozing in their dens — their metabolism drops to some extent, but the fall in bodily activity is not sufficient for their sleep to be considered true hibernation.

Raccoon dogs have established themselves in Europe in many habitats very different from their original home, including reed beds, where they hunt frogs, terrapins and even fish.

Soon after they become active in the spring, mating takes place between pairs which probably met in the time of plenty towards the end of the previous year. When she is ready to mate, the female scent marks the area in which she lives with urine. The litter usually consists of six or seven cubs born after a gestation of 54 days. The cubs are blind at birth, and are covered with dense, dark-coloured fur. In their early days the cubs are given solid food, including frogs and insects, but they are not fully weaned until they are about 2 months old. Even after this the male remains with his family, sleeping in the same den and sometimes staying with them through the winter.

Unlike many other introduced animals, raccoon dogs seem to have fitted into an otherwise unoccupied niche in the European environment. In spite of the fact that they may take some crops, they are not generally regarded as pests.

The female raccoon dog scent marks the area in which she lives to announce her readiness to mate.

The raccoon dog's den is usually at the end of a tunnel up to 2 m long. It generally has at least one bolt hole through which the animals can escape in times of danger.

The raccoon dog was brought to Europe from eastern Asia because of the value of its fur. Escaped animals have established themselves and, unlike many introduced animals, they do not appear to have displaced any native mammal.

POLAR BEAR and BROWN BEAR

Family Ursidae

The polar bear *(Thalarctos maritimus)* is essentially a creature of the pack ice which surrounds the northern shores of Europe, Asia and America. It has been seen at 88 degrees north, but it is more commonly found in the open ice further south where seals, which are its main food, are abundant. It is resident around the shores of Spitzbergen and Novaya Zemlya, and it may swim long distances or be carried on ice floes as far as the coasts of Iceland and northern Scandinavia. In the water it uses the forelimbs as paddles. On land or over ice it has a shambling gait which led old-time sealers and whalers to nickname it the 'farmer'. However, its ungainliness is deceptive and a polar bear can cover vast distances over land and, if necessary, can gallop at about 30 kph for a short distance.

A male polar bear measures up to 2.5 m long and weighs up to 450 kg, females being somewhat smaller. The head seems small for the huge body, but the limbs are, if anything, even more massive than those of the brown bear. The long, dense fur is often yellowish in adult bears, and is a good heat insulator on land, while the heavy layer of fat under the skin helps to keep the animal warm in the water. The fur on the underside of the huge feet also prevents it from slipping as it moves through its frozen environment.

Because they do not have a rich variety of food available to them, polar bears have become the most carnivorous members of the bear family, and this is reflected in their teeth. The canines are longer than those of the brown bear and the molar teeth are smaller, with flesh-cutting crests. Polar bears will eat almost anything available, and have often raided the stores of Arctic travellers, devouring such unlikely items as tobacco, sailcloth and engine oil, and they regularly raid the rubbish dumps of some coastal Alaskan and Canadian towns and would doubtless do the same in Europe if offered the same opportunity. They may occasionally congregate round the carcass of a stranded whale, but seals form the major part of their food, and on land or fast ice these may be stalked. If the seals are on the edge of an ice floe, the bears will swim cautiously towards them until they can emerge almost beside the prey, which has scant chance of escape. In spring, they dig ringed seal pups out of the snow caves in which they are born. At certain times of the year they will wait beside the breathing hole of a seal which they kill with a tremendous swipe of a paw as it comes up for air. Even small whales, such as the white whale, may be killed in a similar manner if they are trapped in an area with only narrow leads of water through the ice. Such is the power of the polar bear that it can drag the whale, which is several times its own weight, out of the water.

In late summer when much of the ice has melted, polar bears may be found on land, feeding on berries, grasses, mosses and lichens, as well as lemmings and birds. When the Arctic winter closes in such food becomes almost unobtainable. While male bears may continue to be active throughout this time, adult females over 4 years old burrow into deep snowdrifts to make a den in which the temperature may be over 20°C above that of the outside air. Here they give birth to two or three cubs, about the size and weight of guinea pigs (about 350 g). Early development is slow and the cubs do not leave the den until the weather begins to break when their mother leads her family to the sea. The cubs remain with her for their first year and become independent before their second winter.

Heavy bodied and shaggy coated, the brown bear *(Ursus arctos)* is the largest land carnivore and, having no serious rival until the coming of Man, it was widespread in woodlands with good undergrowth across Europe, Asia and North America. In Europe it has now been reduced to a tiny

The front foot of polar bear (upper) *and brown bear* (lower). *Both bears are plantigrade, having five long-clawed toes on each foot, but the underside of the polar bears feet are thickly furred for warmth and to prevent slipping.*

Female polar bears make deep winter dens on slopes, where drifting snow will close the entrance but will not be difficult to break through if necessary.

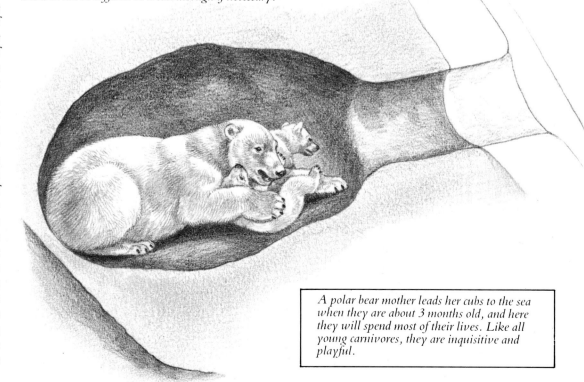

A polar bear mother leads her cubs to the sea when they are about 3 months old, and here they will spend most of their lives. Like all young carnivores, they are inquisitive and playful.

fraction of its former abundance, occurring in the remote mountainous areas of northern Spain, the Pyrenees, Germany, Poland and the Balkans. Only in Scandinavia and Russia does it become at all common.

So widespread an animal is bound to vary, both in size and colour, and even the giant American grizzly bears are thought to belong to the same species as the European forms. In Europe the male is about 2 m long and weighs up to about 265 kg, the female being slightly smaller. The colour is variable, ranging from almost creamy to very dark, while juveniles often have a collar of fur paler than the rest of their coat.

Its large size and lack of visible tail are usually sufficient clues to this bear's identity. Where its presence is suspected, large footprints, shaped roughly like those of a man, but showing marks of long, strong claws, may be found. Like human beings, bears are plantigrade, and walk on the whole length of their feet, rather than on the toes, in the manner of dog and cats. Although it normally travels on all fours, the long feet can support it easily if it stands upright to get a better scent of something suspicious. Bears have a very sharp sense of smell and excellent hearing, but are short-sighted.

Although their bulk has enabled brown bears to be immune from all predators except Man, it has brought with it restrictions, especially in speed, and they are slow moving compared with most other flesh-eaters. Active hunting is therefore less easy and the brown bear has become largely herbivorous. However, virtually anything edible will be taken, including carrion, mammals, ground-nesting birds, fishes and even insects. To cope with this varied diet the shearing teeth have developed broad surfaces suitable for crushing plant food, the canines are relatively small and the intestine is comparatively longer than that of animals with diets consisting solely of flesh. As with other omnivores, the abundance of autumn food allows a build up of fat which enables brown bears to be inactive through the winter, although they do not hibernate.

Brown bears are solitary for the greater part of their lives, each occupying an area about 15 to 20 km in diameter. This territory usually overlaps that of neighbouring bears. Each marks certain points where paths cross or specially favoured feeding places, so that others are warned of their presence. Marking may be with urine, or by rubbing the neck and chest against a tree trunk which has been stripped of its bark by the bear's powerful claws and teeth. Young bears are said to be reluctant to approach trees which have been marked in this way by their elders. In spite of this, bears may occasionally congregate in places where food is particularly abundant but they take care to avoid close contact and if conflict threatens, all give way before the largest males, even females with cubs, who are otherwise respected by the rest of the group.

In the early summer, there is a brief courtship period; after mating the pair part. It is said that in the Pyrenees the same pair come together in successive years, but elsewhere they are reputed to be promiscuous. Implantation of the embryos is delayed and the cubs are not born until the following January or February, when the female is drowsing snugly in her winter den. Compared to their mother, the cubs are minute, measuring only about 22 cm in length and weighing about 350 g. Such tiny infants make small demands on their resting dam, who uses little of her winter resources in suckling them. The family stays in the den for 3 months, by which time spring is well advanced. Weaning starts when the cubs are 4 months old. The female is a devoted but strict mother, watching over the cubs as they play, but cuffing them into the trees if danger threatens. They are not fully independent until their second year and so the females can only produce a litter every other year.

Man has always viewed with deep suspicion such obviously powerful carnivores as the bears. However, a brown bear usually flees at the sight or smell of Man, although there are certainly accounts of humans being attacked. Attacks by polar bears are better documented, for they have little contact with people and will approach with less fear than most other wild animals.

Humans have killed bears since ancient times for their pelts, fat, teeth and claws, and, more recently, for sport. Much of the brown bear's habitat has been destroyed. In these ways, Man has reduced the numbers of bears dramatically. The world population of polar bears is estimated at no more than 12,000 animals in some millions of square kilometres of ice. It is among the world's endangered species, and hunting it for sport is forbidden by law through most of its range.

Seals, which are hunted on land and when they are resting on ice floes, are a major part of the polar bear's food.

Polar bears eat carrion when they can find it, such as this carcass of a stranded whale.

Some Arctic seals remain under the ice during the winter, coming up to breathe at holes which they have gnawed. Polar bears wait at these holes, hoping to make a kill.

The skull of a European brown bear is about 34 cm long. Although the jaws are powerful with large canines, the molar teeth are flat topped, for much of the bear's food consists of plants which need to be crushed rather than sliced. Polar bears have longer, more slender canines (below, left) to cope with their diet of flesh.

Young brown bears are able to climb trees with ease, for their claws are much more curved than those of the adults.

A brown bear burying carrion. In the spring they search out the remains of animals which have died during the winter. Anything which they cannot eat at once is lightly buried with sticks and earth.

A new-born brown bear is about one five hundredth of the body bulk of its mother. The brown bear feeds her cubs in her winter den until they are about 3 months old. She normally suckles them while lying on her back.

RACCOON
Family Procyonidae

The destruction of bears and other flesh-eaters over much of Europe has left niches open for other opportunist carnivores. One is the raccoon *(Procyon lotor)*, a native of the warm forests of North America, which was brought to Europe in the 1930s, probably for fur farming. Some escaped from captivity, or were released, and their descendants have spread from the Eifel district of Germany where they were first reported. They are now in the Low Countries and the valley of the Mosel, and are likely to reach much further in the future, for they are highly adaptable and can live in both open country and forests. It will be interesting to see how it reacts to the raccoon dog, with which it shares many requirements of habitat and food. They are already both present in some areas, but so far numbers are probably sufficiently low for peaceful coexistence.

Raccoons are nocturnal and are not often seen. Should one be glimpsed, the pointed ears and the dark ringed, bushy tail distinguish it from the raccoon dog, which it resembles in the black mask across the upper face. Signs of their presence include scratch marks round holes in trees and five-toed plantigrade footprints. Those of the forefeet are particularly distinctive, for the toes are very long and widely separated, leaving a print almost like that of a baby's hand. Raccoons range in size from 70 to 90 cm, including a tail up to 20 cm long, and weigh up to 25 kg. They may be solitary or live in family parties. The range, which overlaps with that of other individuals, is at least 40 hectares. Most of their hunting is done on the ground, but they are good climbers, and the den in which they spend most of the day is usually in a hole in a tree.

Raccoons' teeth are broader-crowned than those of carnivores which feed exclusively on flesh. They eat a wide variety of food, including molluscs, crayfish, fruit and grain. One reason for their success may be their willingness to live close to Man, scavenging from dustbins and rubbish dumps, and taking eggs and even chickens if possible. During the winter raccoons do not hibernate but their level of activity is low, and they den up for long periods relying on fat deposits formed during the late summer.

In the spring, raccoons leave their winter dens to search for food and for mates. Ovulation is stimulated by mating and the young are born 63 to 65 days later. At birth they have a coat of woolly fur with the distinctive black mask already evident. Their eyes do not open until they are 2 to 3 weeks old. At about 7 weeks they make their first forays from the nursery den and they begin to take solid food, although they are not fully weaned until about 9 weeks later. The cubs remain with their mother through their first summer and learn from her many of the techniques of hunting and escape.

Raccoons are reputed to wash their food in any water available, however dirty, a habit commemorated in their scientific name. Recent studies of wild raccoons have shown that this does not happen in nature. It has been suggested that captive raccoons dabble their food to recapitulate hunting because all the effort of catching their own prey has been eliminated.

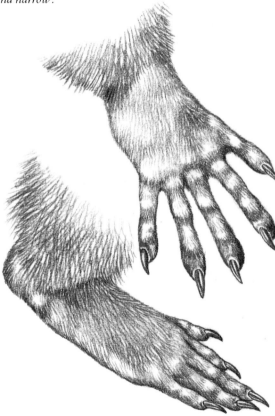

The forefoot of a raccoon (upper) *is hand-like and enables the animal to handle food and other objects with great dexterity. The hind foot* (lower) *is long and narrow.*

Raccoons climb well and the den is usually in a hole in a tree. The entrance hole is often deeply scratched by the animal's sharp claws.

Raccoons feed on many things, including fish and plant food, and when living near villages they may learn to kill chickens.

Female raccoons suckle their young in a sitting position.

The American raccoon is now established in parts of central and western Europe, thriving in many types of habitat, such as this riverside where it is fishing. The young are learning by accompanying the mother on her hunting expedition. In some places it lives alongside the raccoon dog and, in spite of needing similar food and living places, the two seem to coexist peacefully.

STOAT and WEASEL
Family Mustelidae

Almost half of the carnivorous mammals in Europe belong to the weasel family. Most of the animals in this large group are small, with long, lithe bodies and short legs. A bounding, hump-backed gait is normal and the five-toed feet are usually plantigrade. They have short muzzles containing powerful teeth, including well-developed carnassials for they almost all feed entirely on flesh. The smaller members of the family are general hunters, but the larger species tend to be more specialized. For example, the otter has taken to the water, the marten to the trees, the glutton has become a powerful scavenger, while the badger is a heavyweight digger feeding largely on vegetation. In most of the smaller species there is a considerable difference

in size between the males and the females, which in some cases results in different prey being taken by the two sexes.

Stoats and weasels, the smallest of this family, need little cover to protect them. So, where there is suitable food, they occur in a wide range of habitats from lowland forests to upland moors and even towns. In some areas they are quite common and, since they hunt by day as well as at night, they may sometimes be seen working their way along a hedgerow or scuttling across a road. They are wary creatures, but curious, and if anything attracts their attention they may come back for a second look, sometimes standing up on their hind legs to get a better view.

They are perplexing animals for they are so variable in size and coloration that they have sometimes been thought to belong to several different species. However, it is now generally agreed that there are only two. The stoat (Mustela erminea) is found in Great Britain and Ireland and throughout mainland Europe north of the Alps and the Pyrenees, and extends across

Asia and much of North America, where it is called the short-tailed weasel. The weasel (M. nivalis) does not occur in Ireland or most of the Scottish islands, but extends to the southernmost parts of mainland Europe and across Asia and North America, where it is known as the least weasel. The stoat is usually larger than the weasel, has a black-tipped tail, and its colour changes from brown on the back to creamy white on the underparts along a straight line. In the weasel, the very short tail never carries a black tip, and the junction of the bright brown of the back and the white underside is irregular, often with islands of brown fur in the white, particularly in the throat area. Each individual is so distinctive in its colour pattern that behaviourists have used it as a means by which they can recognize individuals in the field.

Both the stoat and the weasel moult in spring and autumn, and in the colder parts of their range both turn white in winter, although even then the stoat never loses the black tip to its tail. When white furred the stoat is referred to as an ermine. Where the winters are warmer both retain their brown

A stoat will often dance about near to rabbits, which seem to be so curious that they allow the predator to come within striking distance.

Stoats and weasels are inquisitive animals and often raise themselves on their hind legs so that they can get a better view.

A weasel enticing a blackbird. Weasels have similar habits to stoats, dancing to attract their prey.

A rabbit attacked by a stoat seems paralysed with fear and allows the predator to approach it, making no effort to defend itself. The stoat usually kills with a strong bite to the base of the skull.

colour throughout the year. In Britain an adult male stoat measures about 29.5 cm plus an 11 cm tail, and weighs about 320 g. The female is about 26 cm plus an 11.5 cm tail and weighs about 210 g. The European mainland, Asiatic and North American stoats are considerably smaller. Where the weasel lives alongside the stoat it is distinctly smaller but in southern Europe where there are no stoats, the weasel may exceed it in size. In Britain a male weasel is likely to be about 22 cm long, with a 6.5 cm tail. The female may be as small as 15 cm plus a 4.5 cm tail, and weigh only 45 g.

Apart from family groups, stoats and weasels are solitary, each maintaining a territory marked by musky smelling droppings. The size of a stoat's home range depends on the type of environment and the availability of food and varies from 10 to 200 hectares, the female's being smaller than the male's. It may contain several dens and is divided up into hunting areas, each of which will be worked for a few days in turn. Weasel territories are smaller, sometimes less than 1 hectare and rarely more than 15, and are marked by musk from the scent glands as well as droppings. The whole territory is worked over regularly, and the distance travelled in a hunting expedition may be up to 2.5 km.

The long, slender shape of stoats and weasels is inefficient in terms of conservation of energy and both species need to eat 23 to 33 per cent of their body weight each day. Their prey consists mainly of small mammals. The weasels specialize in voles and mice, while stoats take larger prey where possible, particularly rabbits, rats and water voles. They also eat frogs, lizards, small birds, carrion, insects and, if they are very hungry, shrews, earthworms and even some vegetation. The method of hunting varies, for weasels are small enough to pursue their prey into their burrows and runs, while stoats hunt almost entirely above ground. Both can climb quite well and may rob nest boxes of nestlings although weasels probably find this easier, since they can more easily squeeze through the small entrance holes. Stoats may stalk their prey, but they often rely on the curiosity of rabbits and birds towards any thing unusual. A hunting stoat may make itself very obvious, gambolling and leaping or rolling on the ground, and the prey, seemingly amazed by such antics, stands watching until the stoat is close enough to make a fatal dash. It kills by a powerful bite at the base of the skull, which causes almost instantaneous death as the long canines penetrate the brain. Extra large prey is gripped at the neck, and raked by the long-clawed hind feet. Any blood spilt is likely to be licked up before the stoat starts its meal, which has, perhaps, given rise to the legend that it sucks the blood of its victims. When killing small prey, weasels employ the same methods but they may have a long struggle with a large animal before it is sufficiently weakened for the kill to be made. Again the weasel licks away any surface blood before dragging its meal under cover. When prey is very abundant, the stoat and weasel kill more than they can eat.

Although so similar in many ways, these two species have very different breeding behaviour. In areas where there is plenty of food, weasels can produce young at almost any time, but they usually mate in March and produce four or five kittens in late April or early May. A second family may be born in July or August. The young of the first litter grow very fast, opening their eyes at 4 weeks and able to kill at 8 weeks, and may themselves be among the breeding population of the late summer. The kittens born at this time grow much more slowly and are not mature until the next year.

Stoats mate during the summer but, due to delayed implantation, the six to twelve kittens are not born until the following spring. They grow very rapidly and even before they are fully weaned the females may mate with the adult males, although the litters so produced are not born until the mothers are mature. The kittens first open their eyes at about 5 to 6 weeks and can kill at about 12 weeks.

In both species, family parties may remain together and sometimes, particularly in winter, weasels may hunt communally, giving rise to usually exaggerated accounts of packs terrorizing the countryside.

As with all small mammals, weasel and stoat populations tend to fluctuate, largely reflecting the abundance of prey. In the mid 1950s after myxomatosis had destroyed almost all the rabbits in Europe, stoat populations fell drastically and they have not yet fully recovered their former numbers.

Stoats and weasels fall to a variety of predators, particularly the larger owls and birds of prey and, sometimes, larger mammals. Through much of Britain and Europe they are relentlessly persecuted by Man, who ensures that few survive to their second birthday. They sometimes destroy the eggs and chicks of game birds, and can do a great deal of damage to domestic birds. However the fact that a family of weasels can destroy about 2,000 mice and voles in a year should stand in their favour. Unfortunately, it rarely does so.

In the colder parts of Europe, stoats change their coat colour to white in the winter, although the tip of the tail remains black. In warmer areas the coat may not change completely (right).

The pattern of pads on the forefoot (upper) *and the hind foot* (lower) *of a weasel is distinctive.*

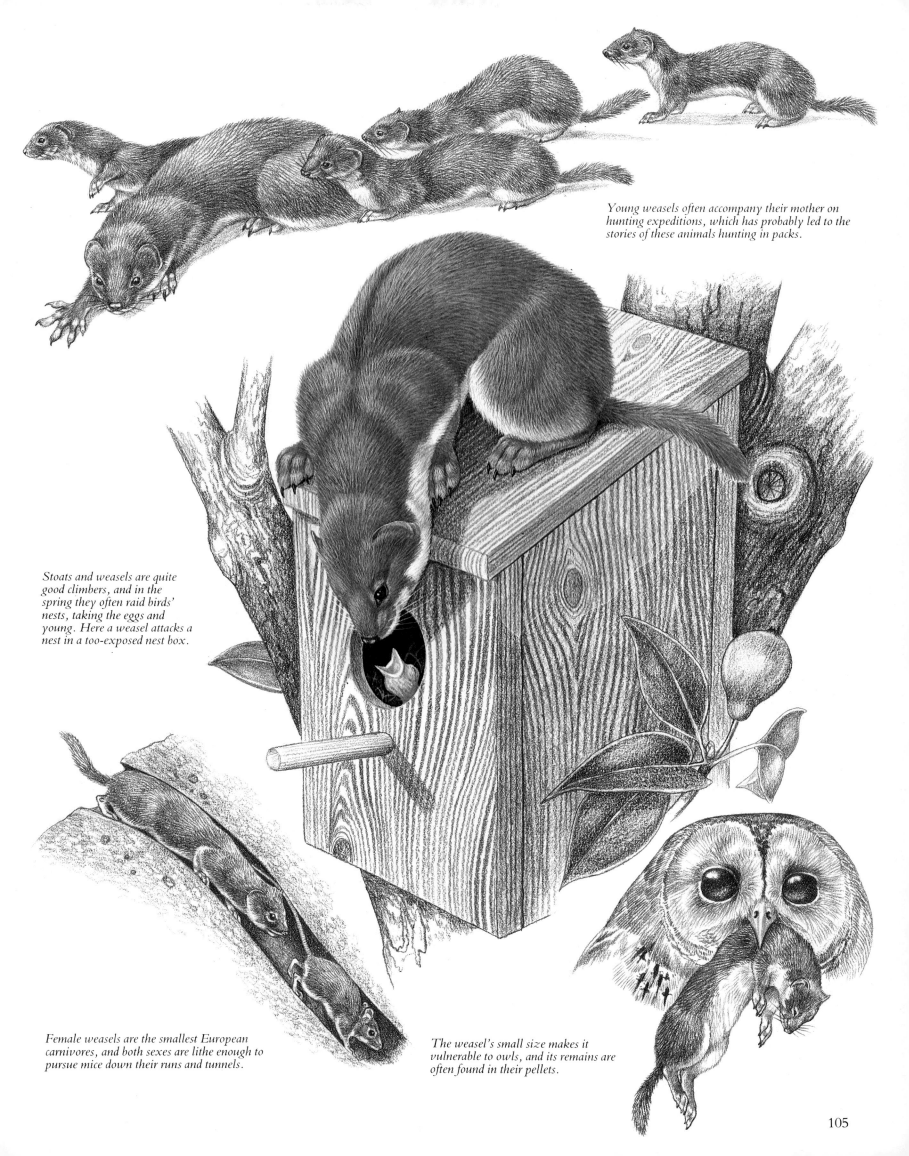

Young weasels often accompany their mother on hunting expeditions, which has probably led to the stories of these animals hunting in packs.

Stoats and weasels are quite good climbers, and in the spring they often raid birds' nests, taking the eggs and young. Here a weasel attacks a nest in a too-exposed nest box.

Female weasels are the smallest European carnivores, and both sexes are lithe enough to pursue mice down their runs and tunnels.

The weasel's small size makes it vulnerable to owls, and its remains are often found in their pellets.

POLECATS
Family Mustelidae

Polecats are medium-sized, ground-living animals with a distinctive black 'robber's mask' across their eyes. The western polecat *(Mustela putorius)* is found throughout the lowland areas of Europe south of the taiga and west of the steppes. The steppe polecat *(M. eversmanni)* as its name suggests, lives in the dry grasslands of eastern Europe and Asia north of the Himalayas. The marbled polecat *(Vormela peregusna)* is a creature of even drier habitats from eastern Europe to Peking.

The relationship of the western and steppe polecats is uncertain, and some authorities regard them as geographical races of the same species. They are similar in size and habits but vary in colour and detail of skull structure. Moreover, where they overlap the two exist side by side without intermediates. To complicate matters the domestic ferret can breed with the western polecat, but has skull features which appear to link it with the steppe polecat.

Although polecats are very widespread, they are rarely seen, for they are nocturnal and secretive. The western and steppe polecats are 32-44 cm long plus a tail of up to 18 cm long and the marbled polecat is slightly larger.

A polecat's gait is generally less sinuous than other members of the Mustelidae, for as it follows a scent the body is usually held low and quite straight. Eyesight does not seem to come into play until the end of the hunt, when the prey is seized and bitten at the base of the skull in a typical stoat manner. Since they favour damp habitats polecats may include quite large numbers of amphibians and water voles in their diet, as well as rabbits, ground-nesting birds and their young, and rodents. It is not known whether polecats maintain hunting ranges, but it is likely that polecats seen fighting were establishing territorial boundaries. These are probably marked by the strongly scented droppings and by musk produced by the large anal glands. This secretion is increased when the animal is excited or frightened, although only the marbled polecat appears to use the threat of it as a defence against enemies.

Steppe and marbled polecats often take over the burrows of sousliks or other rodents for their dens. Western polecats may use rabbit burrows, or dig a hole under the roots of a tree or in a bank. Here, early in the summer, the females give birth to up to 10 kittens, each about 7 cm long and weighing up to 10 g. They are covered with silky white hair, but by the time their eyes open at 5 weeks, this has been replaced by dark-coloured, woolly fur. After this the males grow faster than the females, and adult males are larger.

Their secretive ways protect polecats from other carnivores, although they may sometimes fall to the larger birds of prey or owls, but without doubt Man is their main enemy for they often live in farmland where chickens are an easy source of food for them. Also their pelts are important to the fur trade, in which they are sold under the name of fitch, and few polecats are likely to survive beyond 4 or 5 years, although in captivity they may live to be 14 years old. They were exterminated in most of Britain by the 1930s but in some mainland European areas, polecats have learned to live alongside Man, even becoming scavengers in towns, and it may be that survival for these species will depend on this ability.

The marbled polecat, so named because of the handsome pattern of its fur, is a creature of dry habitats from eastern Europe across much of Asia.

Although a polecat's lair may be in any sheltered place, it is often excavated under the roots of a tree.

A polecat's wide food spectrum includes snakes, even adders, which are killed in a typical stoat manner, by a bite to the base of the skull.

Polecats are rarely seen in Britain, for they live mostly in remote moorland areas, often occupying damp places where they hunt amphibians, voles and sometimes wading birds, such as this curlew.

BADGER
Family Mustelidae

The thick-set, stumpy-legged badger *(Meles meles)* is one of the largest of the weasel family. A male is up to 80 cm long and, in Britain, may weigh nearly 17 kg. The weight varies greatly with the time of the year and the area, and in eastern Europe in autumn may reach 27 kg. The sow is usually smaller and slimmer with a narrower head.

Usually badgers take care to avoid human company. If seen they are easily recognized by the bold black and white stripes on the face. These probably allow the short-sighted badger to recognize another of its own kind, and may also act as a warning to any predator. Few animals, other than a wolf or lynx, would dare to tackle an adult badger. If a young one is attacked, it turns towards the aggressor, growling, the fur of its body fluffed out so that it looks bigger and fiercer than it really is. This, combined with the stark facial markings, is enough to make most attackers retreat, and it may well be that the survival value of the black and white head is at its greatest in young badgers.

The badger occurs from southern Scandinavia to the Mediterranean and from Ireland and Britain eastwards into Asia. It can survive in most areas other than high mountainous country, deserts and water-logged places, but it prefers deciduous woodland with adjacent farmland. In such environments, densities of up to 58 per 1000 hectares may occur.

Although they may start foraging while it is still light in the summer, badgers are mainly nocturnal, and so they are difficult to observe in the wild. However, their presence is often obvious, for they are highly social animals and groups of up to 12 may occupy a communal underground home called a sett. This is usually dug into the side of a hill, and is easily recognized by the size of the entrance hole, which is at least 20 cm in diameter and may be considerably larger. Badgers seem to be compulsive diggers and setts are constantly enlarged with new tunnels and chambers being dug, so that outside most entrance holes there is a spoil heap of excavated earth, often mixed with discarded bedding and hair. Generations of badgers may live in the same sett, which after some years, or even centuries, will have many entrances and tunnels, and may extend 100 m or more along a hillside with chambers up to 90 cm in width and 60 cm high.

Badgers often move from one part of a large sett to another or even leave temporarily for a different sett, so the number of setts in an area is not necessarily an indication of the density of the species. Signs of an occupied sett include scratch marks on tree trunks, which are often mud-covered up to a height of a metre or more. Coarse grey hair caught in barbed wire or brambles and their broad, five-toed footprints show where badgers have passed. Dung pits, about 15 cm deep, are often found within about 20 m of the sett, although droppings may also be deposited to mark territorial boundaries.

Paths from the sett to feeding grounds lie within a large, loosely defended territory. These are often so well trodden that they may be mistaken for human trackways until they pass uninterruptedly under a fallen branch. Badgers are very conservative in their habits and the same paths are used for generations. Where their paths cross roads, badgers often become traffic casualties and in some places special tunnels have been built to prevent this.

The most important item in the badgers' diet is earthworms, which are consumed in vast numbers. However, they are prepared to eat a wide range of food, including small mammals and their young, occasional ground-nesting birds and their eggs, reptiles and amphibians, especially frogs, and they have even been seen flipping fish out of the water, bear-fashion. Among invertebrates, slugs, snails and insects are taken, especially large beetles, and a badger has been recorded waiting underneath a lamp and snapping up the

Badgers' front feet (upper), *which are used for digging, have longer claws than the hind* (lower).

The badger's sight is poor, but it has a superb sense of smell. The turbinal bones, seen inside the large nasal opening, provide an ample support for tissue carrying sensory cells.

Badgers' claws often become clotted with mud. This is cleaned off by scratching a tree, which also enables the animals to keep their claws in good condition.

The flat-topped molar teeth in the badger's skull are very different from those of most of its relatives. These crushing teeth are part of the animal's adaptations to a largely herbivorous diet.

A badger which feels itself threatened by an enemy fluffs up its fur to make itself look bigger and fiercer.

Badger cubs are born very early in the year, but they do not emerge from the sett until they are at least 2 months old, and they are watched by their mother as they play. Should one stray, the bold stripes on its face may make it look fiercer than it really is and it is possible that the facial markings have most survival value to young badgers.

cockchafers which blundered into it. Large amounts of vegetation are eaten, especially fruit in the late summer and autumn. Early in the year, when other food may be scarce, they dig up the starchy, nutritious roots of the wild arum.

Badgers are often accused of killing poultry and lambs. Usually this is the work of a fox but when true it is generally an old animal which cannot find enough of its normal food and is prepared to risk the proximity of Man for an easy meal. Badgers eat carrion and many of the lambs taken are probably already dead. Some live in built up areas, surviving in urban parks, where they are relatively undisturbed. These animals, although wary, often enter gardens to rummage through compost heaps and dustbins in search of food.

The basic social unit of badger life is the sow and her cubs, which remain with their mother for their first year and sometimes longer. One or more boars may live in the same sett but, for most of the time, occupy different dens. Except for mothers defending their young, there seems to be mutual tolerance and friendship between members of the same group, although an intruder is rarely welcomed. Clan members recognize each other mainly by scent. They have a musk gland beneath the tail and with the oily secretion from this, they anoint everything in their environment including each other.

Badgers furnish their setts with large amounts of bedding. This varies according to circumstances; dry grass, bracken, straw and dead leaves may be used, and when the cubs are half grown the green leaves of bluebells are often taken into the nursery. In winter bedding may start to rot inside the sett and this may help to keep it warm but in spring and autumn the old bedding is thrown out and replaced with new.

At the end of the summer when food is plentiful, badgers feed heavily and become very fat. In mild climates they may be active throughout the winter, but in eastern Europe they retreat to their setts for long periods, although they do not hibernate. During this time of prolonged inactivity the sows give birth. In Britain, this is likely to occur in late January or early February, while further north and east it is likely to be later and in the south it may be earlier. Up to five young are born, but often no more than two survive the summer.

At birth, the cubs are about 12 cm long and weigh up to 130 g. They are blind and helpless but their facial stripes are usually apparent. Their mother does not stay with them all of the time, but comes in to feed them and to check that all is well. They snuggle together in the deep bedding of the nursery chamber until they are 6 to 7 weeks old, when they start exploring the sett. At about 8 to 10 weeks they make their first, usually brief, venture into the outside world. Soon their forays are longer and more adventurous and there is much boisterous and noisy play. This ceases instantly if the sow detects danger and calls them to return to the safety of the sett. At a very early stage, their play foreshadows many of the activities of the adult. They learn the moves of attack and defence, and quite tiny cubs musk sticks and other objects close to the sett. They make snuffle holes as though looking for food, and collect and drag bits of dead vegetation well before they are 3 months old, although at this age their concentration soon wanes and they are easily distracted to play some other game.

Badger cubs are suckled for at least 3 months but have shed their milk teeth and are fully weaned within another 3 to 4 weeks. At this time food is usually plentiful, and by the late summer the cubs weigh nearly as much as a small adult, although they are not sexually mature until they are at least a year old. They live for 10 years or more.

Very soon after her cubs are born a sow mates again, and may do so several times through the summer and into October. Implantation is delayed so that all wild cubs are born in the winter after a 7-week gestation. Under circumstances of exceptional stress, implantation may be abnormally delayed, for there are records of badgers in captivity giving birth to cubs over a year later.

Although Man has persecuted badgers for many centuries, it is now realized that they do little harm and may, in some places, be useful in destroying pests. Where they occupy the same ground as cattle carrying bovine tuberculosis they may catch this disease and become a reservoir from which further cattle infections can occur but it not known how long badgers can maintain the disease in an area once the cattle are free of it. The pleasure which badger-watching has given to increasing numbers of people in recent years should, however, be weighed against this limited harm.

The badger's thick fur and heavy skin protect it against wasp stings, when it digs out a nest to feast on the grubs.

A badger's strong claws can quickly dig out young rabbits from their nursery nests.

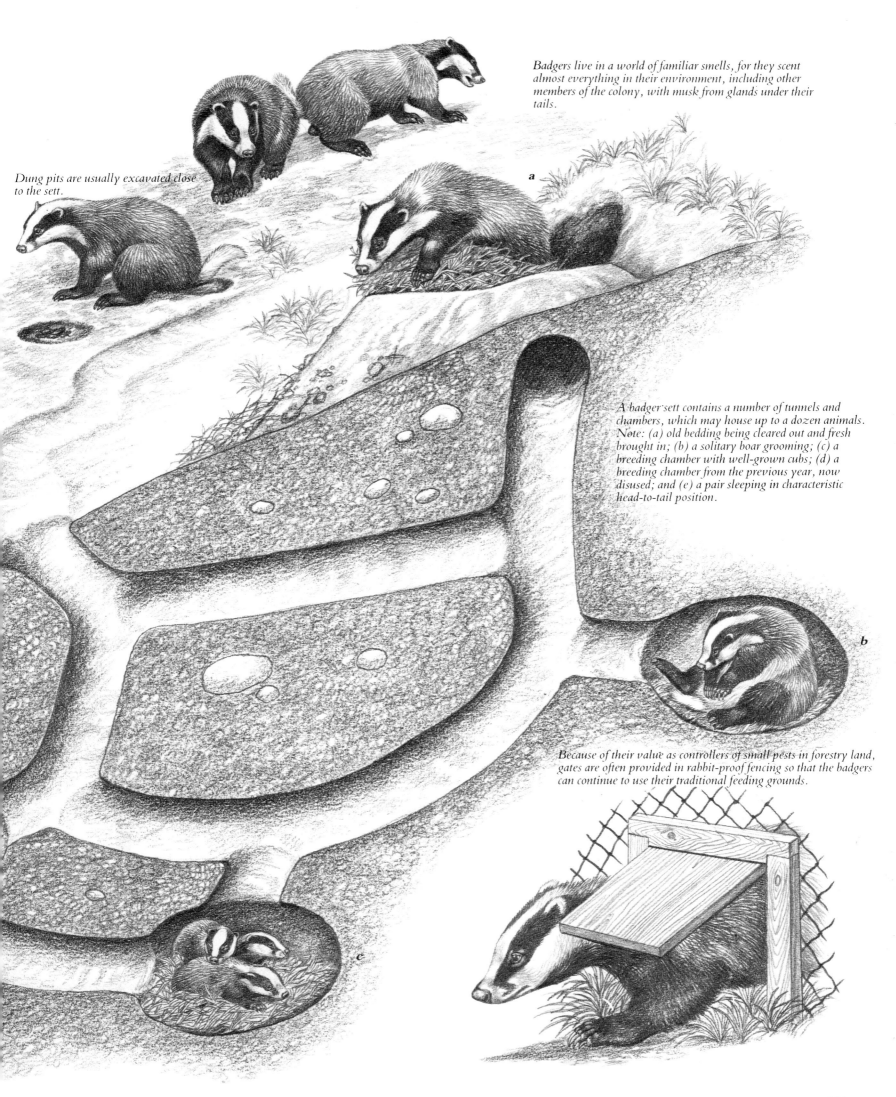

Badgers live in a world of familiar smells, for they scent almost everything in their environment, including other members of the colony, with musk from glands under their tails.

Dung pits are usually excavated close to the sett.

a

A badger sett contains a number of tunnels and chambers, which may house up to a dozen animals. Note: (a) old bedding being cleared out and fresh brought in; (b) a solitary boar grooming; (c) a breeding chamber with well-grown cubs; (d) a breeding chamber from the previous year, now disused; and (e) a pair sleeping in characteristic head-to-tail position.

b

Because of their value as controllers of small pests in forestry land, gates are often provided in rabbit-proof fencing so that the badgers can continue to use their traditional feeding grounds.

c

OTTER and MINK
Family Mustelidae

A steadily spreading V-shaped wake may be all that the otter watcher sees, yet the otter *(Lutra lutra)*, with eyes placed high on its flat head, may well observe the watcher on the bank, and dive silently. It does well to be wary, since for centuries it has been persecuted for its pelt and because it sometimes damages stocks of salmon and trout. Nowadays the dangers of pollution and disturbance of once-peaceful waters are added to an otter's hazards and it is no longer seen in places where it was once plentiful. However, it is still among the most widespread of carnivores, being found from Ireland across Europe and Asia north of the Himalayas, to Japan and North America. It can tolerate a range of climates from the Arctic tundra to the coast of the Mediterranean.

Otters are among the largest of the weasel family. A dog otter will probably measure at least 115 cm, about one-third of which is the heavy, tapering tail. It will usually weigh 10 to 15 kg, occasionally 20 kg. The bitch otter is much smaller than her mate, seldom weighing more than 10 kg.

An otter's streamlined shape and webbed feet enable it to swim with a grace and agility matched only by the seals and dolphins. When swimming slowly on the surface, the paws are used to paddle like a dog. Underwater, the legs are held against the body, except when they are needed for steering, and the hind end of the body is flexed in a series of vertical undulations. In this way it can reach speeds of up to 12 kph. The otter's very large lungs allow it to remain underwater for up to 4 minutes if need be, although it is not usually submerged for more than a minute, but it often swims 400 m before surfacing.

A dense undercoat of fine hairs traps a blanket of air round the body, and over this long guard hairs clamp down to waterproof it completely. When it comes ashore, a quick shake clumps the guard hairs together and the water runs off very quickly.

The otter's eyes and nostrils are placed high on its head, so that it can see and breathe even when the rest of the body is submerged. The big whiskers, or vibrissae, round the face probably help it to find food in dark water. The ears are small and are protected by special valves which close them against water pressure.

On land, otters tend to look humpbacked because the hind limbs are longer than the forelegs, but they can, if pressed, gallop faster than a man can run.

Where they are harassed by human activities, otters become very secretive and are active only during twilight hours and at night. Evidence of their presence can be found in the 'seals' or prints of their webbed feet by the waterside, and by piles of droppings or spraints. They are reputed to be nomadic, and studies in Sweden have shown that this may be true of some males and non-breeding females. In general, males occupy large ranges, which may include as much as 14 km of water bank. These overlap with the home ground of neighbours, who are careful to avoid confrontation. This is done by marking prominent spots on the territorial boundaries with droppings, the investigation of which is an important part of an otter's social

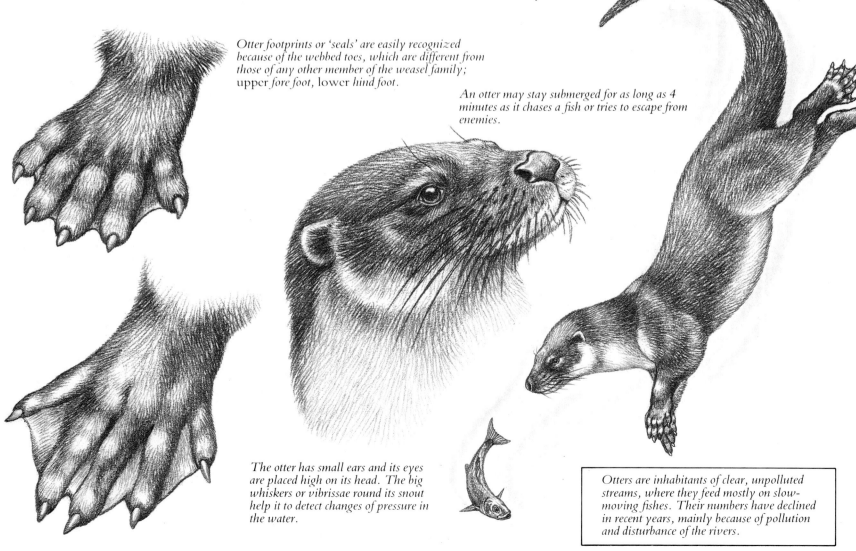

Otter footprints or 'seals' are easily recognized because of the webbed toes, which are different from those of any other member of the weasel family; upper *fore foot*, lower *hind foot*.

An otter may stay submerged for as long as 4 minutes as it chases a fish or tries to escape from enemies.

The otter has small ears and its eyes are placed high on its head. The big whiskers or vibrissae round its snout help it to detect changes of pressure in the water.

Otters are inhabitants of clear, unpolluted streams, where they feed mostly on slow-moving fishes. Their numbers have declined in recent years, mainly because of pollution and disturbance of the rivers.

life. A female with cubs occupies part of the range of a male, presumably her mate.

Otters do not hibernate, but tend to be less active in the winter, spending much time in a den or holt. Usually, this is excavated under the roots of a large waterside tree or a similar protected spot. In the colder parts of their range they make burrows in the snow. At this time of the year they feed mainly on hibernating amphibians, crayfish or other torpid cold-blooded animals. During warmer weather, they may eat a wide variety of animals, including water insects, snails, young birds, water voles, rabbits and crabs. However, fish always seem to be preferred, particularly slower-moving species which they can catch easily, small fish such as sticklebacks and sickly individuals of faster-moving game fishes.

Otters may produce cubs at any time of the year, although most are born in the early summer. The litter usually consists of two or three young, born after a gestation of about 62 days. At birth, baby otters are about 15 cm long, covered with a fine, velvety grey hair, and are blind and helpless. They begin to become active at 2 to 3 weeks old, but their eyes do not open until they are more than a month old. They do not begin to take solid food until they are about 7 weeks old, and their mother provides milk for them for several more weeks.

One very strange thing about baby otters is their apparent fear of water. As soon as they begin to explore beyond the holt they scramble and climb about the banks, but show no interest in the water. Their mother, who cares for them alone, usually has to encourage them to try to swim. Sometimes they are so reluctant that she has to push them in. A female otter has been seen to swim with a cub on her back and then to dive, leaving the baby to make its own way, which it finds it can do very well. It would be unwise for an otter cub to enter the water before it is 2 to 3 months old, since its baby fur does not have the waterproof guard hairs and until these have grown there is a danger of it becoming chilled or waterlogged. The cubs remain with their mother for their first year, so it is likely that the females do not breed more often than every other year.

As with all young animals otter cubs are playful, and even the adults will make slides on snow or mud and play with sticks or bits of floating vegetation in the water.

A great decline in otter numbers occurred in the mid 1950s. This coincided with the first widespread use of organophosphate and hydrochlorine insecticides, which poisoned many lowland waters and killed not only insects but also fishes and amphibians and the otters which depended on them. In some areas, where they are totally protected and where a clean-water campaign is being waged with sufficient energy, their numbers are showing slight signs of recovery. However, without continued care, the outlook for lowland otters is poor.

The mink *(Mustela lutreola),* another water-living member of the weasel family, is to be found in eastern Europe. A uniformly dark brown animal except for a white flash on the chin and round the muzzle, it is about 54 cm long including a 13 to 14 cm tail. Persecuted for its beautiful fur, it has disappeared from most of its former haunts in the west of the continent. In Scandinavia and Britain it has been replaced by the American mink *(M. vison).* This was introduced as a fur-bearing animal in the 1920s but escaped from captivity and now thrives in the wild, in some areas being the most abundant carnivore. The American mink is slightly larger and heavier than the native species and it has a dark coat with white only on the chin. Controlled breeding has selected for grey and pale brown coats which may sometimes be seen.

When American mink began to increase in numbers, it was thought that they would conflict with otters. However, they are less adept swimmers, normally plunging from the bank for fish, and so tend to take different and even smaller species than the otters. They also feed more on warm-blooded creatures, sometimes causing havoc among breeding water birds, but also taking water voles and shrews, and occasionally raiding farms for chickens or even kittens. They are usually only active at night, although a female with hungry young may hunt by day as well.

Like otters, mink are solitary animals, marking their territory, which may extend for 4 km along a river bank, with spraints. Each territory probably holds several dens, although each one may be occupied for a short period only. European mink mate in early spring, and the American species a little later in the year. Delayed implantation extends the 30-day gestation to 39-76 days. The American mink seems to develop slightly faster than the European species. In both the four to five kittens are independent of their mother by August, when the families break up. The young are mature in their first year and breed the next spring.

Young otters mature slowly and do not take to the water until they are 2 or 3 months old. They seem to fear it and have to be encouraged by their mothers to take their first dip.

Otters may mate in water or on land. They have a less well-defined breeding season than most other carnivores and young otters may be born in almost any month of the year.

The European mink is extinct over most of the continent but the introduced American mink (lower) is spreading. It probably does not conflict with the otter (upper), partly at least because of the size difference.

At all ages otters are playful animals making slides in mud or snow.

American mink spend more time on land than the otter. In some places they have caused havoc among water birds.

An otter's den or holt is often excavated under the root of a big waterside tree.

MARTENS
Family Mustelidae

Most members of the weasel family can climb to some extent, but the martens have perfected the art. With their agile bodies, bushy balancing tails and huge flexible feet, they are nimble enough to hunt and catch squirrels in the trees. Martens are found throughout the northern hemishpere. Two, the pine marten (*Martes martes*) and the beech marten (*M. foina*) occur in Europe. The pine marten lives mainly in coniferous and mixed forests in Ireland, mainland Britain and across much of Europe from Scandinavia to northern Spain, and eastwards into Siberia. The beech or stone marten extends throughout southern Europe and into Asia as far as the Himalayas.

Pine martens' breeding dens are usually among a tumble of rocks on the ground, but the adults often den up in hollow trees.

The two species overlap through most of France, Italy, central Europe and the Balkans, but seem to co-exist perfectly well, perhaps because neither is very common over much of the area and also because they prefer different habitats within it. In the Alps the pine marten is not found above 2,000 m, while the beech marten may live at heights of up to 2,400 m. The beech marten is much more strictly nocturnal while about half of all sightings of the pine marten are made in daylight and it is nocturnal only where it fears disturbance. One observer has noted that pine martens climb with less assurance at night, which would suggest that they prefer to hunt in full light.

Both pine and beech martens are about the size of a çat. The pine marten is slightly larger, with a head and body length of 45-55 cm, and a tail up to 27 cm long. A large male weighs about 1.4 kg. In eastern Europe martens tend to be smaller, and the females are always about three-quarters of the size of their mates, with narrower heads. The pine marten is a rich, dark brown, some having a reddish tinge in summer, while the beech marten is paler. Both species have a bib of light coloured fur beneath the throat, the exact shape of which varies with each animal. The beech marten has larger eyes and its shorter legs give it a squat appearance compared with the elegant pine marten.

A strange difference between them is that the pine marten shuns the presence of Man, while the beech marten is often found close to human habitation and may even make its den in barns or other abandoned buildings. In spite of this, very little is known of the life of the beech marten, although such details as have been obtained suggest that it is very similar to that of the pine marten.

Pine martens are solitary animals, occupying a range which varies from less than 1 to over 20 sq. km, according to the type of country and the availability of prey. Males and females are thought to live in adjacent territories and either may travel 6-7 km in a day's hunting. In Britain they are reputed to occupy extended territories, which run round the lower slopes of mountains. These home ranges seem to be very stable and to survive for years, although the territory holders themselves may change.

Territorial boundaries are defined by droppings deposited on boulders or other

Beech martens have less fear of Man than pine martens. They often live in barns or outhouses close to human habitation.

The beech marten is slightly smaller, has shorter legs and is more nocturnal in its habits than the pine marten.

The pine marten is the master climber of the weasel family. It is agile and fast enough in the trees to catch squirrels, although it often hunts for easier prey on the ground.

prominent points, and by secretions from the anal glands. Where the track runs above the ground, tree branches are marked from abdominal glands. These scented products are not unpleasant, and the pine marten used to be known as the 'sweet mart' as opposed to the polecat or 'foul mart'.

Pine marten dens may be in hollow trees, old birds' nests, squirrels' dreys, or, often, among jumbled boulders of a scree or in clefts in a rock face.

Martens climb like squirrels, by embracing the trunk of a tree and holding on with their sharp claws. They find difficulty in climbing smooth-barked trees, such as ash or beech, and may fall. They can right themselves as they tumble, like a cat, and have been recorded as surviving a drop of 18 m, though their usual method of descent is to scramble head first down the trunk.

Pine martens can move very fast for short distances on the ground, where they find much of their prey. In Scotland they often live on barren moorland, long since denuded of its forest. The beech marten is as much at home in the barren escarpments of southern Europe as in woodlands.

Martens are opportunist hunters, taking whatever prey is available. Field voles seem to be the preferred food of pine martens, which pounce stiff-legged like a fox when they have located one. Other rodents and rabbits are also part of their diet, although they will not normally follow such prey into their burrows. Carrion, particularly dead deer or sheep, and birds and insects may be taken. In the spring they can climb to reach the eggs in birds' nests inaccessible to other hunters. Slugs, when caught, are rolled on the ground to rid them of their slime, which is bitter and unpalatable. The beech marten's diet is similar, but includes a higher proportion of reptiles and amphibians. Both martens feed on fruit in the summer and autumn, and pine martens are particularly attracted to raspberries and may even raid gardens to get at cultivated berries. Seeds are an important part of the diet of beech martens in the late summer and early winter.

Female pine martens are receptive to the male for periods of up to 2 days several times during July and August. They may mate in trees but pairing more usually takes place on the ground. Implantation is delayed until early February and the litter, usually containing three cubs, is born in March, after about 28 days further gestation. The breeding den, warmly lined with sheep's wool or other bedding, is more often on the ground than above it.

The cubs, which are blind at birth, weigh about 28 g and are covered with pale coloured fur. This is replaced by a darker, fluffy baby coat when they are 3 weeks old.

Their eyes open when they are 4 to 5 weeks old, and they are weaned by the time they are 6 to 7 weeks old. Their mother may continue to provide some milk until they are nearly 3 months old.

When they venture into the open at about 8 weeks old they are reluctant to climb and, when they do, they show none of the speed and grace of the adults. Those born in tree dens look extremely uncertain and timid when they make their first forays into the branches, although they soon learn that they are safe above the ground. They are playful at any time and under the watchful eyes of their parents they learn the arts of survival in their games. At weaning the males and females are the same size, but the males then grow faster and, by the time they are 6 months old, weigh about 1.7 kg, while the females only weigh 1.35 kg.

Although they reach adult size and weight in their first summer, pine martens do not breed until they are about 15 months old. Rearing a family takes most of the summer, and so a female only breeds every other year.

In captivity, martens may live for up to 18 years but in the wild they are unlikely to survive for anything like this long. Their few natural enemies include foxes, and where foxes are abundant martens are rare, even if the habitat is suitable. In open country in the north of their range, golden eagles may take a few martens, driving them to be more nocturnal in their ways.

In general, Man is the chief enemy of martens. They have been persecuted relentlessly because they occasionally take chickens or other small stock and, particularly, for their beautiful fur. Recently in Britain, however, the increase in forestry plantations and the decrease in strict keepering has allowed the pine marten to spread from the Scottish highlands, which were its final stronghold, to other parts of the country. It has been suggested that they could be returned to places where they have been exterminated to control voles and squirrels, but this has not yet been attempted. In a few places martens have taken to raiding bird tables, and some people put out food especially for them — eggs and, treat of treats, raspberry jam. On the Continent, where the forests are larger and less fragmented, martens are just managing to hold their own against human intervention.

The colour of the bib of pale fur under the chin of the pine marten (upper right) *is always yellowish, while in the beech marten* (upper left) *it is always white and very variable in size. In Crete the beech martens* (lower) *have only a very small throat patch.*

Their large flexible feet enable martens to cling to thin branches where they may sometimes catch unwary small birds.

Martens use their sharp claws to grip the trunks of trees as they climb. They can descend head first and, should they slip, can right themselves.

Territorial boundaries on the ground are marked by scent from the anal glands, and on tree branches from abdominal glands.

Martens can travel through woodland in the tree canopy, leaping 3m or more from one branch to another.

Seeds and fruit are an important part of the martens' diet. Pine martens are particularly fond of raspberries.

GLUTTON
Family Mustelidae

The glutton or wolverine *(Gulo gulo)* is the largest member of the weasel family. It occurs in the taiga of Europe, Asia and North America, and in Scandinavia it also lives in mountainous country above and below the tree line. During the summer months it wanders northwards into the tundra where, briefly, it can find an abundance of food.

Dark with a pale band across the face and along the flanks, it resembles a small bear, but the bushy tail and erect ears distinguish it. Its movements are far less sinuous than those of most of its close relatives, and it travels across rough country with a tireless, bouncing gait. The male is larger than the female, and may be up to 95 cm long including a 15 cm-long tail and weigh up to 25 kg.

Possibly because of much persecution from Man, gluttons are active mainly at night and except for courting pairs and females with young, they are generally solitary. Within their barren tundra environment, the males occupy huge territories up to 2,000 sq. km in extent, which probably overlap the living areas of neighbours. The females seem to need a smaller living space, and several may live within the territory of a single male.

The gluttons' reputation for greed, coupled with the ability to eat very large quantities of food at one time, has given them their name. They are also renowned for their power and ferocity. This may be exaggerated in many cases, but they are certainly capable of killing animals much larger than themselves. Although wild reindeer are usually safe, domestic herds are in peril in the winter. If an old or sickly animal gets bogged down in the snow it stands scant chance of escape for the gluttons' broad paws carry them safely over the soft surface and their jaws and teeth are powerful enough to deal with the bones of the largest prey. During winter, carrion is an important source of food and they travel long distances in search of creatures which may have died in the harsh weather or have been caught in traps. This habit has brought them into conflict with fur hunters who do their best to destroy animals which raid their trap lines.

For the rest of the year there are few things which gluttons will not eat. Their diet includes hares, lemmings, voles, Arctic foxes, birds and their eggs, and any fish which they can drive into shallow water. This flesh is augmented in late summer by the wealth of fruit and berries. Gluttons are said to follow lynxes and drive them from their kill, and even wolves' prey may be taken by a hungry glutton. Anything which cannot be eaten at once is cached.

Mating takes place between April and August, but implantation is delayed. The next spring the female finds a secure den among inaccessible boulders or excavates a deep burrow in a snowdrift, in which her two or three blind but fur-covered cubs are born. They develop fast, for their eyes open at 3 weeks and they are weaned by the time they are 2½ months old. In spite of this, they remain with their mother, who has the sole responsibility for their upbringing, for at least their first year, and often longer. This must make the glutton one of the slowest breeding of European carnivores.

The glutton is a tireless hunter of Arctic land animals and, although solitary, it is powerful enough to tackle prey up to the size of a sickly deer. Here a glutton surprises a hare in its form.

Uneaten prey may be pulled up into a small tree.

A glutton marks its territory and the remains of the kills with droppings, urine and musk.

Gluttons mark trees by tearing pieces out of the bark, giving visual as well as scent markers to their territories.

Gluttons raid the trap lines of fur hunters and eat the dead or maimed animals which have been caught.

MONGOOSES
Family Viverridae

In the tropical parts of the Old World the weasel family (Mustelidae) is largely replaced by the mongoose family (Viverridae). These animals are all fairly small with long bodies, short legs, and long tails which taper from a broad base. When moving they run close to the ground. Most are extreme carnivores feeding on small game, although a few tropical species eat mainly fruit. Three members of this family occur in Europe, two species of mongoose and one of genet.

Mongooses are native to Africa and India, and the Egyptian mongoose or ichneumon *(Herpestes ichneumon)* and the Indian mongoose *(H. edwardsi)* have been imported into Europe. The ichneumon was almost certainly introduced during Roman times, for it is fairly easily tamed and was among the exotic creatures favoured as pets by Roman ladies. At one time it was widespread in Spain and Portugal, but it is now virtually restricted to the southern third of the Iberian peninsula, although it is fairly common in a few places within this area. More recently it has been introduced to the Yugoslavian island of Mljet.

The Egyptian mongoose is up to 1 m long, almost half of which is the long tail. The shoulder height is about 20 cm and the weight is up to 3 kg. Although it may restrict its hunting to the cooler part of the day, soon after sun-up, it is diurnal except where it is harassed by Man. It may lie in reed beds, but on the whole prefers drier habitats, leaving the bogs and marshes to the polecats. Its claws are sharp but non-retractile and it climbs less readily than genets. By these means it is able to co-exist with the nocturnal polecats and genets, which are potential rivals for food.

In spite of the fact that the Egyptian mongoose has been well known for a very long time, little is understood of how it organizes its life. It is thought that they probably live in pairs or in family groups in a territory defined by scent marks deposited on the ground, rocks or trees. In common with many other close relatives, they have anal glands which produce a powerful scented secretion. They may do handstands to reach a position which they feel should be anointed with their scent.

The food of Egyptian mongooses is varied, including insects, scorpions, fruit and even mushrooms, but where available rabbits are a staple part of the diet. They eat reptiles, including the poisonous Montpelier snake, and rodents and birds also feature on their menu. They have been seen entering the nesting burrows of bee-eaters to get their eggs. Little is known of the family life of wild Egyptian mongooses. In captivity, mating takes place in April and the litter of two to four kittens is born about 60 days later. Nothing is known of their size or appearance at birth, but in closely related species the young are weaned at about 1 month. They are sometimes seen in family groups, with the male leading followed in single file by its mate and the young.

The Indian mongoose, which is slightly smaller with a relatively longer tail, has a similar way of life to the Egyptian mongoose. In the 1960s it was taken into Italy and released about 100 km south of Rome, supposedly to control reptiles and, perhaps, rats. Conservationists are pessimistic about the consequences of this introduction. It has itself become a pest, killing many animals other than those it was supposed to destroy.

The Egyptian mongoose sometimes climbs trees, but does so hesitantly, scrambling down again tail first.

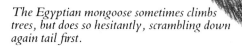

Some eggs, too large or heavy shelled to be broken by the Egyptian mongoose's teeth are bowled between its legs to smash against a stone.

The Egyptian mongoose raids bee-eater colonies, being slender enough to squeeze into their holes to take eggs and young birds.

The Egyptian mongoose feeds on many kinds of small animals including poisonous species such as the Montpelier snake, which is killed with a swift bite in the neck.

GENET

Family Viverridae

The genet *(Genetta genetta)* is sometimes called the small spotted genet, or the feline genet, for its behaviour is somewhat cat-like. It has a head and body length of 50-60 cm and the tail is up to 48 cm long. Its height at the shoulder is about 20 cm and its weight is up to 2.2 kg. It is found throughout Africa, apart from the Sahara and the equatorial rainforest zone.

The genet was probably first brought to Europe as a pet, for not only is it a most attractive creature, but it also becomes tame fairly easily. Some must have escaped from the loose captivity in which they were kept, and they may also have been released deliberately, for at one time genets occurred through western Europe, from the Balearic Islands, through Spain and Portugal, much of France and part of Belgium. Now the numbers seem to be shrinking; they have disappeared from the northerly part of their range and are very rare through most of France.

Although they are so widespread, little is known of genets in the wild, for they are nocturnal, solitary and secretive. They are essentially woodland creatures, for their semi-retractile claws enable them to climb well and their slender bodies can squeeze through even the dense tangles of thorny branches found in Mediterranean scrubland. Two genets in a large cage will ignore each other, so it is probable that in the wild they are strictly territorial. They have powerful scent glands and, if their behaviour is like that of related species, these are used to mark the boundaries of their living area.

Genets have a good sense of smell, and their hearing is excellent. It is likely that they first detect the presence of prey and enemies by sound, for their ears twitch as though they were tuning in to unseen stimuli. Their vision is also good, especially in detecting movement, although it seems likely that they are colour blind.

Recent studies in Spain have shown that the genets' food consists very largely of wood mice, which they hunt by stealth, stalking silently with their bodies almost touching the ground. They take some amphibians, but reptiles rarely figure in their diet. Like cats, genets use their paws to hold their prey and sometimes play with their victims, which are eventually killed by a crushing bite to the head. They are dainty feeders, often biting a mouse into two or three pieces. Considering how well genets can climb, birds form a surprisingly small part of their diet, and are eaten without being plucked. Large insects and scor-

pions are eaten and, in the autumn, berries.

The lair to which a genet retreats may be a hollow tree, or in a squirrel's drey, but is equally likely to be on the ground in a natural crevice, a rabbit's burrow or a badger's earth. Mating takes place usually in February and March, and the one to three young are born after a gestation of 10-12 weeks. At first they are blind and, though they have some hair on their backs, the underside is hairless. They begin to grow hair very quickly and by their fourth day they have a covering of soft, downy fur, on which subdued adult markings can be seen. Their eyes open on the eighth day, although they are still very inactive at this stage. As they grow, their forelimbs develop first, and they use these to pull themselves along. They cannot support themselves on all fours until they are about 3 weeks old and even then their co-ordination is poor for at least another week. When they first leave the nest, the cubs need the help of their mother, especially as they may try to climb into trees from which they cannot descend. They probably leave their mother by the late summer, for a few genets produce a second litter in the autumn, which suggests that they are free to mate again by about July or August.

Genets are strictly nocturnal, sleeping throughout the day in a den, which may be in a tree or on the ground.

Genets' slender bodies allow them to squeeze through the dense thorn scrub among which they often live.

Genets' favourite food is wood mice and, cat-like, they often play with their victims.

Genets are sometimes called feline genets for they have many cat-like habits, including that of grooming themselves fastidiously. Unlike cats, they use both forepaws together when washing the face.

WILD CAT
Family Felidae

Cats are, perhaps, the best known carnivores. Although few people have seen wild cats in their natural habitat, they vary less in their structure and adaptations than any other group of hunting animals, and anybody who has kept, or even seen, domestic cats is aware of the characteristics which make them supremely efficient killers.

All cats hunt by ambushing their prey. They lie in wait, or creep silently as close as they can, before springing on their victims. Sometimes a short sprint is needed, but they are not long-distance runners and seldom pursue prey for more than a few metres. In keeping with their exclusively carnivorous diet, cats have shorter faces and fewer teeth than any other flesh-eaters, for they do not need the crushing dentition of, for example, a dog. Their canine teeth

The paws of wild cats carry sharp claws which can be sheathed in a similar way to those of domestic cats.

have great stabbing force and although some of the delicate, almost pincer-like uses to which dogs may put the incisors are lost to cats, this is compensated for by the sheathed claws, which have a wider function than those of any other carnivore. The shortened face means that cats have a poorer sense of smell than most other hunters, and they rely on their large eyes and excellent hearing to detect prey. Only two wild cats occur in Europe. Both have been greatly reduced in numbers, partly to protect domestic stock from their ravages and partly because both have beautiful fur.

The northern or forest wild cat *(Felis silvestris)*, which was once found through most of Europe except for Ireland and Scandinavia, survives only in remote forested upland regions. In Britain, due to a relaxation in persecution, it is now spreading from the Scottish highlands which were its final stronghold. Beyond Europe, it extends to the western Himalayas and north Africa. In Scotland and other western countries, the males have an average head and body length of 58 cm, a tail length of 31 cm and weigh about 5 kg, females being somewhat smaller. In eastern Europe they are larger and one specimen is said to have weighed over 14 kg.

Because they are scarce and secretive, wild cats are difficult to study. It seems that a pair will normally occupy a territory of 60 to 70 hectares, defined by droppings, urine and scratches on trees, on which the cats probably deposit scent from glands in their

feet. Within this territory, they maintain a series of tracks and several lairs, usually among piles of rocks, although sometimes in hollow trees or even old birds' nests. Wild cats are active mainly at dusk and in the very early morning, hunting for the small rodents which make up the bulk of their food. In some parts of their range, wild cats take large numbers of rabbits and hares and, where they are abundant, birds. Occasionally, they may catch a roe deer kid, or a sickly lamb. However, they certainly do not deserve their reputation of being ruthless killers.

Forest wild cats mate early in the year after a noisy courtship, in the course of which males may fight ferociously. After a gestation of about 69 days, the litter of three or four kittens is born. These are blind, helpless and weigh about 40 g. Their eyes open after 9 or 10 days, and they emerge from the den at 4 to 5 weeks old. Their mother brings them voles and other small mammals soon after this. They do not accompany her on hunting expeditions until they are 10-12 weeks old, and they are fully weaned a month later. They reach adult size at 10 months old and are sexually mature within their first year.

Details of claw structure.

The skull of a wild cat is larger and more robust than that of a domestic cat. It shows the very short face with teeth adapted for an exclusively flesh diet.

In the breeding season, wild cats yowl and fight just as domestic cats do.

A wild cat will try to ambush a rabbit, but if it escapes will not chase it far.

The wild cat feeds almost exclusively on flesh, small rodents making the bulk of its diet, although it may take game birds, such as the partridge shown here.

LYNX
Family Felidae

Like the wild cat, the lynx (*Felis lynx*) has been exterminated from much of Europe and small numbers now survive only in Scandinavia, the Baltic States, the Balkans, Russia, Spain and Portugal. It extends across much of northern Asia and is also found in North America. There is great regional variation in the spots on the coat; in Europe, the Iberian and Balkan lynxes are more heavily spotted than those from Scandinavia, while those from the Pyrenees and the Carpathians are intermediate.

The lynx is a much larger animal than the wild cat with relatively longer legs and a far shorter tail. The female is smaller than the male, and the head and body length is in the range 80-130 cm to which the tail adds 11-24 cm. A small female may be only 60 cm at the shoulder, while a large male may measure 75 cm, and the weight may be 18 to 38 kg. In keeping with its greater size, the lynx occupies a much larger territory than the wild cat. Boundaries are marked by droppings scattered on the surface (they are buried within the territory), sprayed urine and scratched trees. In the old Carpathian forests the lynx's territory is said to occupy about 20 sq. km, while in northern Europe it is four or five times this size. There are likely to be a number of lairs in each territory, situated in hollow trees, natural caves or among boulders. A lynx will hunt through the area adjacent to a den and then move on to another part of its territory. It travels long distances and individuals tracked in the snow have covered 22 km in a single hunting expedition.

Lynxes' sight and hearing are both excellent. They hunt by ambushing their prey, sometimes waiting on a branch or rock overhanging a game track, and sometimes stalking as close as possible before a final sprint, which is rarely longer than 20 m. Many different animals are taken, but lynxes overwhelmingly are hunters of hares. Other, larger prey may be eaten, especially in winter when the snow may develop a thin, frozen crust. At such times the feet of hoofed animals, such as sheep and deer, break through the ice and they flounder in the deep snow. The dense fur round lynxes' paws forms 'snowshoes' which allow them to bound unhampered over the surface. In soft snow, however, lynxes are at as much of a disadvantage as their prey, and they try to avoid such conditions. Although they may devour small prey completely, they are dainty feeders, taking only the choicest flesh and the brains from a deer or other large animal, and rarely returning to the carcass.

In February, males leave their normal territories to look for mates. The litter of up to four furry, blind and helpless kittens, each weighing about 70 g, are born 63-73 days after pairing. Their eyes open at 16 or 17 days, and they leave the den at about 5 weeks old. By this time they have already been fed some meat by their mother, but they continue to take some milk until they are 5 months old or more. They stay with their mother until the next mating season and probably remain for some time beyond this. The females become mature at just under 2 years of age, and the males a year later.

The Spanish lynx is the most heavily spotted of the European forms. It often waits patiently on a branch or rock to ambush its prey.

In captivity, a lynx has survived for 17 years, but it is most unlikely to do so in the wild where man is an implacable enemy. In a few places lynxes have been reintroduced, and there is evidence to suggest that if they are given some respite from persecution the numbers build up again rapidly. Wolves are their most important natural enemies. Apparently the two species cannot co-exist and it is the lynx which gives way. Gluttons are also seen to take precedence over lynxes, although there is probably less competition with the largely scavenging glutton than with the wolf.

The dense coat of the Scandinavian lynx protects it against the bitter winters of its home land. Its huge furry feet prevent it from breaking through crusted snow and so it can hunt hares efficiently even in the winter.

The lynx has the habit, common to many cats, of scratching particular points in its territory and spraying with urine to proclaim its ownership of the area.

Lynx kittens are born in late spring and first emerge from their nursery den in about mid-June, when they are 5 weeks old. These animals come from the Carpathians, and are less heavily spotted than the Spanish form.

FERAL CARNIVORES

Carnivores figure largely among the domesticated mammals, and dogs, cats and ferrets have all been subdued to the extent that they will breed readily in captivity and be more tractable than their wild ancestors. Selection for more manageable stock and the perpetuation of odd varieties produced by accidental genetic change has led to the development of many breeds of dogs and cats, and even ferrets tend to be smaller, weaker and differently coloured from their ancestors, the polecats.

Occasionally, domestic animals escape and establish themselves in the wild, when they are known as feral. The presence of the mongoose and genet in Europe is probably the result of the release of semi-domesticated animals in the remote past, though the numbers now kept are not sufficient to add substantially to the population, should any escape. It is a different matter with cats, dogs and ferrets, all of which are commonly kept and frequently escape or are abandoned. The solitary nature of ferrets probably prevents them from building up viable wild populations. Also they are likely to find chickens easier prey than rabbits or mice, which usually leads to their being recaptured or destroyed quite quickly.

Smaller breeds of dog are so dependent on Man that they are unlikely to survive in the wild. However, larger breeds occasionally become feral. They lose their confidence in human beings and become more furtive in their behaviour and gait, running so that the back slopes. They constantly check for sight, sound or smell of danger by swinging the head from side to side. They do not dig sleeping burrows but nest on flattened long grass, and they are so wary that they change their den site every few days. There are records of them surviving for years, apparently feeding mainly on rabbits, although they may also raid rubbish dumps and human habitations for food. Because of their innate ability as hunters, feral dogs are usually destroyed. Dog catchers are employed in many areas to ensure that stray dogs are dealt with before they can build up packs which might endanger farm stock.

Cats are not only commonly kept as pets, but they are generally little supervised, so it is commonplace for a cat to hunt beyond the bounds of its owner's house and garden. As a rule, comfort and easy food bring them home, but cats can and do survive for many months or years in the wild, and breeding populations can build up. In some urban areas, such as the Colosseum in Rome, there are large cat populations. They feed largely on mice and pigeons, but their survival is ensured by extra food brought to them by human well-wishers.

Altogether different are the cats which run wild in the country. Their inherited hunting skills are used to good effect and they can survive indefinitely on rodents and birds. Breeding populations may build up and take the place of other small carnivores which have been reduced in numbers. Keepers, and others concerned with the preservation of game birds, kill large numbers of feral cats every year. The kittens of feral cats are reputed to revert to a tabby-coat type and to increase in size so that they approximate to the native wild cat in appearance. However, the tabby's coat has blotched markings rather than the stripes of the wild form, and its tail tends to taper. Wild cat kittens have tapering tails but later develop blunt-ended tails.

In areas where wild cats survive, the matter may be complicated by inter-breeding between the domestic and wild forms.

Cats were tamed in Egypt and domestic cats are descended from *Felis libica*, now considered to be a subspecies of the northern wild cat. It differs from that race in its smaller size and tapering tail. Also, the northern wild cat has the long-founded reputation of being difficult to tame while the north African wild cat seem to accept readily an association with humans. These two races can interbreed and some authorities suggest that about a quarter of British wild cats have mixed ancestry.

Even before the principles of heredity were understood, Man kept those animals which reproduced at a faster than normal rate. Dogs, pigs, chickens and cats are all examples of animals where fecundity has been selected for. This trait seems to be retained by cats if they interbreed with wild stock. Cats which are of partly domestic origin may have more than one litter of kittens in a year, while pure wild cats produce only one family during the spring or early summer. In general the crosses retain the characteristic intractability of their northern wild cat ancestors.

Domestic ferrets sometimes escape and survive in the wild. However, it is rare for them to find a mate, and so large populations do not build up.

Escaped ferrets have less fear of Man than most truly wild animals. They may live close to houses or farms, and like this polecat ferret, raid chicken runs.

Feral dogs often find difficulty in obtaining enough food and may be reduced to eating the droppings of herbivorous mammals.

A feral dog is usually a furtive creature. It develops a slinking gait with its tail held low and its head swinging from side to side to test all directions for danger or for possible food.

Feral dogs like to lie up in dry places, often making a bed of trampled long grass. They seem nervous and rarely remain in one spot for long.

Large colonies of feral cats sometimes build up in towns, where they feed on pigeons, mice and rats.

The hunting instinct of feral cats asserts itself very readily and effectively, and they often cause great damage to game birds.

131

PINNIPEDES

Order Pinnipedia

Europe's long and often desolate coastline offers food and living space to many animals, yet mammals are sparsely represented among them. Only two groups have made the sea their headquarters — the whales (pp. 160-9) are totally oceanic, while the pinnipedes divide their time between solid ice or the edge of the land where they rest and breed, and the inshore seas where they feed.

The pinnipedes are related to the carnivores. However, they diverged from the main flesh-eating stock in distant geological times and have followed their own evolutionary paths at least since the Miocene Period. They are now so different from all other mammals that they have been placed in a separate order, the Pinnipedia or 'fin feet'. Two main groups of pinnipedes live in European waters, the true seals and the walrus. Most abundant are the true seals, which are found from the Arctic to the Mediterranean, while the walrus breeds round Spitzbergen and is sometimes seen on mainland coasts.

The pinnipedes' adoption of an aquatic lifestyle has led to great adaptations of shape and bodily functions. The density of sea water has demanded the development of a highly streamlined shape, with a short neck and smooth body devoid of projections such as external ears. Their legs are short and their hands and feet have become fully webbed flippers. In true seals the hind limbs are turned back so that the feet project behind the body. In swimming these are used with a side-to-side motion, with the toes extended on the power stroke and folded together on the recovery movement. The forelimbs are held against the body, except when used for steering. In water, the seals' movements are marvellously sinuous, but on land they are very clumsy. The hind limbs cannot carry any weight, and so the animal has to hitch itself along caterpillar fashion.

Internally, a pinnipede is adapted for swimming and diving in cold water. Unlike most freshwater mammals, which are kept dry by their thick fur, pinnipedes have relatively thin coats and a layer of oil-filled cells, or blubber, beneath the skin. In the walrus and other giants this layer may be up to 15 cm thick. It is a poor conductor of heat and prevents the loss of warmth from the body and also acts as a food reserve.

Like all mammals, the pinnipedes must hold their breath when diving, but they can do this more effectively than land dwellers. Their tissues need oxygen in the same way, but they can work without it for a short time, building up an 'oxygen debt' which must be repaid when there is a chance to breath again. Also they can tolerate a far higher amount of carbon dioxide in the tissues than land animals. The brain must have a constant supply of oxygen and to ensure that this is maintained, pinnipedes have a complex of blood vessels which, under pressure, serve it alone. The heartbeat rate can also drop to about ten beats or less per minute, so that their blood circulates very slowly. Their bodies contain an unexpectedly large amount of blood, highly charged with haemoglobin. The muscles contain large amounts of myoglobin, another compound capable of carrying oxygen. In these ways a diving pinnipede is well prepared to function without breathing for a number of minutes.

Although they may mate in water, pinnipedes must come ashore or on to ice to give birth. Each female has only one pup in a season and in some species they only breed every other year. A baby seal is relatively large and well furred, sometimes with a soft white coat, but in some species this has been shed before birth and replaced by a juvenile pelage. At first the young pup has a wrinkled appearance, but pinnipedes' milk is very rich in fat and the baby fills out in a few days to roly-poly plumpness. They are suckled for a very short time, as little as a fortnight in some cases, after which they strike out on their own.

Many, but not all, pinnipedes are polygamous. In those that are, the males, which tend to be much larger than the females, arrive at the breeding rookeries and take up territories there before the heavily pregnant cows come ashore. The pups are produced within a few days and the next mating takes place shortly after this. Implantation of the ovum and development of the foetus is delayed, sometimes for several months, so that the total length of the pregnancy is one year.

Their diet varies; some species are fish eaters, while others feed largely on crustaceans or bottom-living organisms, or strain larger plankton from the water.

The harp seal is an Arctic species, which hauls out on to the pack ice in spring when the pups are born. Like all North Atlantic seals, it has to hitch itself along caterpillar fashion because it cannot put any weight on to its hind feet.

For much of the year when they are at sea, seals rest hanging vertically with only the head above water, as shown in this grey seal.

The ringed seal is the commonest Arctic seal. It has small teeth and feeds on krill and similar planktonic animals, and on small fish. The young are born in April in dens in the snow.

The hooded seal is an Arctic species in which the male has an enlargement of the nasal cavity which it blows up when angry. It can blow a 'balloon' out of one nostril (right) with part of the elastic tissue between the nostrils. The function of this is unknown.

In the water seals keep their nostrils tightly closed, often opening only one nostril on land.

The bearded seal can be seen close to the Arctic coasts where it rests in summer.

The rare monk seal in the process of moulting.

The common seal lives in shallow water close to estuaries containing sandbanks.

133

SEALS

Family Phocidae

The grey seal *(Halichoerus grypus)* inhabits temperate Atlantic waters and coasts. Its most northerly rookeries are near Murmansk and colonies are also found on the south coast of Iceland, part of the Baltic and the Norwegian Fro Islands, but the major strongholds are round western and northern Britain. On the other side of the Atlantic, the grey seal is found in the Gulf of St Lawrence and round the coasts of Newfoundland.

The grey seal is a large animal, a male measuring 3 m, while a female is usually at least 0.5 m shorter. It overlaps geographically with the much smaller common seal *(Phoca vitulina)* but is separated ecologically since it normally hauls ashore on rocky coastlines, whereas the common seal prefers sandy beaches. The two may be distinguished if visibility is good by the roman-nosed profile of the larger species.

Grey seal pups have been recorded round the British coast in virtually every month, but the majority of births take place between October and December. At the start of this time, the bulls fight to establish territories. Although the battles look and sound terrifying, the contestants are rarely seriously damaged. In time, however, most bulls become heavily scarred round the head and shoulders. A cow may pass through several territories without being molested or herded by any of the bulls, before she finds a place, usually well above the tide line, which suit her for the birth of her pup, which weighs 14-15 kg. She suckles it four or five times a day for 2 or 3 weeks. In this time, it grows to a weight of about 45 kg, sheds its white baby coat and makes its first attempts at swimming.

When first deserted by their mothers, the pups are ready to swim and feed on their own and they strike out with no special direction. Pups from British breeding colonies have been found only a few weeks later on Scandinavian or French beaches. The cow will probably mate first with the bull in whose territory she settled to give birth, but she may mate with others later. The bulls return to the sea after the cows, having fasted for the 2 months that they have been ashore.

The large facial whiskers or vibrissae of grey seals give them an excellent sense of touch. Well-fed blind seals are sometimes found, for they can apparently detect fish by the changes in water pressures as they move. They also have very good hearing, and are highly vocal both in and out of the water. The sense of smell is less well developed, but seals have a characteristic musty odour, and mothers and cubs appear to recognize each other, at least partly, by scent.

Grey seals feed mainly on fish, although cuttlefish and sea birds are also eaten. They can take 7.5 to 11 kg in a single meal, but they may not feed every day. This predilection for fish brings them into conflict with Man. Recently, the population in British waters has been growing and yearly culls are now made to try to keep numbers down to an acceptable level. Pup mortality is very high in the first few weeks of life. Having survived these, a seal may look forward to a long life, a female of 46 years having been recorded.

Left: *The rear flippers of true seals have five webbed toes, each bearing a nail which does not reach the end of the foot.* Middle left: *The front flipper of true seals is much smaller than the hind. It has long nails and is very flexible, and so can be used to scratch a large part of the body.* Bottom left: *The front flipper of the bearded seal is unusual in that the third digit is longer than the others.*

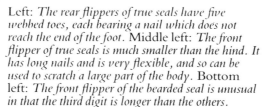

On land, seals always seem to be crying. They are not sad, but have no duct to carry away the tears which are constantly being formed in the eyes, so they run down the face instead.

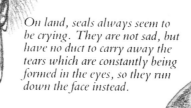

Baby monk seals are born in autumn on secluded sandy beaches where they may be free from disturbance by holidaymakers or persecution by fishermen.

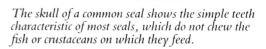

The skull of a common seal shows the simple teeth characteristic of most seals, which do not chew the fish or crustaceans on which they feed.

The majority of the world's population of grey seals comes to secluded rocky beaches on the north and west coasts of Britain during the winter months to produce their pups.

WALRUS
Family Odobenidae

Apart from Spitzbergen, the walrus (*Odobenus rosmarus*) is rare in European waters, although individuals are seen regularly on the coast of Iceland and sometimes further south. The largest of the pinnipedes, a bull may measure 3.7 m in length and weigh 1,350 kg, while a cow will be about 3 m long and weigh 900 kg. Its size, its wrinkled, almost hairless skin and huge tusks make the walrus unmistakeable. A young walrus has a scanty coat of reddish hair, which decreases with age. The skin continues to thicken until it measures more than 5 cm in an adult, and below it is a layer of blubber, about 7.5 cm deep.

The tusks, which are perhaps the walrus's strangest feature, are hugely enlarged canine teeth. These grow throughout the life of the animal and in males may be more than a metre in length, while those of females are more slender and are unlikely to exceed 60 cm.

The walrus is structurally linked to the sea lions and, like them, has the ability to turn the hindfeet forward to take some weight when it is on land. A unique feature is the possession of a pair of pouches formed from the flexible skin of the throat.

These can be inflated from the lungs, and act as a built-in life jacket to support the animal when it rests in the water.

Walruses live in areas of shallow water, usually where they can haul ashore on to sea ice. They seem to be intolerant of other species and although they share their habitat with some Arctic seals, it is very rare to find the animals together. Most of their food is taken from the sea bed at depths of less than 75 m. The snout and tusks are used to stir up molluscs and other sedentary creatures. These are then manipulated by the flexible, whiskery upper lips into the mouth, where the flesh is usually sucked from the prey. Fish may be eaten occasionally and some walruses kill and devour seals. There are even records of a narwhal being eaten, although it is not known whether this was taken as carrion or prey.

Like most pinnipedes, walruses are social. The males are polygamous, although there does not seem to be any definite harem system. Less than half of the females in any herd pup in April or May, after a gestation of 15 months including a short delay in implantation of the embryo. At birth, the pup is over a metre in length and weighs about 40 kg. For the first year of its life it is entirely dependent on its mother's milk. It remains with her for at least another year, possibly because while its tusks are still very small it cannot get enough food on its own. Females are mature at about 5 years and produce a pup every 3 years, breeding less frequently as they age.

In the wild, the walrus's only enemies are polar bears and killer whales, and they probably survive to the age of at least 30 years. Man, however, has hunted walrus since at least the ninth century, and within the last 200 years has decimated the previously stable populations, mainly to obtain the ivory from the tusks. Within recent years, this exploitation has been greatly reduced and the numbers are beginning to increase again.

Sea ice forms in the walruses' habitat in the winter. They keep breathing holes open by chipping at the ice with their tusks.

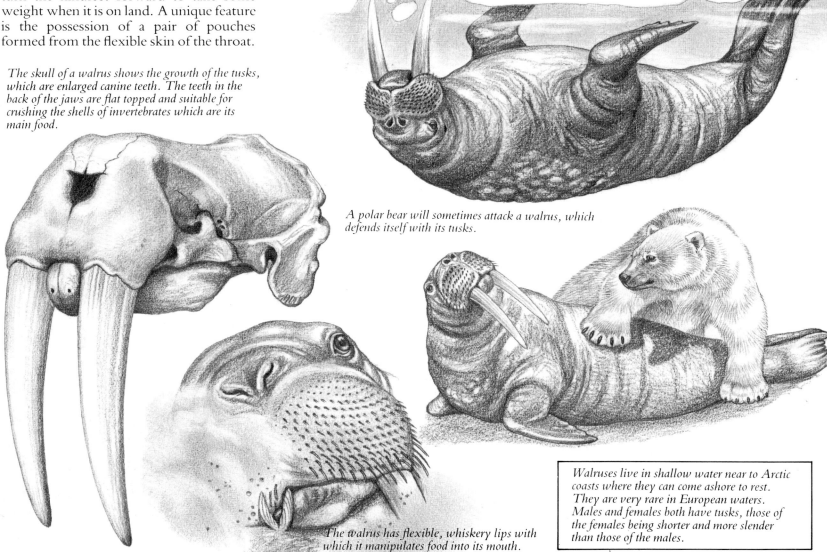

The skull of a walrus shows the growth of the tusks, which are enlarged canine teeth. The teeth in the back of the jaws are flat topped and suitable for crushing the shells of invertebrates which are its main food.

A polar bear will sometimes attack a walrus, which defends itself with its tusks.

The walrus has flexible, whiskery lips with which it manipulates food into its mouth.

Walruses live in shallow water near to Arctic coasts where they can come ashore to rest. They are very rare in European waters. Males and females both have tusks, those of the females being shorter and more slender than those of the males.

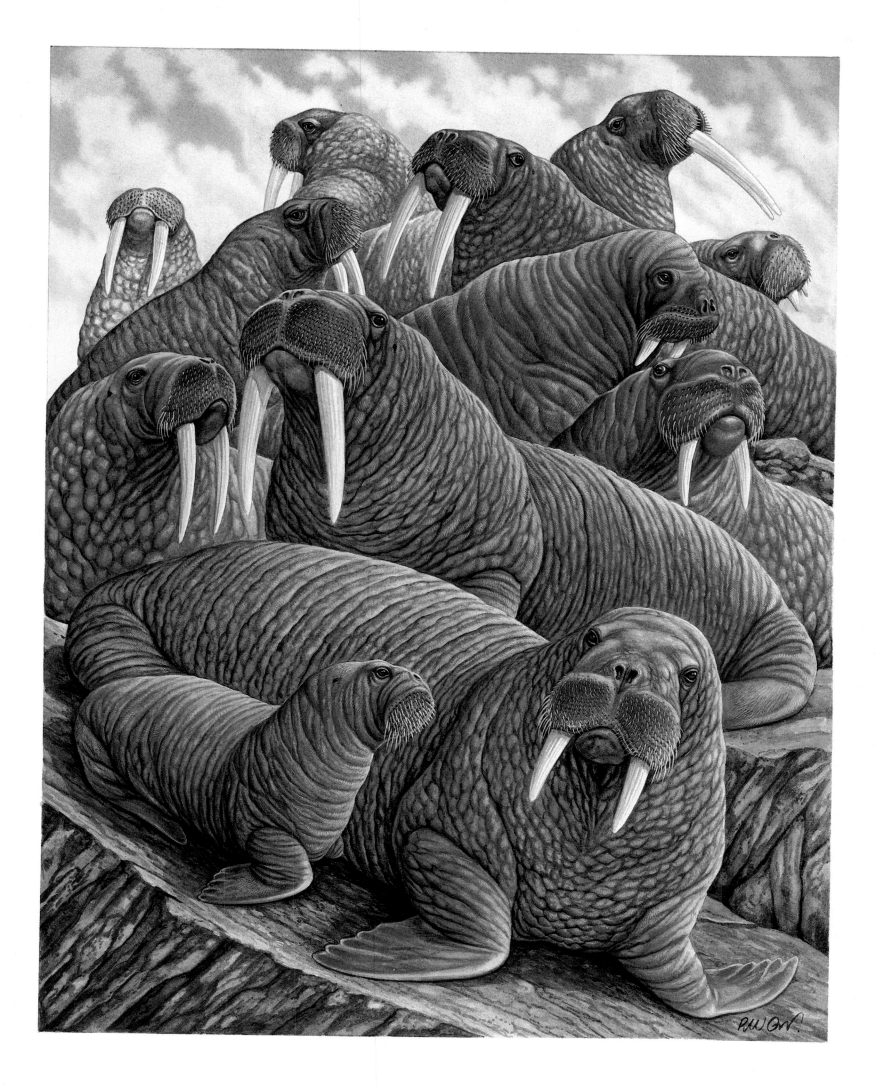

HOOFED ANIMALS

The term hoofed animals or ungulates is one that has little scientific meaning for, on a worldwide basis, it includes creatures with very different body structures and ways of life. However, in Europe it has some validity for only one major group of hoofed animals is native there, although a second, including the wild horse, survived until recent times.

Many species among the hoofed animals are long-distance runners. Their slender limbs contain the same basic bone structure as those of slower animals such as hedgehogs or beavers, but their speed is increased largely because they stand on the tips of their toes and thus add the length of their foot bones to each stride. Almost all have less weight in their feet than other types of mammals, for the five toes possessed by their primitive ancestors have been reduced in number and the hand and foot bones – the carpals and tarsals – have become fused to form a single, strong cannon bone. This has the advantage of adding rigidity to the limb and preventing it from twisting under the stress of running. The toes are protected by a large, horny nail, or hoof, which wraps round the tender sole of the foot and prevents it from making too much contact with the ground. At its outer edge, the hoof is formed of dead cells, which are constantly worn away but are replaced by continuous growth from the living part, or quick, of the nail. Hoofed animals are herbivores and the European species are all large, for their plant food is abundant and easy to come by.

The one surviving native ungulate order in Europe is the Artiodactyla or even-toed ungulates, which are sometimes known as the cloven-hoofed animals. In the feet of these creatures there is no thumb or great toe. The weight is carried on the equally developed third and fourth toes, behind which lie the second and fifth toes. These are referred to as dew claws, for they are usually small and so placed that they do not touch the ground. However, if the going is very soft and the main toes sink into the mud, the dew claws come into play to spread the animal's weight.

The other ungulate group is called the Perissodactyla and in temperate parts of the world it includes only horses. In these animals, the burden of weight is carried on the greatly enlarged third toe, although in some members of the group the second and fourth toes are also present. They, there-fore, have one or three toes on each foot and are called the odd-toed ungulates. From the end of the Ice Age, the horse was the only perissodactyl native to Europe. It was exterminated over a century ago, but feral ponies and donkeys, none of which is truly wild, exist in a number of places.

Of the two orders, artiodactyls seem better able to survive in the modern world for there are at least 18 wild and several feral species of cloven-hoofed animals in Europe, including pigs, sheep, goats, cattle and deer. There are very many differences between the two groups besides that of the structure of the feet. In general, horses inhabit open country where they feed on grasses, while most cloven-hoofed animals are woodland browsers. Their method of eating differs as well as their food. Horses crop grass with incisor teeth, which lie in the front of both the upper and lower jaws, and grind it between a long row of pre-molars and molars in the back of the mouth. All of the teeth of a horse are open rooted and continue growing throughout the animal's life, an adaptation to a diet of grass, which is one of the harshest of all foods. Horses spend a considerable part of each day feeding, for each mouthful has to be chewed thoroughly before it is swallowed. Moreover, their stomach capacity is not, for their size, very great, and they cannot take in a day's supply of food at one time. Pigs, which are cloven-hoofed animals, also have upper incisor teeth and a way of feeding which is comparable to the horses. However, the rest of the European artiodactyls have a very different feeding regime, which is probably the major factor in the success of this group of animals. In cattle, deer and their relatives, the incisors of the upper jaw are replaced by a horny pad against which the lower incisors and the tongue work. Food is gathered very quickly and swallowed without chewing into the first compartment of a large and complex stomach. Later it is returned in small amounts to the mouth, where it is masticated thoroughly. It is then re-swallowed into a different part of the stomach for digestion to continue. An advantage of this system, which is called ruminating, or chewing the cud, is that animals which might be exposed to predators while taking in large amounts of relatively unnutritious food can telescope this dangerous period. They can then find a safe place to lie up while they chew and digest their meals.

The ruminants tend to carry outgrowths from the head. These may take the form of deciduous, branched, bony antlers, or permanent horns in which an internal core of bone is surrounded by a sheath of toenail-like material. The functions of these include defence, sexual fighting and the spreading of scent on to vegetation.

With the exception of the wild boar, all European hoofed animals live in herds. The females produce one, or at most two, large and well-developed young in each breeding period. The babies are able to stand soon after birth and can follow their mothers within a few days, joining the herd soon after this. In common with most animals which are the prey of others, they have sharp senses but are less intelligent than the predators.

Man has hunted the hoofed animals for their palatable flesh, their hides, and sometimes for prestige, since the earliest time. The aurochs, the ancestor of domestic cattle, was brought to extinction in the seventeenth century, to be followed by the wild horse in the nineteenth century, while wild sheep and goats are now among Europe's rarest mammals. Domestication has been no help to the wild stocks, for where they had the potentiality of breeding with tamed animals, they were regarded as weeds to be exterminated, as a cross between wild and domestic animals would almost certainly be less tractable and less strong than a creature selected for these qualities over many generations. Only recently has the value of these relatives of domestic animals been recognized, and today most are carefully protected in nature reserves.

HORSES
Family Equidae

Towards the end of the Ice Age, many wild horses and tarpans roamed the cold plains of Europe. They were an important prey of early Man who painted them on the walls of caves in France and Spain. As the ice retreated, changes in climate and vegetation caused a great decline in their numbers. Both donkeys and horses were domesticated shortly after this in western Asia, and through trading their descendants had spread over the whole of Europe by about 2000 BC. The few wild horses which survived on the eastern steppes were harried into extinction by farmers who could tolerate neither their depredations to crops nor their inter-breeding with domestic stock and the last European wild horses are reputed to have been killed in 1851.

Ponies of the wild type, almost certainly the result of crossing wild and domestic horses, have been put into forest reserves in Poland. Those hardy, independent and intractable individuals which survived the catastrophe of war now form herds approximating very nearly to the original wild stock. Two other Polish breeds with much tarpan blood are the Hucul of the Carpathian Mountains and the Konik of the plains. These are strong, tough, thrifty beasts, able to survive to a great age on poor fodder.

In many other parts of Europe, there are small populations of feral horses, living in remote and often mountainous areas. These are the descendants of tame horses which escaped or were set free. All are ownership can be established. In general, they are rounded up regularly so that ownership can be establishd. In general, they are small, standing less than 145 cm at the shoulder. The Shetland, which is the smallest, measures only about 100 cm at that point.

All ponies are canny and sure footed, capable of finding forage in poor country, and hardy enough to survive harsh weather without shelter. The original ancestors may have been bred for a particular purpose but subsequently natural selection has played a part in shaping their form and character. Mountain ponies tend to have narrow hooves, while those of the Camargue are broad footed, which helps them as they splash through the swampy hollows. It is claimed that a few, such as the Exmoor ponies of western England and the Pottocks of southern France, are the descendants of very ancient breeds, perhaps the first domesticated horses in western Europe. Attempts have been made to 'improve' many other ponies by running stallions of larger breeds with them. However, today efforts are usually made to maintain the regional variety.

Wild ponies generally live in small herds, which include a stallion, several mares and their offspring, although once they approach adulthood, the young males are driven out of the group. Horses are essentially grass eaters and a herd will roam over several hundred hectares through the year to get all the fodder they need. Foals are usually born in early summer, when the weather and feed are at their best. Although they can nibble grass soon after they are born, they are partially dependent on their mothers for about a year. Scent is not important in horses, their excellent eyesight enabling them to communicate largely by body language and expression.

In southern Europe, feral donkeys occur in some places. These show far less variability than the pony breeds.

The foot of a horse from below shows the almost circular hoof, which is protected in working animals by an iron shoe.

The Konik pony from Poland is very like early wild horses. It is strong, wary and independent.

The horse has only one toe on each foot, protected by a large wrap-around toenail, or hoof.

The skull of a horse shows the cropping teeth (incisors) in the front of the mouth and the flat-topped premolars and molars at the back. These are open rooted and grow throughout the life of the animal, but they are continually worn down by the tough food which it eats.

Although there are no truly wild horses in Europe today, a number of populations of feral horses survive in remote regions. Some of them have features thought to be similar to those of early horses. The Exmoor pony is considered to be the most primitive of the British breeds of feral small horses or ponies. It is usually dark bay in colour with a mealy nose and a pale ring round the eye.

WILD BOAR
Family Suidae

The wild boar *(Sus scrofa)* is the only wild member of the pig family found in Europe. It is the ancestor of domestic pigs, but unlike the forerunners of almost all other domesticated animals, it is still fairly abundant. Originally it was an inhabitant of broadleaved and mixed forests from Britain (though not Ireland) eastwards through much of Europe and southern Asia. It became extinct in Britain during the seventeenth century, and over much of Europe its numbers have declined greatly with the destruction of forests. In spite of heavy persecution, its numbers have been increasing in recent years. It has been reintroduced into some areas and has even been taken to places, such as southern Scandinavia, where it had never occurred naturally. It is highly adaptable, and today is often found in more or less open agricultural land. It may be a considerable pest, raiding such diverse crops as grain, potatoes, melons and grapes. Apart from the food actually consumed, it causes so much damage to the rest of the growing plants that the enmity of farmers is easy to understand.

Wild boars have an average head and body length of 1.5 m, a tail 25 to 40 cm long, and the height at the shoulder is about 1 m. However, the size tends to vary with the habitat. In the great forests of eastern Europe a boar may weigh between 300 and 345 kg, but in France 100 kg would be regarded as a good weight. The sow is generally slightly smaller than her mate, and is usually rather fatter. The colour of the harsh, bristly coat is variable, ranging from grey to russet, and is always darker in the winter. In general, the wild boar is a solitary animal, although the sow is usually accompanied by the young of her last litter and sometimes by the nearly full-grown young of the year before.

The size of a wild boar's territory varies greatly with the richness of the environment. It is likely that mud wallows made by males, and possibly by sows also, have territorial significance. Since pigs are well endowed with scent glands on the face, body and forelegs, these probably play a part in the definition of the living areas. The acid smell of wild boar, like that of damp oak leaves, is sufficiently strong for a human nose to detect their presence. Within its territory, a wild boar will have several lairs. These may be among a tumble of rocks, but are often no more than shallow trenches dug under the shelter of a fallen tree or branch. They may be lined with dead leaves or grass, or devoid of bedding.

Wild boars eat almost anything which can be obtained from the ground. The powerful snout, protected by a small bone not found in other animals, allows them to dig for underground roots, tubers and bulbs and to search for small animals, from snails to helpless young mammals, such as rabbits or rodents. They are selective to some extent, for while wild garlic and the bulbs of martagon lily are eaten with relish, those of wild daffodils are avoided, even when they are growing abundantly alongside the other plants. In the autumn, acorns and beech mast form an important part of their diet and wild boars become very fat. In spite of this, they remain fully active throughout the winter. During this time, males seek out females and mating takes place, the pairs separating again after a few weeks.

After a gestation period of about 4 months, the sow prepares a rough nursery. Up to 10 piglets are born, which remain in the nest for a few days. They follow their mother for up to 2 years, by which time they are sexually mature, and the next winter they are ready to find mates of their own.

The cloven hoof the wild boar has two well-developed dew claws, which lie behind the main toes and help to support the animal on soft ground.

The wild boar gets most of its food on the ground, rooting with its powerful snout for plant or animal food.

The tusks of the female (upper) are smaller and less angular than those of the male (lower).

The snout is protected by a small bone, not found in other animals.

The skull contains 44 teeth, the maximum number normally found in placental mammals. These allow the animal to eat almost any food, for it is one of the few true omnivores.

> Wild boar piglets are less fully developed at birth than the young of most cloven-hoofed animals, and follow their mothers for longer. In their early months they are camouflaged in the woods by their striped coats.

DEER
Family Cervidae

Deer are the most important of the cloven-hoofed animals in Europe. There are five native species augmented by five introduced species, which have established themselves firmly in suitable habitats. They are cud-chewing herbivores, which, except for reindeer, were originally woodland dwellers. Today the largest populations and heaviest animals are still found in forests. They are, however, highly adaptable and many can survive in open parkland or even on moors. In recent years, some of the smaller species have invaded suburbs and towns, relying on the food and cover to be found in parks and gardens. These little animals can survive in such areas because they are solitary for most of their lives. The larger deer are social and normally live in herds, which could not be supported by urban environments.

Scent plays an important part in a deer's life, and all species are well provided with scent glands on the face, legs and feet. As might be expected, the sense of smell is acute, not only to the nuances of the herd's own odour, but also to that of strangers, and a whiff of a hostile scent will alarm them faster than anything else. The sense of hearing is also good, but while a strange sound will alert the deer, they are not likely to run until they get confirmation of the presence of an enemy from their nose. Although their eyes are large, sight is comparatively unimportant and a deer will often not observe a stationary object, although it may be close by.

The feature which distinguishes deer from all other animals is their antlers. These bony outgrowths from the head are the prerogative of the male of all species, except for the introduced Chinese water deer which has none and the reindeer, in which the females also have small antlers. They grow from projections on the frontal bones, called pedicles, which are a permanent feature of the skull. The antlers are shed yearly, in most cases at the end of the winter, and almost immediately new antlers begin to grow.

The first antlers grown by yearlings are usually just simple spikes. In successive years, they tend to grow bigger and to be more complex in shape until the animal reaches full maturity. Subsequently, as it ages, they regress in size. The yearly growth is not necessarily a steady one for, although it is hormonally controlled, it may be affected by adverse living conditions. Antler growth is rapid, taking 2 to 3 months in early summer, during which time they are covered with a densely haired

skin, called velvet, which provides the growing bone with an abundant blood supply. At this time, the antlers can be harmed easily and a slight knock can cause abnormal growth. When the antler has reached full size the blood supply is cut off; the velvet skin dies and is cleaned off by the deer, leaving the antlers ready for use.

This growth period is a difficult time, particularly for those species with large antlers, for they require large amounts of minerals which, especially in poor habitats, are hard to come by. Deer often obtain the necessary substances by eating their antlers as soon as they are cast. They may also assuage their craving for minerals by chewing bone or any other animal tissue which they come across, even destroying axe handles impregnated with sweat to get at the vital salts.

The most obvious functions of antlers are fighting for mates and indicating social status within the herd. However, another use is spreading the scent produced by the facial glands, and it is thought that this may have been their original function.

Wherever they live, deer are in danger from predators, the most severe of which is Man. Large-scale destruction of forests has reduced numbers, and hunting has further exterminated them from some areas. However, deer have been protected as game animals for many centuries. Now, in some parts of Europe, the taking of deer is controlled by law, and so their future seems secure in the remaining forests.

Chinese water deer buck

White-tailed deer buck

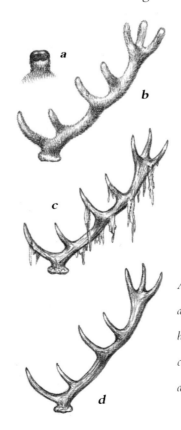

Antler growth in red deer.

a)   APRIL. Pedicle with antler beginning to grow.
b)   Late JUNE to early JULY. Antler fully grown but still in velvet.
c)   Mid JULY to mid SEPTEMBER. Velvet dries and is cleaned off by deer.
d)   Mid SEPTEMBER to mid FEBRUARY. Antler fully functional and can be used for spreading scent or fighting.
e)   Mid FEBRUARY to MARCH. Antler cast; pedicle only on head.

Red deer stag

Roe buck

Fallow buck

Muntjac buck

In spite of protection, deer are often poached, sometimes being killed by most inhumane methods and at others being allowed to escape when wounded. This jawbone was part of a red deer skeleton found in a nature reserve in Scotland. It had been shattered by a poacher's bullet and subsequently healed in two pieces. The animal died later from other wounds.

RED DEER
Family Cervidae

The red deer *(Cervus elaphus)* is the largest truly wild animal to be found over most of central and western Europe. Only where it overlaps with the elk in southern Scandinavia and the bison in Poland is it exceeded in size. In Britain it tends to be thought of as a highland species, for herds which are direct descendants of prehistoric stock survive on Exmoor and on the Scottish hills. However, red deer grow to a far larger size on the rich old lowland forests of eastern Europe, where animals weighing over 225 kg have been recorded, compared to an average stag from the island of Rhum, Scotland, which weighs, when gralloched (gutted), about 85 kg. The head and body length of these continental beasts is up to 260 cm, compared to a maximum of 201 cm on Rhum, while the height at the shoulder is up to 150 cm compared to 122 cm.

Territory size varies according to the type of habitat and may be up to 800 hectares for a highland stag, although it may be as little as half this for a hind, while the size of home ranges for woodland deer are unknown. Herd size also varies with the habitat, very large numbers having been recorded in open places, while smaller herds are usual in forests. Food also varies with the living place, from tree bark and shoots to grasses, sedges and farm crops.

Red deer are at their most obvious in October, for then the stags enter the territories of the hind herds and announce their readiness to mate by roaring—a moaning bellow which rings through the woods and hills to attract females and warn rivals. They fray small trees as they spread the scent from their facial glands with their antlers. The older stags are first in the field, and soon other stags challenge by roaring and thus assess the strength of the opposition. A weak animal will not attempt to usurp a harem master. If a powerful adversary arrives on the scene, after careful preliminaries during which either animal can retreat, they will suddenly lower their heads and lock antlers, wrestling for dominance. When one of the contestants is finally unable to push back, a quick sideways movement of the head disengages the antlers and the loser turns and runs. The winner rarely follows him for more than a few paces, because to do so might mean the loss of his harem to another stag. It would, in any case, be harmful to the species if the loser were to be seriously injured or killed, since he may win a battle with another stag later in the season or sire calves in subsequent years. Although accidents do occur and a stag may be hurt or killed, the defeat is mainly psychological and the loser will not challenge the winner again in the same year. The harem owner spends its time guarding, fighting and mating, with little left over for feeding or resting, so he soon has to relinquish his females, which have no apparent preference for mates.

The single calf is born in May or June, and for the first week or more it lies hidden in the undergrowth, protected by its dappled baby coat. It then begins to follow its mother in the evenings, but will return to hide during the day until it is about a month old. By this time it is capable of keeping up with the adult herd, although it will suckle until it is about 10 months old.

Red deer society is basically matriarchal and a young stag will remain with the hind herd until he is 2 or 3 years old. Stags are, in general, more or less solitary, although they may be forced together for lack of shelter or food during the winter. They tend to stay apart from the hind herds, which are more stable and usually take the richer grazing and shelter. Calves may be attacked by almost any large predator including eagles, but adult red deer are immune from almost all enemies other than wolves and Man. They can live to the age of 20, but few survive for this long.

In its first year a red deer stag's antlers will begin to grow, forming simple spikes. As it matures, each year's growth of antler will tend to be larger and more complex.

The pedicles from which new antlers will grow remain on the stag's head after the old antlers have been cast.

Red deer use wallows at all times of the year, partly to spread their scent and partly to ease the itching caused by biting flies.

Stags fight by locking antlers and pushing against each other. Even young animals, such as those shown here, will practice fighting in this way.

Red deer are essentially forest animals, but they can survive in a wide range of habitats including the barren uplands of Scotland. In the autumn a master stag challenges other males and attracts hinds with his roaring.

146

FALLOW and ROE DEER
Family Cervidae

Fallow deer *(Cervus dama)* were probably originally native to woodlands of the Mediterranean, but they have been introduced to many other places further north and are now found in suitable lowland areas from Scandinavia to northern Greece and the Pyrenees, with isolated populations in Italy, Spain and Sardinia. The Romans are reputed to have brought them to Britain, but the archaeological evidence suggests that the Normans were responsible. They were often kept in parks and enclosures, and were selected for attractive colours, with the result that their coats now show a far greater range than is normal in wild animals, varying from near black to milky white. The normal form has a bright chestnut coat with white spots during the summer months, which is moulted for a drab grey-brown in the winter.

Fallow are closely related to red deer, but are a little smaller, with a length of about 150 cm and a shoulder height of 120 cm. They have similar life cycles but there are important differences during the rut, which is a little later in the year than the mating season of the red-deer. Rutting fallow bucks rub their antlers in urine and transfer this to vegetation as they fray. They often dig up the ground as they rub their antlers and plaster the stinking mud on to their flanks. Later, the males stay with the herd, which is usually led by an old doe.

The fawns are born in May or June and are ready to follow their mothers soon after birth. Fallow are cautious and cunning, and tend to be more active during the daytime than other deer. They graze more, although they also feed on acorns, beech mast and many cultivated crops.

Roe deer *(Capreolus capreolus)* are the smallest deer native to Europe, with a head and body length of about 120 cm and a shoulder height of up to 75 cm. They are the most widespread of the deer, occupying deciduous and mixed woodland with plenty of cover throughout the continent, apart from Ireland. In places where they are undisturbed, roe deer may be seen feeding during the day, their brilliant chestnut coats gleaming among the foliage in the summer, although their greyish brown winter pelage disguises them well. They are less social than the larger deer, and they are unusual in that they retain territories throughout the year, although non-territorial males may wander over large areas. They may be forced by winter conditions into loose herds of up to 30 animals, in which dominance seems to be decided by the distance of any male from his territory and by the order of arrival at the feeding grounds of the females.

The roe deer rut occurs in mid-July to mid-August, with a second 'false rut' in October. In the rutting area, a buck will fray and mark vegetation with scent and scrape the soil with his forefeet. The roe is the only European hoofed animal in which delayed implantation occurs, for rapid development of the embryo does not occur until the end of the year and the kids are born in May or June. At first well camouflaged with spots, they are left hidden by the doe which feeds close by. About 20 per cent of does produce twins, but it is rare for both young to survive for they are small enough to be the prey of many predators, including domestic dogs. Those that remain are suckled throughout the winter and are sexually mature at 14 months, breeding yearly after this. Their lifespan is unknown, but animals estimated to be 10 years old are found occasionally.

Paths, running in circles or figures of eight round trees or bushes, are known as rutting rings and may be made by pairs in courtship chases,

During the rut, the roe buck makes conspicuous scrapes in the ground. These are probably strongly scented to other deer, for the roe has scent glands in its feet.

The rump patch of the roe doe is white and shaped like an inverted heart (upper), *while that of the buck is yellowish and kidney shaped.*

Like all deer, the roe stands on the tips of its toes and the long foot bones enable it to increase its stride. The whole foot, from toe to ankle, is shown here. The dew claws are placed so that they rarely touch the ground except when it is very soft.

Like all deer, while this roe buck's antlers grow, they are covered in a coarse hairy skin called velvet.

While their antlers are still in velvet, fallow deer often stand on their hind legs and box with their forefeet. Fallow show a wider range of colour than any other deer.

This fallow deer fawn, dappled to match its background, lies hidden in the undergrowth for the first two weeks of its life, after which it is able to follow its mother.

Although they can jump well, fallow deer often prefer to go under an obstacle, such as a wire fence, rather than over it.

When running away, but not desperately alarmed, fallow deer often leap for a few paces, then stand. At other times, they may jump as they run.

The pellets which make up the **droppings** of fallow deer are generally adherent but separate easily. Those of the male are up to 16 mm long and indented at one end, while those of the female are smaller and more rounded.

149

ELK and REINDEER
Family Cervidae

Reindeer and elk are found across much of Asia and into North America, where the reindeer is known as the caribou and the elk is called the moose. The elk *(Alces alces)* is the largest of all deer, with a head and body length of 280 cm and a shoulder height of up to 220 cm. It lives in wet woodlands, broken by rivers and lakes, where it browses by day or night on aspens, willows or herbaceous waterside vegetation. It often wades into the water to reach aquatic plants and ducks its head beneath the surface to take the stems and rhizomes of water lilies. In the autumn, as the deciduous trees lose their leaves, the elk turn to eating the shoots and bark of coniferous trees.

Elk are usually seen singly, for they are less social than other large deer. By the end of the summer, when they are fat with good feeding, the males' trumpeting bellows signal their readiness to mate. Fights are common between the bulls, which do not accumulate a harem but pair with a succession of females. The rut lasts through most of September during which time the males do not feed and since they cannot face the winter with depleted resources, many from the northern part of the continent migrate to forests further south.

The gestation period is about 8 months and in May the females produce their calves, usually twins. Unlike the young of most other deer, they are unspotted, but like all other animals their early days are the most perilous and many are killed by predators, especially bears and wolves. Adult elk have few enemies except for wolves and Man. Largely as a result of human activity, the species is no longer found in Germany or France. However, hunting is now strictly controlled throughout its European range, and the elk is increasing in numbers to the extent that it is regarded as a traffic hazard in parts of Scandinavia.

The reindeer *(Rangifer tarandus)* is the most northerly of all deer, and is a more migratory species than the elk, vast herds making their way south from the inhospitable trundra as winter approaches. The migrants are food for many predators including Man, who in part of the reindeer's range is nomadic, following the herds and being totally dependent on them for meat, milk, hides and transport. Some selective breeding has taken place and the domesticated forms are smaller than the truly wild animals, which are about 210 cm long and up to 120 cm at the shoulder. Tamed reindeer tend to depart from the normal grey-brown of ancestral forms, but the very different breeds which have been developed in other domestic animals do not exist yet.

Reindeer differ from other deer in that the cows carry antlers, although these are smaller than those of the bulls. After the rut in September to October, the males shed their antlers and do not start to regrow them until the spring, while the females retain theirs until after the birth of their single calf in the early summer. The young are suckled for 12 months and become sexually mature at the end of their second year.

The food of reindeer varies with the environment and includes, during the summer, grasses, sedges and many broadleaved plants. During the winter the buds and shoots of trees, and lichens, especially that known as reindeer moss, are important.

Female reindeer carry small antlers and are the only female deer to do so.

In the winter, reindeer need to dig for their food, which may be deeply covered in snow.

When antler growth is complete the velvet skin dies and has to be removed. Here an elk is cleaning his antlers against a branch.

The feet of reindeer spread to take the animals' weight in soft conditions. The loosely jointed hooves make a characteristic 'clack' as the feet are lifted.

The largest of all deer, the elk is an inhabitant of wet woodland. During the summer it often wades into the water to feed on aquatic plants and to escape the torment of biting flies.

EXOTIC DEER
Family Cervidae

During the last century there was a widespread notion that the world's food supply could be increased by introducing species to new environments. 'Acclimatization societies' were formed, with the idea of bringing animals from other continents to Europe and exporting European animals. Deer were in the forefront of these plans and were among the relatively few species which thrived in alien habitats. They sometimes did too well; the red deer for example is now regarded as a pest in New Zealand. During this time, deer were also imported to add to the attractions of great estates. It was inevitable that some of these exotic animals should have escaped, and they have now established themselves thoroughly in European woodlands and are, in many cases, increasing in newly planted forests of alien conifers.

The sika deer *(Cervus nippon)* which originated in eastern Asia, is found in many parts of western Europe, including Great Britain and Ireland. With a body length of only about 120 cm and a shoulder height of 85 cm, it is smaller than the red deer to which it is closely related and with which it occasionally hybridizes. The smaller antlers are similar in shape, and the coat is spotted in summer, moulting to greyish brown in winter. If any confusion arises, the two species can be distinguished by the colour of the rump which is pure white in the sika and yellowish in the native species. Sika normally live in small herds, remaining in dense cover by day and emerging at night to feed in glades or open country close to the woods.

The chital or spotted deer *(Cervus axis)* is another Indian species which is often seen in game parks and has established itself in woodlands in various parts of mainland Europe, including northern Yugoslavia. It is slightly smaller than the fallow deer, which it resembles in its way of life and its brightly spotted coat, although this is retained through the year. There is less white on the rump than in the fallow and the slender antlers are never flattened.

The white-tailed deer *(Odocoileus virginianus)*, which is the most widespread species in North America, has been introduced into a number of places in Europe, including Britain and Finland. It is about the size of a fallow deer, with a bright, unspotted, brown coat in summer, which moults to a greyish colour in winter. The white of the rump is inconspicuous when the animal is browsing peacefully, for the broad tail conceals it almost completely. It is only when it leaps away in alarm, with the tail raised, that the white area is obvious. The antlers have a forward slope to their upper half and are quite unlike those of any native European deer.

Two very small species of deer, the muntjac *(Muntiacus reevesi)* and the Chinese water deer *(Hydropotes inermis)*, from eastern Asia, have been introduced to Great Britain. Both are shy and solitary, and so rarely seen. The Chinese water deer is smaller than a roe, while the muntjac is hardly larger than a fox. The muntjac has tiny, toothpick antlers set on very long pedicles, and the water deer buck has no antlers but sports instead large canine tusks. Both feed on a wide range of shrubs and fruit, including acorns, and both have a greater potential for increase in numbers than most deer. The muntjac has no special breeding season; the does mate within a few days of dropping a fawn and usually produce at least two young in a year. The Chinese water deer doe usually produces twins in May or June, which she is well able to rear. Alone among deer, she frequently gives birth to three or four young, while up to six have been recorded in a single litter.

Over the centuries the legal status of deer has changed greatly. In medieval times they were the quarry of kings but later they came to be regarded as little better than vermin, to be destroyed in any way at any time. Now it is recognized that, although deer may damage growing trees, in a well-grown woodland their actions do little harm and they may be thought of as part of the forest's resources. In many areas deer are now protected by conservation laws, which may seek to control numbers so that the habitat is not damaged, but at the same time to prevent inhumane or wholesale slaughter. As a result of these policies the numbers of deer are growing over much of Europe. There has been a recent move towards domestication for meat, hides and milk. Elk have been domesticated in Russia, and in Britain red deer are being selected for tractability and a readiness to live in a small area, which are important aspects of domestication.

Most deer have scent glands on the hind legs and feet and below the eyes. Roe have an extra scent producing area between the pedicles, with which they anoint twigs during the rut.

In the early part of the year, when other food is in short supply, deer eat the bark of trees. Since they have incisor teeth in the lower jaw only, they dig these into the bark and tear long strips from the side of the trunk.

a

A roe buck with insufficient male hormone fails to shed the velvet from its antlers which are not cast, eventually forming a heavy growth on the top of the head. Such animals are known as perruques.

Antler malformation may be due to damage during the period of growth.

The skull of the roe buck shows the long pedicles from which the antlers grow. Very occasionally roe does also grow small antlers.

The characteristic target patch on the rumps of deer serve to identify them as they run away. a) Red deer stag. b) Fallow buck. c) Sika stag. d) White-tailed deer buck. e) Roe buck.

Père David's deer, originally a native of China, was saved from extinction by captive breeding in Europe and now herds may be seen in many game parks. Rutting stags increase the impression of their bulk by gathering vegetation in their antlers.

Deer normally regain the minerals lost in cast antlers by eating them as soon as they are shed. In Britain it is more usual to find antlers chewed, as shown here, than not.

CATTLE
Family Bovidae

The horned ruminants of Europe have never been so varied or abundant as the deer, and today all the surviving species are extremely rare. The musk ox *(Ovibos moschatus)*, which was widespread in Europe at the end of the Ice Age, became extinct there in prehistoric times but survived in Greenland and North America. In 1929, a small herd was released on Spitzbergen, and in 1932 another group was introduced into southern Norway from where it has spread over the border into southern Sweden, but it is unlikely ever to become widespread on the continent. It is small and heavy-horned with a dense, shaggy coat which enables it to withstand the hardest winter weather. Throughout the year the bulls and cows mingle in small herds, which may amalgamate in more sheltered ground during the

When threatened, musk oxen gather in a tight circle, heads outwards, to present their bulk and horns to the aggressor. Their tight-packed bodies cause a heat haze in the cold air above them.

winter. The rut is in the summer, and calves are born the following May.

The aurochs *(Bos taurus)*, which was the ancestor of domestic cattle, became extinct in the mid-seventeenth century, although back-bred animals, physically resembling the aurochs, may be seen in a few places. In the protection of parks, a small number of herds of primitive cattle breeds remind us of the early stages through which today's milk and beef breeds have passed. These animals, which are predominantly white, are large, long-horned and of uncertain temper.

The European bison *(Bison bonasus)* has fared slightly better. Closely related and similar to the American bison, it was never so numerous for it is a woodland-living, rather sedentary animal. Its original range included most of the deciduous forest areas of Europe, excluding Britain. It had been reduced to very small numbers by the beginning of the twentieth century and the majority of these animals, living in eastern Poland, were destroyed during the First World War. The remaining tiny herds in Lithuania and the Caucasus had died out by the middle 1920s. However, the species was not completely extinct, since a few animals survived in captivity in zoos and parks. Cooperation among the owners of these made it possible to return the nucleus of a herd to the great Bialowieza Forest in Poland. At first they were enclosed and guarded, but they have now been freed and are thriving. A second small herd exists in Lithuania. Numerous bison remain in captivity, and a stud book is maintained to chart their progress and to enable excessive

The musk ox has the compact shape of all Arctic animals, and its long, dense fur protects it against the harsh climate. The outer coat is coarse, but beneath lies a mat of fine woolly hairs, which may be used by Eskimos as clothing.

inbreeding to be prevented. The latest edition shows that the world population stands at about 2,000 individuals.

The social organization of bison is much like that of red deer. Females live in small herds throughout the year, while mature males are solitary, except for the mating season in August. At this time, the bulls batter trees and churn up the ground with their horns, to mark their rutting areas. The cows leave the herd briefly in May or June when their single calf is born. It soon follows its mother and is weaned by the autumn. It is sexually mature at 3 years old, but its growth is comparatively slow. It does not reach full stature until it is about 6 years old, when it measures up to 250 cm in head and body length and up to 190 cm at the shoulder.

Bison normally rest throughout the day and are mainly active at dusk and during the night, when they browse on the leaves and shoots of many broadleaved trees. In the autumn their diet is supplemented by acorns and beech mast, and in the winter they turn to heather and evergreens, but they rarely graze.

Male musk oxen normally live at peace with each other, but spar to establish precedence during the rut in July and August.

European bison can be seen in many zoos, and herds descended from captive animals now roam forest reserves in Poland and Lithuania, where they are carefully protected. Dust baths are an important part of their summer grooming.

SHEEP and GOATS
Family Bovidae

At one time wild sheep probably inhabited steppe country across much of south and eastern Europe, but they now survive as truly wild animals only in mountains from western Asia to Mongolia. The mouflon *(Ovis musimon)* is a sheep found in Corsica, Sardinia and Cyprus. Its origin is a mystery, and it may be descended from early domesticated sheep which were taken to the islands by Man. It is little altered from its wild ancestors, for its coat is hairy, rather than woolly.

In recent years, mouflon have been released in France, Germany and a number of places in southern and eastern Europe. They have demonstrated their ecological versatility by generally settling in dense, scrubby woodlands, where they graze in clearings rather than browsing the woody vegetation. The rutting season takes place just before winter and the lambs, often twins, are mostly born in April. They are sexually mature by the age of 18 months and, when full grown, have a head and body length of up to 120 cm and a shoulder height of about 70 cm.

The wild forerunners of domestic goats are found in some Mediterranean islands and herds survive in the barren mountains of Turkey, Iran and southern Russia. Wild goats *(Capra aegagrus)* can be distinguished from ibex and domestic goats by their long beard and their swept-back horns, which scarcely diverge over a length of 60 cm or more in the males, although they are much shorter in the females. They are active but wary creatures, protected more by the remote environments to which they have been driven than by the law, which is frequently flouted, so that wild goat numbers are almost certainly declining.

The rut occurs in November, and the kids, usually twins, are born in May. A kid can follow its mother within 3 days and will probably stay with her for up to a year, although it will have been weaned to the harsh, tough fodder of the dry hills long before this. It is thought that most of the wild populations are to some extent of domestic origin, for wild and domesticated goats are fully interfertile.

Domesticated goats tend to be thrifty, self-sufficient beasts which often escape

Adult male mouflons have large horns and a pale patch on the reddish brown sides. Females and young males have no flank patch, and the females, (except in Corsica) also lack horns.

from captivity, so that feral flocks now occur in many remote areas. In Britain, they are to be found in the uplands of Wales, Scotland and Ireland, where they usually occupy ground too rough and craggy even for the highland sheep, although in the absence of competition they will feed in lower meadows. Almost all British feral goats are extremely shaggy, skewbald animals.

At one time widespread in the mountains of central and southern Europe, the Alpine ibex *(Capra ibex)* is among the success stories of the conservation movement. This impressive animal measures up to 150 cm long with a shoulder height of up to 80 cm, and has curving, knobbly horns up to 75 cm long. It generally lives above the tree line where it is an easy target for hunters who had, by the early years of this century, exterminated all but a handful in the Italian Alps. Careful and strict conservation measures in Italy have ensured their survival, and the species has now been returned to some areas of France, Switzerland and Germany.

Ibex tend to form flocks of separate sexes, the males occupying even higher ground than the females. Both descend to lower ground at night, although they rarely come below the treeline. They feed on a wide range of Alpine shrubs, and in the winter may subsist largely on a diet of lichens. The rut takes place in December and January, and the kids, often twins, are born after a gestation of about 6 months.

The slightly smaller Spanish ibex *(C. pyrenaica)* is found in small numbers in Spain, where it is now totally protected by law and its numbers are beginning to increase. Should there be a setback, it is possible that zoo specimens could provide the nucleus of herds to be returned to the wild.

The Spanish ibex lives in isolated groups in various parts of Spain. Its horns may have developed their present shape as a result of interbreeding with domestic goats.

Wild goats have swept-back horns and dark stripes on the back and over the shoulders.

Feral goats have outward-spiralling horns which differ from any of their relatives.

Herds of male Alpine ibex usually live on higher ground than the nannies. Although the rut is in mid-winter, the males may clash their horns in mock battle at other times of the year.

157

CHAMOIS
Family Bovidae

The button-hook horns and the strongly striped face of the chamois *(Rupicapra rupicapra)* distinguish it at once from other mountain-dwelling, goat-like animals. Smaller and more slender than the ibex, it has a head and body length of up to 130 cm and a shoulder height of up to 80 cm. Small populations are found widely on European mountains as far north as the Tatras. Although they have been heavily persecuted, they have fared better than their relatives, for they frequently take refuge in forests, where they escape not only the worst of the weather but also the attention of hunters.

In an Alpine study, each chamois occupied a home range of about 4.5 sq. km. Since they are social animals, small groups would together use areas far larger than this. The society appears to be an open one with no special bonds except that between mothers and young, which made up about four-fifths of the total. The imbalance between sexes was apparently caused by heavy winter mortality among the males, which were probably weakened by the excesses of the rut and were, furthermore, heavily infected with parasites. In summer chamois keep mainly to high ground, where their agility, second only to that of ibex, allows them to graze on a wide variety of mountain plants on dizzy ledges and cliffs. Unlike ibex, which seem to enjoy warmth, they avoid the heat of exposed rocks, often resting in the shade or on icefields. The light-coloured summer coat is shed in autumn and replaced by a darker, denser pelage. Once the moult is complete, the rut starts, and the males mark out territories with scent from occipital glands at the back of their heads. They attempt to gather small herds of nannies into these mating areas, but the groups do not survive for long.

Males display to each other sideways on, raising a crest of hair along the midline of the back to make themselves look bigger and keeping their heads erect so that each adversary can see the other's striped face. Complex threat behaviour, which includes panting, stamping, bleating and bounding, reduces the need for actual conflict in places where fighting could result in both contestants falling to their death.

The gestation period is about 25 weeks after which the female groups split up as each one finds a secluded place to bear her lamb. These are usually dropped soon after dawn, and are very soon able to stand. Little and often is the rule for the kids, and they are soon taking 14 to 16 feeds a day.

The mother keeps a sharp watch for enemies, especially eagles. Within a few days, the nanny returns to the group, where each mother nurses only her own kid, which she smells carefully to be certain that she has the right baby, although each kid seems to recognize its mother by sight. The mothers are extremely solicitous, searching for 6 to 8 days if a kid is lost and remaining for several days by its body should she find it dead.

The kids start to become independent at the age of about 3 weeks, when they begin to graze. They play king of the castle and other fighting games together, the mothers sometimes joining in as well. By the time that they are 6 months old, they have learned all the paths in their part of the mountains and are almost independent of their mothers, taking a little milk only once or twice a day. By the time of the rut, they form separate sex herds on their own. The young females mate 1 to 2 years after this. If the winter is hard, they descend to lower levels of the mountain slopes but, even so, a high proportion of the young die each year. In some parts of Europe, food is put regularly on the mountain slopes to help the chamois survive the rigours of their environment.

Male chamois display to each other sideways on, to show the stark facial pattern of dark-and-white stripes to its best advantage. They also raise a crest of long hair on the midline of the back, to make themselves look bigger and more alarming.

During the rut, chamois scent twigs and sometimes rocks with musk from glands lying behind the horns.

Chamois' feet have narrow, pointed hooves. When going uphill, the tip can be used to get some purchase on the smallest of footholds. When travelling downhill, the back part of the hoof makes contact with the rock and the dew claws give extra support.

Chamois mothers seem to identify their young by smell, while the babies recognize their mothers by sight. Very young chamois go through a brief phase of eating earth, which probably gives them vital additional minerals.

Chamois live at a lower level than Alpine ibex but are almost equally agile on precipitous slopes. In deep snow a flock travels in single file, each stepping exactly into the footprints made by the leader.

WHALES
Order Cetacea

For most people the word 'whale' conjures up a monster of the deep, but the group, scientifically known as the Cetacea, contains many quite small species, usually referred to as porpoises or dolphins. Whatever their size, they contrast greatly with all other mammals for their streamlined bodies are fitted to live in water, which is the only habitat in which they can survive. Yet in spite of their extreme adaptations to an aquatic life, whales are mammals — air-breathing, warm-blooded and bearing and suckling their young.

Living cetaceans are rarely seen and the best view an observer usually obtains is only a glimpse of the back or side as the animal rises to breathe. However, if a whale becomes beached, it can be seen to have no legs, and instead broad, horizontally-set tail flukes provide the sole means of locomotion. A pair of flippers lies behind the head, supported by bones comparable to those of the forelimbs of other mammals, but these are used almost entirely for steering and balance in the water. The skin is smooth and virtually hairless with at most a few bristles round the jaws. In life a high body temperature is maintained by a layer of oil-filled cells, or blubber, which lies just below the skin and in some large species is up to 60 cm thick. The blubber is more than just an insulating layer, for it is shot through with tiny blood vessels. Normally these capillaries are closed, but when a whale generates heat through a burst of activity they dilate so that it can lose heat through the skin. The flippers, back fin and tail flukes have no blubber, and these areas are kept warm because the veins carrying deoxygenated blood back to the lungs are packed round the arteries which are taking fresh, warm blood to the tissues. The structure looks like a multicore cable, but has the effect of keeping the venous blood near to the normal temperature.

The nostrils of whales are set in a depression on the top of the head, referred to as the blow hole. This can be closed by powerful valves, for cetaceans breathe only when they have access to air and would drown, just like any other mammal, if they were to get water into their lungs. The idea that whales produce a fountain of water from their blow holes as they breathe doubtless arose because most observations of them have been made in polar regions. Here, the water vapour in the breath condenses on contact with the air to form the cloud of droplets of moisture known as the blow. In fact, large whales throw up a little water as they breathe if there is some lying in the blow-hole depression. Also, they may blow out a fine jet of fatty mucus, which would add to the impression of a cascade rising from the top of the head.

The eyes of whales are rather small and widely spaced, and they are used to see objects both below water and in the air. However, vision is of no use in the darkness of the sea depths, nor in the polar winter and there is no doubt that whales' most important sense is that of hearing. They use direct sound for communication, and echo location to detect obstacles and prey. This was only discovered fairly recently for, although it had been known since classical times that many whales are noisy animals, producing a wide range of clicks, squeaks and whistles, it was thought that they were deaf. The reason for this is that there are no external ears and the very narrow passage leading from the outside of the head is blocked with a substance which looks like wax; since wax is an effective barrier to sound, deafness in whales seemed a reasonable supposition. However, it has now been discovered that the ear plug is made of a horny substance which is capable of transmitting sound very well. Three types of sounds are used: low-frequency clicks give the whale information about its surroundings; higher frequencies are for conversation and in some species, the sperm whale for instance, it seems that individuals identify themselves with a signature sound; the highest frequencies, which are well above the threshold of human hearing, are used for the location of food.

The brain of cetaceans is large and complex, and all of the species studied in recent years seem to be strikingly intelligent. In common with most intelligent animals, the cetaceans are social creatures, swimming in groups which may be as small as a single family unit or may number many hundreds of individuals. In most instances, there seems to be a definite social structure within the school.

The breeding patterns of whales vary with the species, but mating is preceded in all observed species by displays of fast swimming, and sound and flipper signalling. The length of gestation is normally about a year and the single young is born tail first. There is often a second female in attendance to help the mother lift her baby to the surface, where it takes its first breath. In captivity 'aunties' have been seen helping to care for young dolphins when their mothers, which are normally very solicitous, are otherwise engaged. Baby whales must swim within minutes of their birth, and so they are always very large and well developed. At birth a baby blue whale weighs 8 tonnes and a baby common porpoise is half the length of its mother.

Cetaceans can be divided into two large groups, the whalebone whales and the toothed whales. Most whalebone whales are very large and include the blue whale *(Balaenoptera musculus)*, which is the biggest animal ever to have lived on the earth. Their jaws are quite toothless, and triangular plates of horny material, often called whalebone but better known as baleen, hang from the palate. These are used to strain vast numbers of small marine creatures, such as shrimp-like krill, from the water which the whale takes into its mouth. The toothed whales, which include many quite small animals, mostly have a long row of similar-shaped, pointed teeth in the mouth, which forms an efficient trap for fish and squid. In some toothed whales the teeth are reduced in number to a few small pegs or may even be completely absent. It has been suggested that these animals, and perhaps all whales, confuse and stun their fast-swimming prey by bombarding them with streams of underwater sound. This would account for the healthy survival even of individuals with grossly deformed jaws.

It is likely that Man's first encounters with whales were with individuals which had run aground. Later, shallow-water species were frightened into places where they could be caught, and whaling grew from this. In the nineteenth and early twentieth centuries, this became one of the most destructive industries that the world has ever seen, reducing the once huge schools of great whales to scattered small numbers and bringing whole species to the brink of extinction. Now that very few large whales are left, whaling has virtually ceased in the North Atlantic, and it is to be hoped that in time the whale stocks will recover their former numbers.

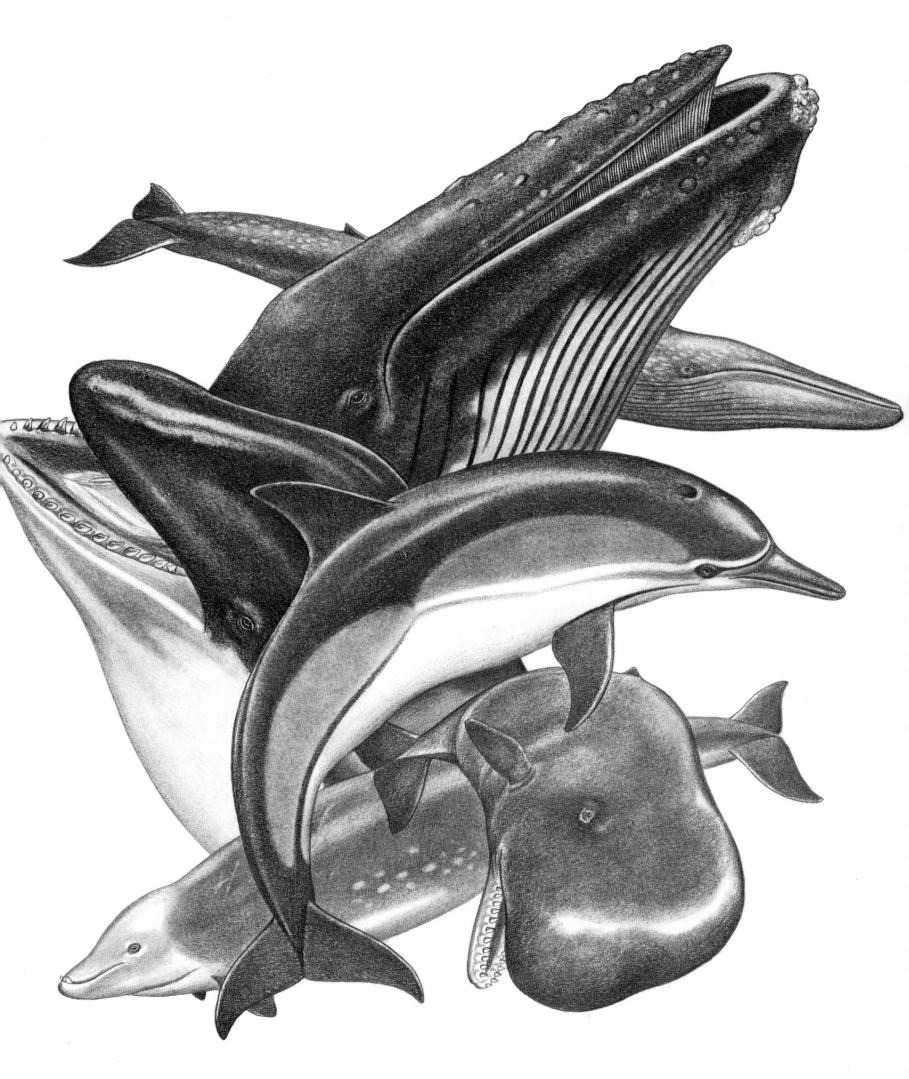

COMMON PORPOISE

Family Phocoenidae

All that most people ever see of a common porpoise (*Phocoena phocoena*) is a blunt, black fin and dark shining back, cartwheeling through the waves. Generally it is a slow swimmer, rarely riding in the bow-waves of ships, and hardly ever leaping clear of the water. Even so, it has given its name to the method of swimming used by many air-breathing marine animals. When it takes a breath it rises so that its head comes briefly into the air and then with closed nostrils it dives below the surface, so that it can only be seen intermittently. It is the smallest of all the Cetacea, growing to a maximum length of 2 m, and probably weighing less that 80 kg. Compared to other species, its body is thickset, with a broad, low fin on the back, and rather small, oval flippers.

Common porpoises may be seen in in-shore waters round all European coasts from the White Sea in the north to the Mediterranean and Black Sea, and they sometimes venture considerable distances up rivers. They are more affected by pollution than other cetaceans and are now very rare in the Baltic, North Sea and the Mediterranean, although quite large groups may still be seen in other European waters.

They are very timid animals, avoiding humans, and are rarely caught alive. Individuals caught in deep water often die of shock as they are lifted from their element. Some have been taken alive from shallow depths, and are said to be docile in captivity.

Their hearing is reputed to be extremely acute, and in the past they were herded into nets by beating the water with sticks. They were netted for their dark flesh, which was a well-liked table delicacy, particularly relished on Fridays in the

Porpoises frequently become stranded on shelving sandy beaches. Unless they can be returned very quickly to the sea they are doomed, for their bodies need to be supported by water and they cannot expand their lungs in air.

centuries before their mammalian status was recognized. They are still the most frequently caught cetaceans in European waters, although they are no longer an important item of human diet.

Common porpoises become beached more often than other cetaceans though the reason for this is unknown. It generally happens on a shelving sandy shore where it is thought that the animals' echo-location system cannot detect the decreasing depth of water. It has also been noted that many beached cetaceans suffer from heavy infestations of parasitic worms, especially in the ears and lungs, which may destroy their ability to ascertain depth.

The short jaws of porpoises house between 88 and 100 small, spade-shaped teeth, with which they catch small fish such as herring and whiting. They may also take cuttlefish and crabs. When hunting, they normally stay submerged for 5 to 10 minutes, after which they rest at the surface, panting deeply at a rate of about 6 breaths a minute. The sound of their breathing can carry a long distance and has given them the name pufferfish among fishermen.

In common with all other cetaceans, female porpoises give birth to only one calf a year. The gestation period is 11 months and the young are born in July or later. The baby comes into the world tail first, for

The nipples of cetaceans are long enough for the young to take in the corner of the mouth, while the rich milk is pumped in by muscular action on the part of the mother. Suckling often takes place on the surface, the mother rolling on her side, so that her baby can breathe as it feeds. There is frequently an 'auntie' in attendance, especially when the calf is very young.

otherwise it would probably drown before it was clear of its mother's body. It is very large, measuring almost half the adult length at birth. It is sexually mature at 3 to 4 years old.

Once mature, it has few enemies other than the killer whale and sharks. It may be attacked by lampreys but can apparently rid itself of these pests, for although many bear the mark of the parasite's mouth on their skin, there are no records of a common porpoise being seriously debilitated or even killed by them and it may survive for 15 years.

Cetaceans' tail flukes are not supported by bone. As the end of the body moves down, the tips of the flukes are higher than the central part of the tail. The reverse is true on the downstroke. The resulting movement of the water is comparable to that caused by the propeller of a boat, and the animal is thrust forward.

Young porpoises have spade-shaped teeth which wear, by the time they are old, to flat pegs in the mouth.

The common porpoise, like all other cetaceans, normally gives birth to only one calf a year from July onwards. The exact breeding areas are unknown, but large numbers of adults and young are found in inshore waters on both sides of the North Atlantic until October.

DOLPHINS
Family Delphinidae

Most small whales belong to the dolphin family. They are the most familiar cetaceans, since some species are very abundant and a few of them are inquisitive about humans, following ships and sometimes even coming inshore to play among small boats and swimmers. Most dolphinaria are stocked with the bottle-nosed dolphins (*Tursiops truncatus*) which seem to be intelligent and playful, and to enjoy co-operating with their captors in learning tricks, even to the extent of attempting to imitate human speech. Much of the detailed knowledge which we have about whales is based on studies of this animal.

At least six species of beaked dolphin occur in European waters, besides some larger, non-beaked forms. The two best known species are the common dolphin (*Delphinus delphis*), which is worldwide in temperate and tropical waters, and the bottle-nosed dolphin, which is found mainly in the temperate and warm areas of the Atlantic and the Mediterranean. Common dolphins are more easily recognized, for they usually travel in large schools, swimming fast and often leaping clear of

the water, showing the yellow patch on their flanks. They are very inquisitive and often play around ships, keeping up a speed in excess of 20 knots. They rarely exceed 2 m in length and 114 kg in weight, although they may grow to 2.4 m. Bottle-nosed dolphins are larger, growing to a length of up to 3.7 m, and an adult weight of 394 kg. They are usually seen in smaller groups, and are slower swimming than common dolphins, reaching 20 knots only during an exceptional burst of speed.

Both species produce a wide range of whistles and clicks which are used in echolocation and communication. Schools seem to have a hierarchical system and those of the common dolphin may even synchronize their breathing and diving. As with many other social animals, sick or infant members of the group are helped in times of need. Bottle-nosed dolphins are particularly fearless towards people and have on many occasions aided swimmers in distress. Possibly they have recognized that the floundering humans are in need of the sort of help which they would give to one of their own kind.

Common dolphin schools usually contain both sexes and all ages of individuals but outside the breeding season bottle-nosed dolphins form single-sex groups. The gestation period for common dolphins is about 10 months, and most of the young are born in July or the later summer months. The larger, bottle-nosed dolphins have a gestation of 12 to 13 months, and in European waters the young are all born in summer. Bottle-nosed dolphins are sexually mature at about 12 years and both species may survive to about 30 years of age.

Both species feed on a wide variety of fish and cephalopods. Adult dolphins have few enemies, although common dolphins often carry scars indicating encounters with sharks. Man is generally tolerant towards them, except where they are seen as competitors for fish.

The members of a dolphin school try to help others of their group who are injured or sick, lifting them to the surface so that they can breathe.

Common dolphins usually swim in large schools, often leaping clear of the water simultaneously. They can be recognized by the yellow on their fore-flanks (which may be absent), and the figure-of-eight pattern of dark lines on their flanks.

The skull of a dolphin shows the large numbers of similar teeth in the jaws, which make them efficient fish traps. It does not indicate the exact shape of the head, for in front of the blow hole is a large area of soft tissue, called the melon. This is thought to control the quality of the animals' sonar, and it also contains many nerve endings sensitive to water pressure.

Cetacean sonar employs short bursts of ultrasonic sound produced through the blow hole. Sound travels well in water and the echo from food or obstructions is picked up by the animals' ears. Whale sonar is sufficiently refined for different species of fish to be identified in total darkness.

Bottle-nosed dolphins usually swim in small schools of up to about 20 animals. In European waters the young are born in summer; the American populations have two main birth seasons, the spring and autumn.

KILLER WHALE
Family Delphinidae

The killer whale *(Orcinus orca)* is found throughout the seas of the world, and in European waters it may be seen from Spitzbergen to the Mediterranean. It is one of the larger dolphins, with males growing to a length of 9 m and females rarely exceeding 6 m. This is a reversal of the usual situation among the cetacea, in which females are normally slightly larger than

Before attempting to tilt an ice floe a killer whale will lift its head out of the water to see if there are any seals on it. They do not seem to regard humans as prey, and explorers have even patted killer whales on the snout as they rose to inspect the ice.

males. It may be recognized by the very long dorsal fin, which in an old male may be as high as 1.8 m; females and young males have smaller, more curved fins. Its flippers are large and rounded, and in ancient males are disproportionately large, as are the tail flukes. Both sexes and all ages have a bold pattern of black and white on the head, side and flanks.

Among the cetacea, the killer whale has an unrivalled reputation for ferocity. Occasionally a solitary individual may be seen but usually they travel and hunt in packs, ranging in size from a family group of three up to 40 or more animals. They have up to 13 sharply pointed, conical teeth on each side of both upper and lower jaws, which mesh together as the animal bites. They cannot slice or chew their prey and prefer, if possible, to swallow their victims whole. Large fish and squid, birds (especially penguins in the Antarctic), seals, porpoises and dolphins all fall prey to them. Working as a group they will harass young and even adult large whales, tearing at their lips, tongue and throat. Apparently, large whales make no attempt to defend themselves or flee, perhaps because killers can swim at up to 35 knots and nothing is immune from them unless it can dive to great depths.

In polar regions killer whales congregate near to seal breeding grounds. They may stick their heads out of the water to check whether seals are resting on the ice floes. They are reputed to use the dorsal fin to check the thickness of the ice. If the floe is small, thin or unstable, the killer whales

swim hard up under it, either breaking or tilting the ice by hitting it with their head. In either case the seals end up in the water, where they are easy prey. Their appetites seem to be insatiable; records show that the stomach of one contained 14 seals, while another had the remains of 27 porpoises and seals. Strangely, they do not seem to regard Man as either an enemy or prey, and there are many records of killer whales ignoring humans who have fallen into the sea. When taken into captivity, they rapidly become docile and learn tricks readily, so that they are among the favourite exhibits in dolphinaria.

The great discrepancy in size between the sexes suggests that killer whales are polygamous. They can breed throughout the year, although in the north calves are usually born around the shortest day. The calf, which is born after a gestation of about 12 months, measures about 2.1 m. Most toothed cetaceans suckle their young for about a year and mating takes place again some time after this, so the female killer whale only produces a calf every 2 or 3 years. Protected during its early days in the family group, it may survive for 40 years. Man is its only enemy and his hunting, which was never on a very large scale, has now practically ceased.

Groups of killer whales may band together to attack the slow-swimming baleen whales, which they harrass by tearing at the flippers and lips.

In polar waters, killer whales may tilt ice floes with their heads to tip resting seals into the water, where they are no match for this cetacean

OTHER WHALES
Order Cetacea

Most whales seem to exist in two populations, one in the northern hemisphere and one in the south, and despite long migrations made by many species, it is rare for individuals to cross the equator. Many North Atlantic whales have migration routes which take them through European waters as they travel between their cold-water feeding areas and their warmer breeding grounds. Identification at sea is likely to be difficult but baleen and toothed whales may be distinguished by their blow. In baleen whales, the blow forms a double cloud, for both nostrils emit water vapour. In the toothed whales, there is only one nasal opening, so the blow is a single stream.

The large whales include seven baleen or plankton-feeding species. These range in size from the Minke whale *(Balaenoptera acutorostrata),* which is only 10 m long, to the blue whale, which may reach a length of 30 m and is the largest creature ever to have lived on this planet. The right whales are slow swimmers, rarely exceeding 8 knots. The humpback whale *(Megaptera novaeangliae)* also travels at a leisurely pace, but it has the habit of leaping clear of the water when its long, wavy-edged flippers can be seen. The other members of the rorqual family are slender, fast-swimming animals, travelling in schools at speeds of up to 30 knots. Most of them are paler on the underside than on the back. The common rorqual or fin whale *(Balaenoptera physalis)* has a curious asymmetry, for the right side of its head is always far lighter in colour than the left. Like all cetaceans, the baleen whales are noisy creatures, communicating through a wide range of sounds, from low to high pitched. Perhaps the best known are those of the humpback whale, whose moaning songs are said to carry for 200 km underwater.

The sperm whale *(Physeter catodon)* is the largest of the toothed whales, with males reaching a length of 18 m, although the females are rarely more than 10 m long. They can be recognized at sea by the forward-pointing blow, and, if they rise from the water, by the square-shaped head. A group of sperm whales generally consists of a dominant male, his harem and their offspring. The young do not reach maturity until they are 9 or 10 years old. As with many polygamous animals, the old males are solitary. If they escape the attentions of whalers, they survive for 60 or more years, which is about the maximum age reached by the large whales in general.

They are normally slow swimmers, and feed almost entirely on squid, including very large, deep-sea species. They may have to dive to depths of over 1000 m for their prey, and they can remain underwater for up to an hour. We can only guess at the battles which take place at such depths, but the skin of many sperm whales is scarred with the marks of the clawed suckers of their prey.

The beaked whales are intermediate in size between the giants of the whale world and the small dolphins and porpoises. The largest is the bottle-nosed whale *(Hyperoodan ampullatus),* which measures up to 9 m long. Beaked whales are fast-swimming, deep-diving animals, which feed mainly on cuttlefish. Only the males have visible teeth, and then only two at the very tip of the lower jaw. In at least one member of this family, the jaw muscles suggest that a sucking action is used in gathering food.

Two species of smaller whales are normally found only in Arctic waters. These are the white whale *(Delphinapterus leucas),* which is most often seen in shallow areas, or even ascending rivers, and the narwhal *(Monodon monoceros).* Both are highly gregarious and vocal, the White whale whistling so much like a bird that old time sailors called it the 'sea canary'. Both feed on squid and fish. The white whale holds its prey with up to 40 pointed teeth. The narwhal has no normal teeth, although the males have the left (and occasionally also the right) upper incisor prolonged into a twisted tusk, which may measure up to 3 m. The function of this tooth is unknown. It is unlikely to be used for fighting since it has a very long pulp cavity, though it may be used to stir flat fish from the sea bed.

Our knowledge of whales is based partly on observations made at sea. However, much detailed information on sizes, shapes and weights has been obtained from whales which have run ashore, or from animals killed by whaling. Most species of whales become beached occasionally. Large numbers of some species, particularly pilot whales *(Globicephala melaena),* regularly meet their end in this way. It has been suggested that this apparent determination to commit suicide is, in part, an attempt to help those members of the school which are already beached and are dying, demonstrating the close cooperation which is found among members of most whale schools.

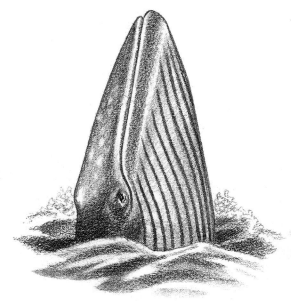

Whales, such as this blue whale, sometimes adopt a vertical position in the water so that they can push their heads into the air and scan the surface of the water.

All toothed whales have one nostril suppressed, so that the blow is produced as a single spout. This distinguishes them from the baleen whales in which there are two functional nostrils and a double spout.

The long tusk of the male narwhal always has a left-handed twist, even when, as rarely happens, two tusks are present in the jaw. The fragile tusk is not used for fighting, but possibly for stirring up fish from the sea bed. The females never have tusks.

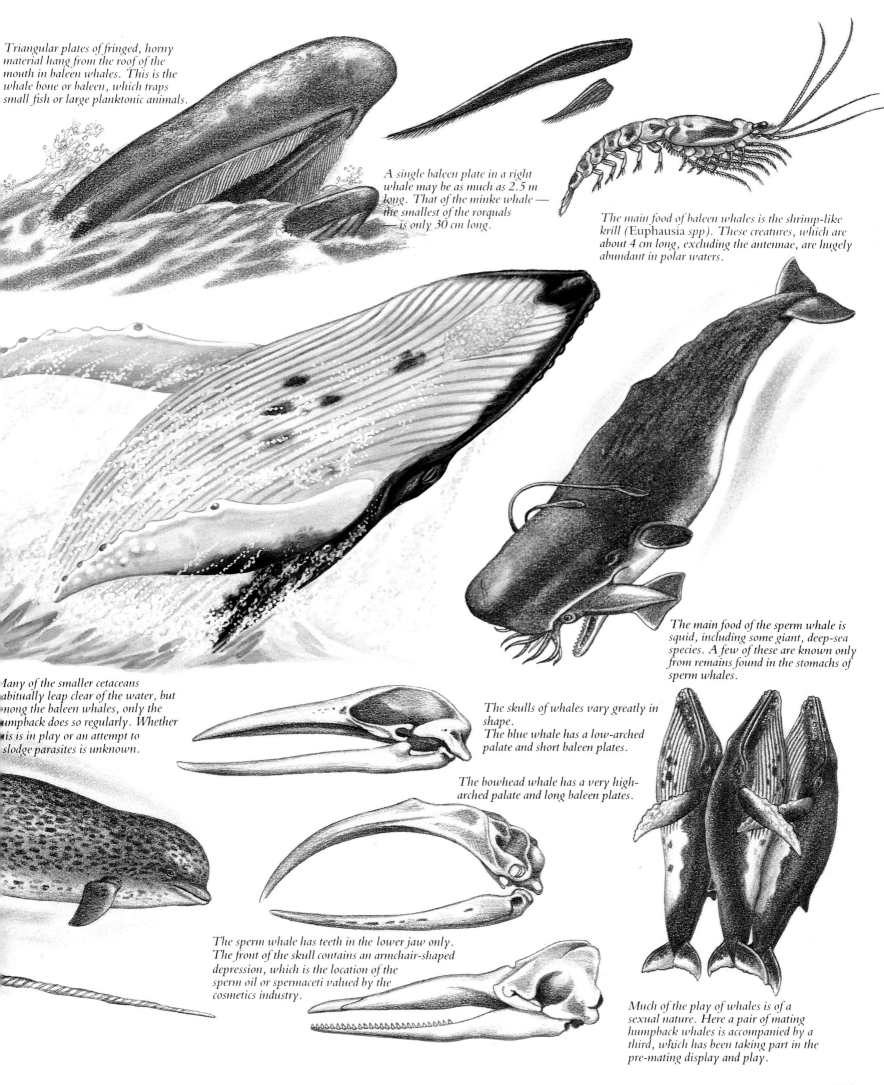

Triangular plates of fringed, horny material hang from the roof of the mouth in baleen whales. This is the whale bone or baleen, which traps small fish or large planktonic animals.

A single baleen plate in a right whale may be as much as 2.5 m long. That of the minke whale — the smallest of the rorquals — is only 30 cm long.

The main food of baleen whales is the shrimp-like krill (Euphausia spp). These creatures, which are about 4 cm long, excluding the antennae, are hugely abundant in polar waters.

Many of the smaller cetaceans habitually leap clear of the water, but among the baleen whales, only the humpback does so regularly. Whether this is in play or an attempt to dislodge parasites is unknown.

The main food of the sperm whale is squid, including some giant, deep-sea species. A few of these are known only from remains found in the stomachs of sperm whales.

The skulls of whales vary greatly in shape.
The blue whale has a low-arched palate and short baleen plates.

The bowhead whale has a very high-arched palate and long baleen plates.

The sperm whale has teeth in the lower jaw only. The front of the skull contains an armchair-shaped depression, which is the location of the sperm oil or spermaceti valued by the cosmetics industry.

Much of the play of whales is of a sexual nature. Here a pair of mating humpback whales is accompanied by a third, which has been taking part in the pre-mating display and play.

169

OBSERVING EUROPE'S MAMMALS

Much is known about the appearance and lifestyle of Europe's mammals. A few, such as squirrels in municipal parks and the Barbary apes in Gibraltar, live so much under the protection of humans that they show no fear and are easily observed. Sadly, most other species are rarely seen, for almost all of the large animals are either very rare or restricted in their distribution, while the smaller ones are elusive, secretive and nocturnal. However, they are present in the environment, sometimes in large numbers, and since each modifies its habitat to some extent, learning to read the signs of this will lead to the animals themselves.

Most mammals are creatures of habit, and travel the same routes each day about their territories, making well trodden trackways. Some, such as those leading to badgers' setts, are so well-established that they may be mistaken for human paths. All the land mammals occupy dens or lairs of some kind. These may be in holes in the ground or in hollow trees or built among vegetation, while martens and some rodents may even take over old birds' nests. Recognizing a hole as belonging to a fox or marmot, or a nest as being that of a harvest mouse or dormouse, confirms that creature's presence even though the animal cannot be seen.

Most animals leave traces of their meals when they eat. The way in which bark has been stripped from a tree may betray the work of a pony, deer or squirrel, while the way in which holes have been dug for roots may indicate a wild boar or badger, among others. Interpreting these signs with certainty is an aspect of the study of mammals beyond the scope of this book, more particularly since mammals are flexible in their behaviour and may change their types of living place and their way of feeding under stress or abnormal conditions.

Footprints and droppings, on the other hand, are an extension of the animals' physical entity and cannot be modified in the same way, although in the field both may be difficult to identify. In soft mud or snow the details of footprints may become blurred, while on firmer ground they may be incomplete. The tracks of very small animals are rarely seen, for their light weight hardly marks the soil and they often tunnel under rather than run over snow. The footprints of larger animals may be difficult to interpret because of their habit of placing the hind foot in exactly the same place occupied by the forefoot in the previous stride, a feature known as registration. An animal's droppings may also vary, both with its state of health and its diet, but tend to be characteristic of the species. Typical examples of the footprints and droppings of a number of European mammals are shown on pages 172-173.

While a few mammals, such as rats and foxes, have learned to live in close proximity to human beings, most have not. The spread of Man's influence across the continent has meant for many that there are fewer places to live each year. Mammal populations have also been reduced by farmers who killed them to protect crops and stock, and by hunters for food, furs or sport.

Towards the end of the last century, it became clear that both landscape and wildlife were at risk and various voluntary bodies were set up to protect them. In Britain the National Trust and the Royal Society for the Protection of Birds were among the first and they are paralleled by comparable bodies in the rest of western Europe. European governments, however, showed little interest in conservation, although they may have been impressed by the setting up of Yellowstone Park in the United States in 1872. The first European national parks were established in Sweden in 1909, and this example was slowly followed by a number of other nations. To begin with, most of the areas designated as national parks were chosen for their natural beauty and conservation of the animals living in them did not follow automatically. It was not until after the Second World War that most European countries began to enact legislation setting up networks of reserves and protecting their animal inhabitants by law.

Many countries are still in the process of establishing primary habitat reserves, where plants and animals can live undisturbed. Not surprisingly, the easiest places in which to do this are areas not wanted for agriculture or industry, and so most of Europe's conservation areas are in the mountains. These mountainous regions are, in any case, the last strongholds for many species which were once widespread, such as bears and wolves. Unfortunately, money for an adequate number of wardens is almost always lacking and mountain reserves are difficult to patrol; and so, despite governmental goodwill, animals towards which man has had a traditional enmity may still be in danger. Poaching is widespread in many reserves, for even when the animals have been specifically protected by legislation, farmers who fear that their stock may suffer are likely to take the law into their own hands. Wolves particularly have suffered in this way.

A viable population may need more space than a sanctuary can afford and, should they stray beyond the boundary of the reserve area, they are likely to be destroyed. To combat this risk, many reserves are now surrounded by peripheral zones, which afford protection to straying animals.

In this book the range of country through which the various species may be found has been indicated. However, it must be remembered that within that area they will usually occupy only one type of habitat, and they may be very rare over much of it. The best—and in some instances the only—places in which to see European mammals are reserves and national parks. Only in these, with very few exceptions, do the large and rare animals survive.

One of the most important conservation areas in the Alps is the Gran Paradiso National Park in north west Italy. Like many places where animals have been preserved, it used to be a hunting reserve. In 1856 it was declared a special preserve by the Italian royal family, because it was here that the last of the Alpine ibex, numbering only a few dozen animals, survived. Victor Emmanuel II and Victor Emmanuel III both took great interest in building up the stocks of ibex, and in 1914 it was estimated that the numbers had grown to 3,000 animals. In 1922 an area of 62,000 hectares lying between 2,000 m and 4,000 m high was declared a national park and presented to the nation. Unfortunately, inhabited valleys cutting into the mountains are not included and many animals have been killed when they descended to lower levels in the winter. However, the establishment of peripheral park areas should alleviate this problem.

In 1963 the Vanoise National Park, which abuts on to the Gran Paradiso along a 7 km frontier, was declared a protected area by France. This adds 52,839 hectares of strictly protected national park and 144,000 hectares of peripheral zone, and has meant that animals moving into the Vanoise from Italy are no longer at risk. Despite losses during the last war, the numbers of ibex were estimated to be 3,500 in 1961, and some have been exported to other mountain areas from which they had long since disappeared. Bears and wolves no longer occur in the Gran Paradiso-Vanoise area, but chamois, marmots, hares, foxes, badgers, pine and beech martens may all be seen there. There are information centres and tracks in both parks, and in Vanoise there are nature trails which may be followed in the summer months.

Other great highland reserves are situated in the Pyrenees, where bears and Pyrenean desmans may be seen; in the Tat-

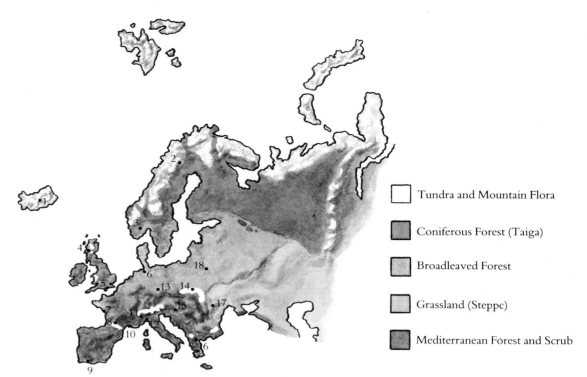

Tundra and Mountain Flora

Coniferous Forest (Taiga)

Broadleaved Forest

Grassland (Steppe)

Mediterranean Forest and Scrub

Almost every European nation has numerous nature reserves and parks. This map marks some of the largest and most important.

ras and the Carpathians where bears and some wolves still remain; and in Scandinavia. Access to these parks is variable, but visitors are generally helped to see the landscape and the animal inhabitants.

Lowland reserves are usually less easy to establish, for the land is often highly populated or taken for agriculture. Undrained wetland areas are exceptions and many have become important reserves. The largest is Mývatn og Laxá in Iceland, which covers 600,000 hectares, but the best known is probably the Camargue in southern France. This was established as a reserve in 1975 and has a protected area of 3,279 hectares. The mammal fauna is not spectacular, although it includes the Camargue white horses which are adapted to the wetland habitat. The Hortobágy National Park in eastern Hungary, set up in 1972, gives protection to 43,550 hectares of steppe and marshland. Here most of the smaller mammals of eastern Europe, such as sousliks, mole rats and polecats, may be seen. One of the greatest of the world's national parks is Bialowieza which occupies 125,610 hectares on the boundary between Poland and the USSR. This park is particularly important, for it is part of the original deciduous forest zone which has been largely destroyed elsewhere on the continent. Over 14 species of trees make up the forest cover and give a variety of food and microhabitats to the small mammals, such as squirrels, dormice, voles and insectivores, as well as providing room and shelter to several species of deer. Some attempts were made to control hunting as long ago as 1557, but these failed to save the aurochs which became extinct in 1627. European bison fared rather better, for the last of these was not killed until the early 1920s. A herd based on captive animals was set up in 1929 and now, although a few are kept in captivity so that visitors may be certain of seeing a bison, many more are living wild in the park.

The Mediterranean fringe of Europe is heavily populated and few reserves or national parks are found there. One great exception is the Doñana National Park, where 39,225 hectares were dedicated to the nation in 1969. The money which made the establishment of this reserve possible was largely obtained from foreign sources, via the World Wildlife Fund, which is responsible for the funding and management of many wildlife reserves in Europe. The Doñana lies on the north west of the Guadalquivir estuary in an area which remained isolated and without permanent settlements because it was a royal hunting reserve. It contains a number of habitats, including marshes, woodlands and heaths, and its variety is the key to the richness of its mammalian fauna. The most famous of its inhabitants is the Spanish lynx, which survives in small numbers. Among the large animals are fallow and red deer and wild boar, while the smaller ones include wild cats, otters, polecats, badgers, foxes, mongooses and genets. This area, although protected, is under threat from the excessive use of insecticides and fertilizers higher up the river, and there are plans to build a motorway through it. Although permission must be obtained to visit Doñana and visitors must be accompanied by wardens, it is still possible to obtain a glimpse of the continent's wealth of wildlife, unmatched elsewhere.

Britain, which is one of the most densely populated countries in the world, has already lost most of the large mammals that can still be found in the rest of Europe. Bears, beavers, wild boar and wolves have all been exterminated since the Norman Conquest, and there is little room for the establishment of reserves on the scale seen in other European countries. Although some areas have been designated as national parks, these do not equate with such institutions elsewhere, for although they are mostly areas of scenic beauty, they are often heavily farmed and may contain considerable towns and industries. Most are visited by large numbers of tourists, and wildlife is generally not abundant in them. There is however, a network of habitat reserves in which much of Britain's remaining wildlife can be found. The vast majority of these reserves are privately owned by such bodies as the County Naturalists' Trust or the Royal Society for the Protection of Birds, but by the nature of their funding most are small, amounting to a few hectares only. A few reserves have been set up by local authorities, but the majority of the largest and most of the important reserves in Britain are National Nature Reserves, administered by the Nature Conservancy Council, which is financed by central government.

Beinn Eighe in Torridon, Scotland, is one of the biggest, with an area of 47.6 sq km. Although the hills are largely barren, the valleys contain remnants of the great Caledonian forest which once stretched over much of the country. Here pine martens, wild cats, red squirrels, deer and foxes may be seen, as well as many species of birds, including some rare birds of prey.

Kingley Vale in southern England is only 1.46 sq km, but it is important because it contains the finest ancient yew forest remaining in Europe. Its hill slopes also carry a flora typical of the chalk downs, including many species of wild orchids. Over 70 species of bird have been recorded there and deer, foxes and badgers can be seen. The roe deer are particularly interesting in that they have developed the ability to feed on yew, which is normally highly poisonous to browsing animals.

TRACKS and DROPPINGS

Track and droppings can help to identify the kinds of animals occupying a particular area.
The grey prints indicate the forefeet and the black indicate the hind feet.

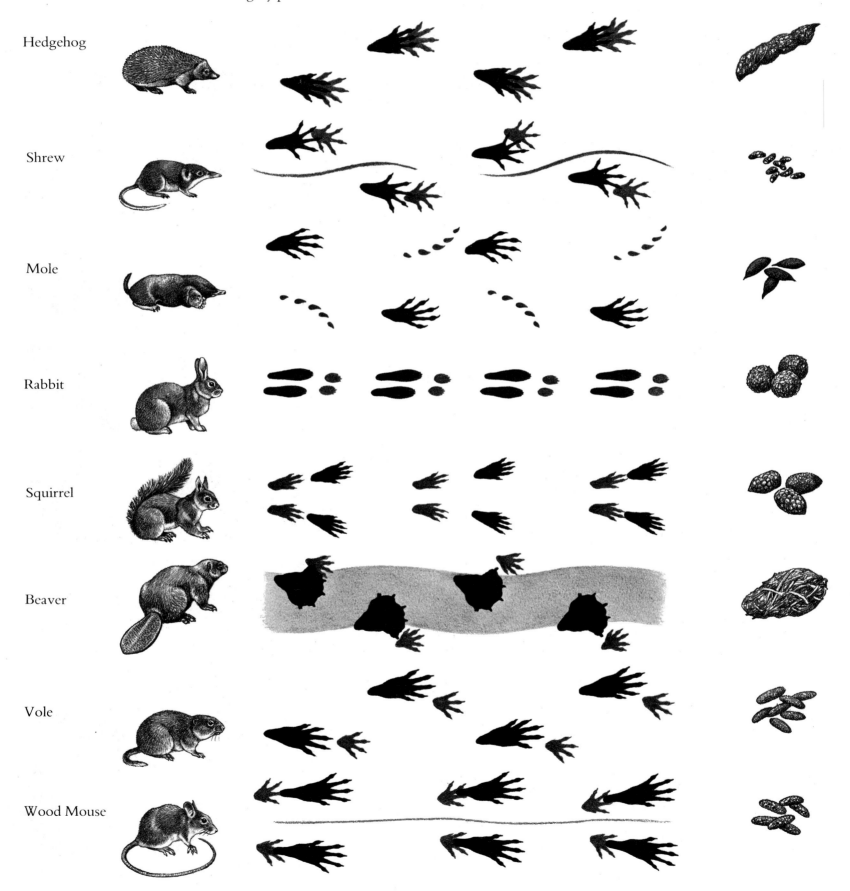

Hedgehog

Shrew

Mole

Rabbit

Squirrel

Beaver

Vole

Wood Mouse

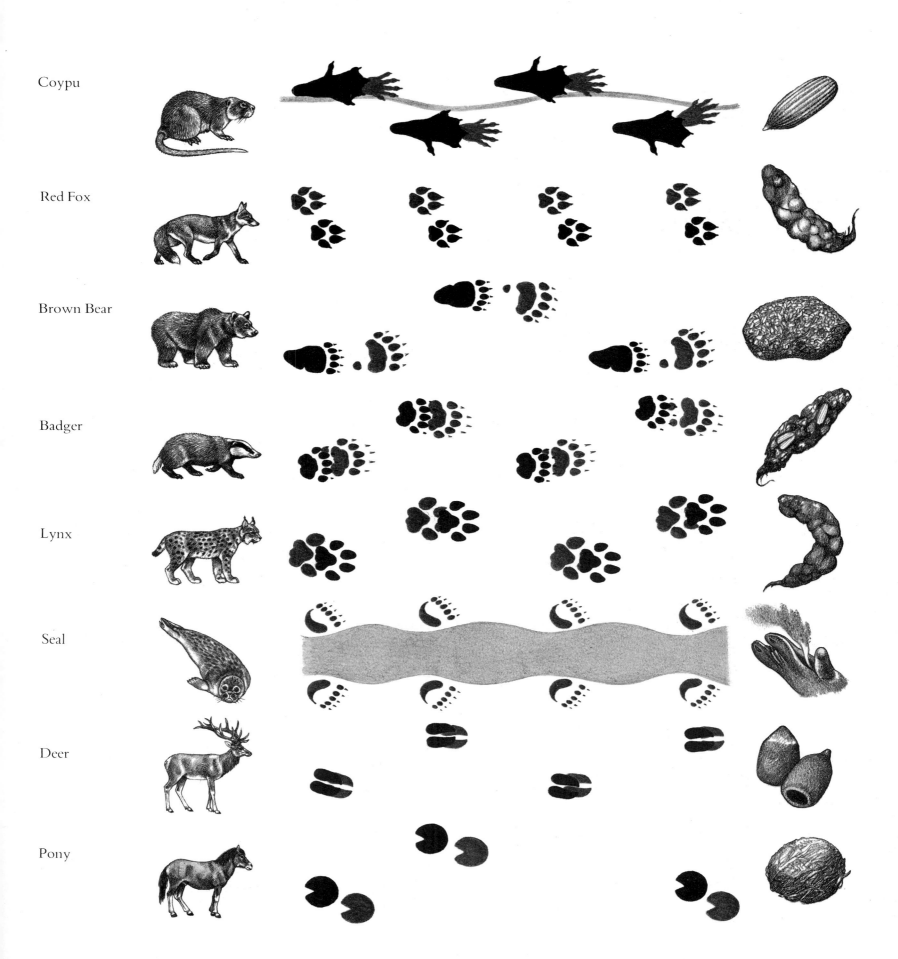

Coypu

Red Fox

Brown Bear

Badger

Lynx

Seal

Deer

Pony

COMPLETE LIST OF EUROPEAN MAMMALS

MARSUPIALS	**ORDER MARSUPIALIA**
Wallaby and Kangaroo Family	**Family Macropodidae**
Red-necked wallaby	*Macropus rufogriseus*
INSECTIVORES	**ORDER INSECTIVORA**
Hedgehog Family	**Family Erinaceidae**
Western hedgehog	*Erinaceus europaeus*
Eastern hedgehog	*Erinaceus concolor*
Algerian hedgehog	*Erinaceus algirus*
Mole and Desman Family	**Family Talpidae**
Northern mole	*Talpa eurpaea*
Blind mole	*Talpa caeca*
Roman mole	*Talpa romana*
Pyrenean desman	*Galemys pyrenaicus*
Russian desman	*Desmana moschata*
Shrew Family	**Family Soricidae**
Common shrew	*Sorex araneus*
Millet's shrew	*Sorex coronatus*
Spanish shrew	*Sorex granarius*
Appennine shrew	*Sorex samniticus*
Pigmy shrew	*Sorex minutus*
Laxmann's shrew	*Sorex caecutiens*
Least shrew	*Sorex minutissimus*
Dusky shrew	*Sorex sinalis (S. isodon)*
Alpine shrew	*Sorex alpinus*
Water shrew	*Neomys fodiens*
Miller's water shrew	*Neomys anomalus*
Pigmy white-toothed shrew	*Suncus etruscus*
Greater white-toothed shrew	*Crocidura russula*
Lesser white-toothed shrew	*Crocidura suaveolens*
Bicoloured white-toothed shrew	*Crocidura leucodon*
PRIMATES	**ORDER PRIMATES**
Old-world Monkey Family	**Family Cercopithecidae**
Barbary ape	*Macaca sylvanus*
BATS	**ORDER CHIROPTERA**
Horseshoe Bat Family	**Family Rhinolophidae**
Lesser horseshoe bat	*Rhinolophus hipposideros*
Greater horseshoe bat	*Rhinolophus ferrumequinum*
Mediterranean horseshoe bat	*Rhinolophus euryale*
Blasius's horseshoe bat	*Rhinolophus blasii*
Mehely's horseshoe bat	*Rhinolophus mehelyi*
Smooth-Faced or Evening Bat Family	**Family Vespertilionidae**
Daubenton's bat	*Myotis daubentoni (Leuconoe daubentoni)*
Nathalina bat	*Myotis nathalinae*
Long-fingered bat	*Myotis capaccinii (Leuconoe capaccinii)*
Pond bat	*Myotis dasycneme (Leuconoe dasycneme)*
Brandt's bat	*Myotis brandti*
Whiskered bat	*Myotis mystacinus (Selysius mystacinus)*
Geoffroy's bat	*Myotis emarginatus (Selysius emarginatus)*
Natterer's bat	*Myotis nattereri (Selysius nattereri)*
Bechstein's bat	*Myotis bechsteini (Selysius bechsteini)*
(Greater) mouse-eared bat	*Myotis myotis*
Lesser mouse-eared bat	*Myotis blythi (M. oxygnathus)*
Noctule	*Nyctalus noctula*
Leisler's bat	*Nyctalus leisleri*
Greater noctule	*Nyctalus lasiopterus*
Serotine	*Eptesicus serotinus (Vespertilio serotinus)*
Northern bat	*Eptesicus nilssoni (Vespertilio nilssoni)*
Parti-coloured bat	*Vespertilio murinus*
(Common) pipistrelle	*Pipistrellus pipistrellus*
Nathusius's pipistrelle	*Pipistrelle nathusii*
Kuhl's pipistrelle	*Pipistrelle kuhli*
Savi's pipistrelle	*Pipistrelle savii*
Hoary bat	*Lasiurus cinereus*
Common long-eared bat	*Plecotus auritus*
Grey long-eared bat	*Plecotus austriacus*
Barbastelle	*Barbastella barbastellus*
Schreiber's bat	*Miniopterus schreibersi*
Free-tailed Bat Family	**Family Molossidae**
European free-tailed bat	*Tadarida teniotis*
Slit-faced Bat Family	**Family Nycteridae**
Egyptian slit-faced bat	*Nycteris thebaica*
LAGOMORPHS	**ORDER LAGOMORPHA**
Rabbit and Hare Family	**Family Leporidae**
Rabbit	*Oryctolagus cuniculus*
Brown Hare	*Lepus capensis (L. europaeus)*
Mountain Hare (Arctic hare)	*Lepus timidus*
RODENTS	**ORDER RODENTIA**
Squirrel Family	**Family Sciuridae**
Red Squirrel	*Sciurus vulgaris*

Grey squirrel	*Sciurus carolinensis*
Flying squirrel	*Pteromys volans*
European souslik	*Spermophilus citellus (Citellus citellus)*
Spotted souslik	*Spermophilus suslicus (Citellus suslicus)*
Alpine marmot	*Marmota marmota*
Siberian chipmunk	*Tamias sibiricus*
Beaver Family	**Family Castoridae**
European beaver	*Castor fiber*
Canadian beaver	*Castor canadensis*
Old-world Porcupine Family	**Family Hystricidae**
Crested porcupine	*Hystrix cristata*
Hutia Family	**Family Capromyidae**
Coypu	*Myocastor coypus*
Dormouse Family	**Family Gliridae**
Garden dormouse	*Eliomys quercinus*
Forest dormouse	*Dryomys nitedula*
Fat dormouse	*Glis glis*
Hazel dormouse	*Muscardinus avellanarius*
Mouse-tailed dormouse	*Myomimus roachi (M. personatus)*
Hamster, Vole, Mouse, Rat Family	**Family Muridae**
Hamsters	Sub-family Cricetinae
Common hamster	*Cricetus cricetus*
Rumanian hamster	*Mesocricetus newtoni*
Golden hamster	*Mesocricetus auratus*
Grey hamster	*Cricetulus migratorius*
Lemmings and Voles	Sub-family Microtinae
Arctic lemming	*Dicrostonyx torquatus*
Norway lemming	*Lemmus lemmus*
Wood lemming	*Myopus schisticolor*
Bank vole	*Clethrionomys glareolus*
Northern red-backed vole	*Clethrionomys rutilus*
Grey-sided vole	*Clethrionomys rufocanus*
Balkan snow vole	*Dinaromys bogdanovi (Dolomys milleri)*
Field vole (Short-tailed field mouse)	*Microtus agrestis*
Common vole (Orkney vole)	*Microtus arvalis*
Sibling vole	*Microtus epiroticus (M. subarvalis)*
Root vole	*Microtus oeconomus*
Snow vole	*Microtus nivalis (Chionomys nivalis)*
Gunther's vole	*Microtus guentheri (M. socialis)*
Cabrera's vole	*Microtus cabrerae*
Common pine vole	*Pitymys subterraneus*
Alpine pine vole	*Pitymys multiplex*
Bavarian pine vole	*Pitymys bavaricus*
Tatra pine vole	*Pitymus tatricus*
Liechtenstein's pine vole	*Pitymys liechtensteini*
Mediterranean pine vole	*Pitymys duodecimcostatus*
Lusitanian pine vole	*Pitymys lusitanicus*
Thomas's pine vole	*Pitymys thomasi*
Savi's pine vole	*Pitymys savii*
North-western water vole	*Arvicola terrestris (A. amphibius)*
South-western water vole	*Arvicola sapidus*
Musk rat	*Ondatra zibethicus*
Mongolian gerbil	*Meriones unguiculatus*
Mole Rats	Sub-family Spalacinae
Greater mole rat	*Spalax microphthalmus*
Lesser mole rat	*Spalax leucodon*
Mice and Rats	Sub-family Murinae
Common rat (Brown rat)	*Rattus norvegicus*
Ship rat (Black rat)	*Rattus rattus*
Wood mouse (Long-tailed field mouse)	*Apodemus sylvaticus (Sylvaemus sylvaticus)*
Yellow-necked mouse	*Apodemus flavicollis (Sylvaemus flavicollis)*
Pigmy field mouse	*Apodemus microps*
Rock mouse	*Apodemus mystacinus (Sylvaemus mystacinus)*
Striped field mouse	*Apodemus agrarius*
Harvest mouse	*Micromys minutus*
House mouse	*Mus musculus*
Algerian mouse	*Mus spretus*
Steppe mouse	*Mus hortulanus*
Cretan spiny mouse	*Acomys minous (A. cahirinus)*
Birch Mouse Family	**Family Zapodidae**
Northern birch mouse	*Sicista betulina*
Southern birch mouse	*Sicista subtilis*
CARNIVORES	**ORDER CARNIVORA**
Bear Family	**Family Ursidae**
Polar bear	*Thalarctos maritimus (Ursus maritimus)*
Brown bear	*Ursus arctos*

Wolf and Fox Family	**Family Canidae**
Wolf	*Canis lupus*
Jackal	*Canis aureus*
Red fox	*Vulpes vulpes*
Arctic fox	*Alopex lagopus*
Raccoon dog	*Nyctereutes procyonoides*
Weasel Family	**Family Mustelidae**
Stoat	*Mustela erminea*
Weasel	*Mustela nivalis*
European mink	*Mustela lutreola (Lutreola lutreola)*
American mink	*Mustela vison (Lutreola vison)*
Western polecat	*Mustela putorius (Putorius putorius)*
Steppe polecat	*Mustela eversmanni (Putorius eversmanni)*
Domestic ferret	*Mustela furo*
Marbled polecat	*Vormela peregusna*
Pine marten	*Martes martes*
Beech marten	*Martes foina*
Glutton (Wolverine)	*Gulo gulo*
Otter	*Lutra lutra*
Badger	*Meles meles*
Mongoose and Genet Family	**Family Viverridae**
Egyptian mongoose	*Herpestes ichneumon*
Indian grey mongoose	*Herpestes edwardsi*
Genet	*Genetta genetta*
Raccoon Family	**Family Procyonidae**
Raccoon	*Procyon lotor*
Cat Family	**Family Felidae**
Lynx	*Felis lynx (F. pardina, Lynx Lynx)*
Wild cat	*Felis silvestris*
Feral cat	*Felis catus*
PINNIPEDES	**ORDER PINNIPEDIA**
Seal Family	**Family Phocidae**
Common seal	*Phoca vitulina*
Ringed seal	*Phoca hispida (Pusa hispida)*
Grey seal	*Halichoerus grypus*
Monk seal	*Monachus monachus*
Harp seal	*Pagophilus groenlandicus*
Bearded seal	*Erignathus barbatus*
Hooded seal	*Cystophora cristata*
Walrus Family	**Family Odobenidae**
Walrus	*Odobenus rosmarus*
ODD-TOED HOOFED ANIMALS	**ORDER PERISSODACTYLA**
Horse Family	**Family Equidae**
Feral horse and pony	*Equus caballus*
Feral donkey	*Equus asinus*
EVEN-TOED HOOFED ANIMALS	**ORDER ARTIODACTYLA**
Pig Family	**Family Suidae**
Wild boar	*Sus scrofa*
Cattle Family	**Family Bovidae**
Bison	*Bison bonasus*
Musk ox	*Ovibos moschatus*
Mouflon	*Ovis musimon (Ovis ammon)*
Domestic sheep	*Ovis aries*
Alpine ibex	*Capra ibex*
Spanish ibex	*Capra pyrenaica*
Wild goat	*Capra aegagrus*
Feral goat	*Capra hircus*
Chamois	*Rupicapra rupicapra*
Deer Family	**Family Cervidae**
Red deer	*Cervus elaphus*
Sika deer	*Cervus nippon*
Fallow deer	*Cervus dama (Dama dama)*
Spotted deer	*Cervus axis (Axis axis)*
Elk	*Alces alces*
Reindeer	*Rangifer rangifer*
White-tailed deer	*Odocoileus virginianus*
Roe deer	*Capreolus capreolus*
Muntjac	*Muntiacus reevesi*
Chinese water deer	*Hydropotes inermis*
Père David's deer	*Elaphurus davidianus*
WHALES, DOLPHINS, PORPOISES	**ORDER CETACEA**
BALEEN WHALES	SUBORDER MYSTICETI
Rorqual and Humpback Whale Family	**Family Balaenopteridae**
Fin whale (Common rorqual)	*Balaenoptera physalis*
Blue whale	*Balaenoptera musculus*
Sei whale	*Balaenoptera borealis*

Minke whale
(Lesser rorqual)
Humpback whale

Right Whale Family
Black right whale

Bowhead whale
(Greenland right whale)

TOOTHED WHALES

Sperm Whale Family
Sperm whale

Pigmy sperm whale

Balaenoptera acutorostrata

Megaptera novaeangliae

Family Balaenidae
Balaena glacialis
(Eubalaena glacialis)
Balaena mysticetus

SUBORDER ODONTOCETI

Family Physeteridae
Physeter catodon
(P. macrocephalus)
Kogia breviceps

Beaked Whale Family
Bottle-nosed whale
Cuvier's whale
Sowerby's whale
True's beaked whale
Gray's whale
Gervais' whale
Blanville's whale

White Whale Family
White whale
(Beluga)
Narwhal

Dolphin Family
Pilot whale

Family Ziphiidae
Hyperoodon ampullatus
Ziphius cavirostris
Mesoplodon bidens
Mesoplodon mirus
Mesoplodon grayi
Mesoplodon europaeus
Mesoplodon densirostris

Family Monodontidae
Delphinapterus leucas

Monodon monocero

Family Delphinidae
Globicephala melaena

Killer whale
Bottle-nosed dolphin
Risso's dolphin
Rough-toothed dolphin
False killer whale
Common dolphin
Striped dolphin
(Euphrosyne dolphin)
White-sided dolphin
White-beaked dolphin

Porpoise Family
Common porpoise

Orcinus orca
Tursiops truncatus
Grampus griseus
Steno bredanensis
Pseudorca crassidens
Delphinus delphis
Stenella coeruleoalba
(S. styx)
Lagenorhynchus acutus
Lagenorhynchus acutus

Family Phocoenidae
Phocoena phocoena

FURTHER READING

Most of these books should be easily obtainable from a bookshop or public library.

Burton, R., *Carnivores of Europe*. Batsford, 1979.
Chaplin, R. E., *Deer*. Blandford, 1977.
Corbet, G. B., *The Terrestrial Mammals of Western Europe*. Foulis, 1966.
Corbet, G. B. and Ovenden, D., *The Mammals of Britain and Europe*. Collins, 1980.
Corbet, G. B. and Southern, H. N., *The Handbook of British Mammals*. Blackwells, 1964 (second edition 1977).
Crowcroft, W. P., *The Life of the Shrew*. Max Reinhardt, 1957.
Crowcroft, W. P., *Mice All Over*. Foulis, 1966.
Curry-Lindahl, K., *Europe: A Natural History*. Hamish Hamilton, 1964.
Duffey, E., *Natural Parks and Reserves of Western Europe*. Macdonald, 1982.
Godfrey, G. and Crowcroft, W. P., *The Life of the Mole*. Museum Press, 1960.
Groves, C. P., *Horses, Asses and Zebras in the Wild*. David and Charles, 1974.
Guggisberg, C. A. W., *Wild Cats of the World*. David and Charles, 1975.
Hainard, R., *Les Mammifères Sauvages d'Europe*. Delachaux et Niestlé, 1948.
Harrison Matthews, L., *British Mammals*. Collins New Naturalist, 1952.

Harrison Matthews, L., *The Life of Mammals*. Weidenfeld and Nicholson, 1969.
Harrison, R. J. and King, J. E., *Marine Mammals*. Hutchinson, 1965.
Herter, K., *Hedgehogs*. Phoenix House, 1965.
Laidler, L., *Otters in Britain*. David and Charles, 1982.
Lawrence, M. and Brown, R., *Mammals of Britain, their Tracks, Trails and Signs*. Blandford, revised edition 1973.
Lever, C., *The Naturalised Animals of the British Isles*. Hutchinson, 1977.
Mallinson, J., *The Shadow of Extinction: Europe's Threatened Wild Mammals*. Macmillan, 1978.
Mech, L. D., *The Wolf*. The Natural History Press for the American Museum of Natural History, 1970.
Morris, P. A. and Yaldon, D. K., *The Lives of Bats*. David and Charles, 1975.
de Nahlik, A. J., *Wild Deer*. Faber, 1959.
Neal, E., *Badgers*. Blandford, 1977.
Perry, R., *The World of the Polar Bear*. Cassell, 1966.
Perry, R., *Polar Worlds*. David and Charles, 1973.
Poore, D., and Gryn-Ambroes, P., *Nature Conservation in Northern and Western Europe*. I.U.C.N., 1980.
Shorten, M., *Squirrels*. Collins, 1954.
Twigg, G., *The Brown Rat*. David and Charles, 1975.
van den Brink, F. H., *A Field Guide to the Mammals of Britain and Europe*. Collins, 1967.
Whitehead, G. K., *The Deer of Great Britain and Ireland*. Routledge and Kegan Paul, 1964.

INDEX

Figures in bold refer to illustrations.